WI

STARTING TO COLLECT SERIES

20TH CENTURY CERAMICS

Andrew Casey

STARTING TO COLLECT SERIES

20TH CENTURY CERAMICS

Andrew Casey

ANTIQUE COLLECTORS' CLUB

ISBN 10: 1-85149-514-2
ISBN 13: 978-1-85149-514-6

Origination by the Antique Collectors' Club Ltd., Woodbridge, Suffolk, England
Printed and bound in China

Endpapers:
Detail from a hand-painted plate manufactured by A.E. Gray and Co. Ltd., c.1933

Frontispiece:
Art Deco figure by Stefan Dakon for Goldscheider, 1920s

Title page:
Earthenware plate decorated with the House and Bridge *pattern designed by Clarice Cliff for A.J. Wilkinson Ltd., c.1930*

ACKNOWLEDGEMENTS

During my research for this book I have come into contact with several important authors, researchers and recognised authorities who have written about twentieth century ceramics. They have advised me about historical facts, given me information and checked through my proofs. I should like to thank: Maria Anderson, Frank Ashworth, Paul Atterbury, Stella Bedoe (Brighton Museum and Art Gallery), Janek Boniecki (Bauer Pottery), Emma Bridgewater, John Clappison, Biddy Cole (Rye Pottery), Tarquin Cole, Tim Colling, Mick and Derry Collins (Sylvac Collectors' Club), Stan Dawe, James Elliot-Bishop, Daniel Gallen (Decorative Arts Dept., Christie's, South Kensington, London), Scott Gillmer (Red Wing), Filipp Goldscheider, Halls Collectables, Leslie Hayward, Paul Hulme (Aynsley China Ltd.), Steven Jenkins, Robert Lunn (Box of Porcelain), David Mann (www.freeformusa.com), Helen Martin, Ian McCallum, Julie McKeown, Peter Meister (Arzberg-Porzellan GmbH), Steven Moore, Simon Moss, Ian Newton, Steen Nottelmann (Royal Copenhagen), Gary Preston (Portmeirion Potteries Ltd.), Beate Reichel (Rosenthal AG), Robin Reilly, Michael Richardson (www.retroselect.com), Alan H. Roberts (Fieldings Crown Devon Collectors' Club), Kim Rowley (Wade), Alan Ruddle, Rob Runge, Linda Salt (The Denby Pottery Co. Ltd.), Schiffer Books, Ester Schneider (Villeroy and Boch), Andrew Scott (Ashtead Pottery), Susan Scott, Greg Slater, Nick Sugden (Myott Collectors' Club), Norman Tempest (Royal Stafford Tableware), Jonathan Thornhill (Churchill Group), Dick and Judy Wagner, Martin Wilkie (Myott Collectors' Club), Vega Wilkinson, and Kathie Winkle.

Many national museums have kindly assisted me with my research. In particular Alun Graves (Ceramics Dept., V&A Museum, London) gave me access to archive material at the start of my research; Miranda Goodby, Julia Knight and Sue Taylor (all from the Potteries Museum in Stoke-on-Trent) allowed me access to their extensive archives and answered my many questions. Several regional and national libraries have been to very kind to me during my research, in particular the British Library in Wetherby Yorkshire, the Leeds Art Library, and the Hanley Library, Stoke-on-Trent, where Chris Latimer and his staff kindly allowed me access to the all-important pottery trade journals and books in the Horace Barks Reference Section.

I am grateful to the various people who kindly gave permission to reproduce images of items from their collections, including Sylvia Baldry, John Barter and Linda Ellis, Linette Cherry, Jenny Beesley, Bob Duarte, Diana Macmillan, Christine Norman, Chris Walker and Jane Simpkin.

Many people have been very generous with supplying images. I am indebted to the generous support from Michael Jeffery (Woolley and Wallis Auctioneers, Salisbury) for his many suggestions and his generosity in supplying images; also to Tennants, who were kind enough to invite me to their auction house to select images from their sales. Shapiro Auctioneers in Sydney, Australia, were exceptionally helpful in supplying me with images I was unable to locate elsewhere; as was Mark Hill from the Price Guide Company. Several museums have kindly allowed me to reproduce images, in particular I would like to thank Jacqueline Smith (Museum Curator) and Lisa Roberts from Royal Crown Derby, and Amanda Savage from Royal Worcester Ltd for all their assistance. In Europe, Villeroy and Boch, and Brigitte Heinrich at Rosenthal AG were incredibly generous in their help: offering original source material, photographs and books. For the American section, I should like to thank Jeff Zilm, from the Dallas Museum of Art, not only for supplying many images but also for organising the various permissions; Dan Farrell (ACC) for introducing me to David Rago, who kindly provided a number of images from his important American auctions; and Ellen Denker (Lenox China), for giving me advice and correcting proofs for my chapter on Lenox China, as well as providing images for the book.

Photographic credits

Aynsley: 26-27.

Bridgewater: 41.

Cameron and Hollins Ltd.: 123.

Linette Cherry: 148.

Churchill Group: 13 (bottom left), 45.

John Clappison: 81 (top), 82 (bottom), 83.

Dallas Museum of Art: 18 (top), 19 (top), 20, 190-191, 194-198, 200, 205-206, 213-215.

Dorling Kindersley/The Price Guide Company (UK) Ltd.: 164

Francis Joseph Publishing Ltd: 46.

David George, Tea and Antiques, Felixstowe: 187 (bottom).

Lenox: 18 (bottom), 19 (bottom), 203-204.

M and H: 59 (bottom), 162 (top left).

Steven Moore: 88.

Myott Collectors' Club: 13 (top centre), 107

Portmeirion Pottery Ltd: 13 (bottom, centre), 114-117.

Potteries Museum: 23, 74 (bottom), 79, 101, 108-109, 124, 149 (top).

David Rago: 192-193, 207-212, 216-17.

www.retroselect.com: 17 (right), 150, 171, 183, 184 (bottom), 188 (bottom right), 189.

Richard Dennis Ltd: 69 (top).

Rosenthal AG: 17 (left), 182, 184 (top left; top right), 185.

Royal Bank of Scotland Group: 151.

Royal Copenhagen: 186.

Royal Crown Derby: 126-128.

Royal Worcester: 133-134.

Rye Pottery: 137 (top).

Shapiro Auctioneers, Sydney, Australia: 153 (top), 156-157, 177 (right), 180-181.

Norman Tempest: 32, 94, 99.

Tennants: 8, 68, 69 (bottom), 97 (top), 105 (top), 111, 112 (bottom), 152.

Villeroy and Boch: 188 (top; bottom left)

Vega Wilkinson: 145.

Woolley and Wallis: 9, 11, 13 (top left), 33-35, 48-50, 61, 63, 66 (bottom), 67 (right), 80 (bottom), 82 (top), 89, 100, 103-104, 105 (bottom), 118, 129-130, 132, 138-140, 141 (bottom), 143 (top), 158 (top), 160-161, 162 (top right; bottom), 163, 173-176, 178-179, 187 (bottom).

The Barratts backstamp is reproduced with the kind permission of Royal Stafford.

All Wedgwood and Royal Doulton backstamps (including William Adams, E. Brain, Clarice Cliff, Susie Cooper, Johnson Brothers, J. & G. Meakin, Midwinter, Minton, Ridgways, Rosenthal and Shelley) are reproduced with the kind permission of Waterford Wedgwood plc., Kilbarry, Waterford, Ireland.

FOREWORD

When I heard that the next volume in the *Starting to Collect* series was to be 20th Century Ceramics, I must admit that my old heart skipped a beat. Surely people don't collect pots that my parents used in London in the 1920s or children's things that were bought for me in Woolworth's (nothing over sixpence) or more rarely at Liberty (nothing under sixpence). However, my spies tell me that 20th century ceramics are among the fastest growing field of collecting, from the sinuous Art Nouveau of 1900 to the flamboyant Art Deco of the 1920s and '30s; the post-war restrained designs of the 1950s and '60s to the exuberance of the 1980s and '90s.

Sadly, all my parents' pots were destroyed in a succession of three bombed-out homes during the War. The only pot to survive was my precious Donald Duck teapot, which was evacuated with me, so I can understand the affection that collectors have for their pots. Hand on heart; my favourite 20th century pots were the superbly painted vases and plates by the great Royal Worcester artist Harry Davis and the splendidly made craft pottery by the many great potters. But there is something for everyone in collecting pottery and this book will give you lots of ideas.

Happy collecting.

Henry Sandon

CONTENTS

Examples of the Lord Of The Rings *figures from the* Middle Earth Series *introduced by Royal Doulton in 1980. Further figures were added with the whole series being discontinued in 1984*

INTRODUCTION

The 20th century offers the new collector a wide range of opportunities to build up a collection, from coffee sets, dinner wares, TV sets, decorative plaques, egg cups and even chamber pots, to a whole range of novelties that were manufactured by the ceramics industry across Europe and America.

The market for collectables (the preferred phrase used for 20th century items rather than 'antiques') has expanded greatly over the last 20 years with many people starting to buy their first examples from local flea markets, car boot sales and auction houses. Also, the ordinary person in the street is now much more knowledgeable as a result of the many popular television programmes and books. More recently, new opportunities to buy and sell collectables have been established via the internet, particularly the very

popular auction sites such as www.ebay.com. This has opened up the international market, enabling collectors to find rare and unusual examples from around the world.

There are, of course, different types of collectors. Not only do budgets and interests vary, but also collecting styles: some may concentrate on types of objects, such as teapots, others a particular maker. Some collectors are interested in a particular style, such as Art Nouveau, or a particular period of design, the '30s and '50s are particularly popular, with many building up the complete 'look' in their homes including furniture, curtains, crockery, accessories and fashions.

This book is for the novice collector of ceramics produced in the 20th century, whether a collector who concentrates on one factory or designer, such as Susie Cooper, or a collector of a type of ware, such as the toast rack, egg cup or preserve pot. Often collectors will naturally tend to a theme, or become more focussed as their collection develops, sometimes selling pieces to fund purchases. This book covers the diverse range of ceramics produced in those 100 years, aiming to provide a starting point for all those collectors.

What to Collect?

With such a wide range of designers and factories coupled with various price ranges it is very much up to the individual person to choose what to collect. Whilst some build up collections for investment purposes, the majority have a genuine passion for their favourite styles or makers. Collectors can gain an appreciation of typical prices by experience, joining the related collectors' club and reading various publications. It is worth 'watching' items on internet auctions, looking around at antiques markets and shops and going to auction houses to get a 'feel' for prices before you start actually purchasing items.

For the most part, the later general wares from the post-war period are still readily available and more affordable than the older, more rare items that a lot more people are searching for and, as a result, that reach much higher prices. For instance, a Susie Cooper hand-painted cup and saucer dating from the early '30s has a much higher value than one of her bone china cup and saucers decorated with a printed pattern from the late '60s. Similarly, a rarer colour variation of a popular pattern or an unusual shape produced by any of the companies featured in this book will fetch a higher price than its standard counterpart. Prices vary hugely within the collectables market, with some of the best examples of Art Deco ware by the well-known Clarice Cliff, for example, being financially out of reach for the general collector.

Big Bad Wolf, *Wade Heath earthenware musical jug, height 10⅜in (26.5cm), c.1935*

Fakes

One of the greatest concerns for the collector is making sure that an item is genuine. There are some quite sophisticated fakes on the market and these are often difficult to spot for the general collector. Always play safe: if you are unsure, buy from reputable dealers or auction houses in your local area. If you are collecting the more common and affordable wares from the '50s, for example, you are less likely to be troubled by this problem. If, however, you are interested in a style or maker that is particularly popular and usually commands higher prices, then you do need to be careful; alarm bells should ring if a dealer offers you something rare for a 'bargain' price. Remember: if it looks too good to be true then, sadly, it probably is.

Of course all 'look-a-likes' are not actually fakes. Over the years there have been a number of official collectors' reproductions that are clearly labelled as such, usually on the base, and so do not pose any concerns; indeed, they can be of great interest to collectors. Whilst some have special individually

numbered certificates of authenticity, other such reproductions are made for certain museums or galleries. Furthermore, some of the most popular best-selling patterns, such as blue and white patterns by Spode, are still in production as a regular line and are purchased to be used on a daily basis.

With regards to attribution, collectors should also be aware that some dealers can easily misrepresent a piece by attributing it to a particular well-known designer or giving it an earlier date to get a better price. For instance, the well-known designer Charlotte Rhead worked over a long period of time. Examples of her work from the '40s are marked with the Bursley Ware mark, however, some dealers, perhaps without realising it, are wrongly dating such pieces to the '20s; of course the earliest wares command the highest prices. The best advice for the collector is to read up on the subject to gain information of the shapes, years of production and, importantly, the range of backstamps. Remember though, that some factories continued to use a designer's name, which they considered to be a brand name for quality, for many years after he or she had retired or moved to another pottery works, as a good marketing ploy. High-quality books and magazine articles should highlight this.

Condition

Ideally any collector would want to buy a perfect example for the right price. However, real life takes it toll and, on occasion, pottery may be chipped, cracked or crazed, which should be reflected in the price. If you see a rare piece by your favourite designer or factory that has a bad chip or crack, but is priced at £10, then you may well decide that it is worth it, especially if the damage cannot be seen when displayed. Collectors should never attempt to restore a damaged piece themselves, doing so can drastically reduce the value of a piece. This is not saying that it is not worth having a cherished piece restored, but it is recommended that you contact an expert or a specialist dealer for their advice.

What about buying a piece that has already been restored? Restoration is probably one of the biggest difficulties for the beginner. If it has been done well it can be very difficult to spot. However, if an item has been restored and is labelled as such and priced accordingly, then there really isn't a problem. In particular, some over-glaze hand-painted pots that were popular during the Art Deco period tended to ware or rub, in particular the blue enamel wore away from the acid in fruit, and as a result is often repainted to make the pots saleable. Reputable dealers will identify the restoration to the customer.

Handling

Collectors should take special care when handling ceramics. Always pick the piece up with both hands, and avoid holding it by a vulnerable part such as a handle, spout, arm or leg. If you need to move an item carry it in a padded box or basket making sure the container is sturdy enough to stand the weight of a heavy piece; cardboard boxes have a nasty habit of giving way.

Cleaning

Even the best pieces will fail to impress if they are dirty and dingy. However, collectors should be very careful when cleaning ceramics as damage is often irreversible: paint and glaze can be removed, gilding simply wiped right off, earthenware can become soft, surfaces stained, and repairs come apart! If an item is particularly old, rare or valuable it is always best to have the item cleaned by a ceramics conservator.

You may find that it is enough simply to remove dust and dirt with a dry artist's paintbrush. If you do think that the item needs a more thorough clean, remember that ceramics come in all sorts of bodies, glazes and decoration, each requiring different cleaning processes, many should not be immersed in water, some, such as painted earthenware, should preferably never even get damp. Never use bleach and never put pottery or porcelain in the dishwasher. Both *Starting To Collect Antique Porcelain* by John Sandon (Antique Collectors' Club, 1997) and *Looking after Antiques* by Frances Halahan and Anna Plowden (National Trust, 2003) contain good advice on cleaning collectable ceramic items.

Tea for two in the Stanford *shape, decorated with the hand-painted* Trees and House *pattern, designed by Clarice Cliff for A.J. Wilkinson Ltd., 1929*

Displaying your collection

The display of a private collection of pottery is rather down to personal taste, though most collectors tend to ensure that the display is appropriate to the style or period of the collection. For instance, a walnut veneered glass cabinet would be ideal to display a collection of Art Deco pottery, as would a Welsh dresser to display blue and white china. If possible, glazed cabinets are advisable as they minimise dusting and keep items safe. Take your time when setting up your display or adding in a new item and think carefully about how the different pieces work together – you may find that an elaborate piece needs to stand on its own.

It is important to be very careful not to cause damage when displaying your collection. Try to keep your collection out of direct sunlight as strong light can discolour any restoration, and avoid any extreme fluctuations in temperature as this can damage pottery. Some wall hangers can place a plate under stress and cause cracks; the key is to use hanging wires that fit the plate exactly and make sure that the wall fixing is strong enough to take the weight of the plate. If a plate is already cracked, it is best displayed on a shelf using plate stands of the appropriate size. Be extremely cautious when removing old display hangers from a plate: never force them off, as you are likely to chip the plate. Never glue or stick any display device to your ceramic item – it may permanently mark the piece.

TRENDS IN THE MANUFACTURE OF POTTERY IN 20TH CENTURY

The story of the production of pottery in Britain, Europe and America during the 20th century is one of great achievement, innovation in design, the development of new shapes, and the devastation caused by conflicts and economic problems. Though the quality of both the design and the manufacture of pottery was dependent on the skilled workforce, it was the machinery, kilns and printing processes that enabled the designs to become realised. Improving the quality of the pottery and the decoration, whilst still keeping prices competitive, was imperative in order to stay in business in an ever-decreasing market.

Manufacturers responded differently to the call for better design, though most relied initially on the experienced designer alongside the general improvements in manufacturing. During the early part of the twentieth century the American customer tended to prefer European pottery, in particular from Britain and France, which held a strong position in the U.S. market for a number of years. In the early thirties, as several American manufacturers became more established in the industry, they developed their own pottery lines to meet the changing needs of the American public. Despite the many debates on modern design and the many important expositions to promote the latest designs, it was, after all, the buying customer who steered the market. Pottery manufacturers could ill afford to invest in expensive lines that would not be commercially profitable.

Fashion through the decades

The prevailing style at the end of the 19th century was Art Nouveau, which took its inspiration from the flowing lines of nature. This elegant new movement, named after Siegfried 'Samuel' Bing's famous Parisian shop, was influential in all aspects of design, even the Metro stations in Paris, and especially ceramics. Art Nouveau began in France in about 1880 and quickly spread across Europe in various guises: Il Stile Liberty in Italy, Jugensdstil in Germany, Secessionist in Austria. In Spain the work of Antonio Gaudi is well known, especially his Sagrada Familia Cathedral; in America the style was represented by the iridescent glass wares and lampshades of Louis Comfort Tiffany. However, Art Nouveau was relatively short lived, probably ending with the breakout of the First World War in 1914.

In the '20s, following the devastation of WWI, a new, simpler, more austere style emerged that was very different from Art Nouveau. With its clean, simple lines, bold geometric patterns and bright colours, Art Deco took the design world by storm. The 1925 Exposition Internationale des Arts Décoratifs et Industriels Modernes in Paris was one of the most influential design events of the 20th century. On display were some of the best examples of interior design, furniture, textiles, ceramics, glass and silverware in the new fashion of the time. The Exposition brought the Art Deco style, and the benefits of hand-painted designs using bright and bold colours, to the attention of designers around the world. The term Art Deco was not coined until the late 1960s following a retrospective exhibition of the 1925 Paris Exposition. At the time this sort of design was referred to as 'Jazz Moderne'.

In Europe the 'International Modern' style was coming to the fore. European designers rejected the more frivolous aspects of Art Deco, and other period styles, in favour of clean, plain, practical forms as typified by the wares manufactured by Gustavberg. An important influence was the Bauhaus School of Art and Design, founded by the designer Walter Gropius in 1919, in Germany. The teachers were all practising artists, architects or designers and included Paul Klee. The Bauhaus promoted a new philosophy towards design, using mass-production methods and

Art Nouveau
(Minton)

Art Deco
(Myott)

Modernism
(Josiah Wedgwood and Sons Ltd.)

Bauhaus style
(Arzberg)

1950s Contemporary
(W.R. Midwinter Ltd.)

Scandinavian
(Royal Copenhagen)

1960s
(James Broadhurst and Sons Ltd.)

1970s
(Portmeirion Potteries Ltd.)

1990s
(William Adams Ltd.)

materials, rejecting decoration and historical influences. The Bauhaus, which became a symbol of modernity, made an important contribution to all forms of design across the world.

Whilst British manufacturers were quick to adopt mass production, thereby keeping costs low, they were aware that the British customer still wanted decoration.

After the Second World War most British and European manufacturers found it difficult to begin again as there was so much hardship and restriction of materials. Some countries, such as those in Scandinavia, continued production developing new shapes and styles that would later dominate the international market. American design prospered; by the late '40s some of the most important American manufacturers employed influential designers such as Eva Zeisel, who introduced a new approach to form and pattern typified by her *Tomorrow's Classic*.

By the early '50s, a new generation of British designers came to the fore, their work was showcased at the 1951 Festival of Britain in London. Having endured so many years of rationing and hardship, and putting up with plain Utility Wares, the British public embraced these colourful new ceramic designs, which were quickly dubbed 'contemporary'.

During the '50s the Scandinavian manufacturers made a significant impact on the British market, featuring extensively in the British trade press as representing good design. In particular, the decorative wares by Stig Lindberg for Gustavberg proved very popular as did a number of stylised vegetable designs by Marianne Westman at Rörstrand. These important designs influenced British manufacturers such as Midwinter Pottery, which led the market through the '50s and '60s with its practical sets. Its modern patterns, such as *Primavera*, reflected a new taste appealing to the younger generation. Midwinter also introduced 'carry home packs', which proved ideal for newly-wed couples and smaller families, and were soon copied by many other manufacturers. Ironically, after the Second World War the American market turned again to Britain for the traditional wares, because of their high quality.

In Britain the '60s and '70s saw many of the larger pottery manufacturers buying out the smaller firms in order to gain a greater share in the market. Despite these often hostile 'mergers' it was the smaller pottery works that were quick to respond to the latest fashions and styles, albeit in an ever-shrinking market. The role of the designer was changing as well. With such a competitive market, pottery manufacturers began to use freelance designers to create a wider range of patterns in order to attract business from overseas.

In America, Europe and Britain, after World War II, the structure of the family changed: more women went out to work, families were smaller and daily life became more informal. Customers tended to buy smaller dinner sets and the increasingly casual approach to dining led to oven-to-table wares, coffee sets and, eventually, to TV sets and the individual mug.

Britain

From the very start of the new century there was concern over Britain's poor industrial performance, coupled with the need to promote good design. Despite great efforts being made to improve both the quality of pottery and the shapes and patterns created, the general market still wanted traditional printed patterns on table wares, toilet wares and fancies.

The pottery industry, based chiefly in Stoke-on-Trent in Staffordshire, was very competitive with larger companies, such as Josiah Wedgwood and Sons Ltd. and Royal Doulton, leading the way in design. In tandem with these important pottery companies were hundreds of smaller, family-run businesses, which produced pottery for the open market, hotels, institutions and the travel industry, both in Britain and abroad. Historically, the industry has always been cautious of change and efforts by pioneering designers and manufacturers to revolutionise design proved difficult. Furthermore, smaller companies could not afford to invest in the development of new shapes.

However, before any major changes in pottery design could take place, the market was devastated by the effects of the General Strike and the subsequent economic slump caused by the Wall Street Crash in 1929. In particular, the export market was badly hit, with leading British and European companies losing important contracts to the decimated American markets, which could no longer afford to import expensive wares.

Emerging from Europe during the late '20s, the Art Deco style proved very popular, many young British couples welcoming the brightly-painted pottery into their homes, as they wanted something that was different to what their parents had had. At this time hand-painted decoration was cheaper to produce than printed ware and many pottery manufacturers adopted the style, although sometimes superficially. As demand grew for British pottery abroad, hand-painted decoration was phased out and replaced by transfer-printed patterns that had improved somewhat over the years.

Commissioned by Woolworth's in 1958, Ridgway's Homemaker *pattern has become the iconic design associated with the 1950s*

The buoyant market was brought to a standstill at the end of the '30s when WWII broke out. The British pottery industry never really recovered from the devastation, with many smaller companies closing down. Austerity measures prohibited the production of any new patterns or shapes until restrictions were lifted in the early '50s. Furthermore, the important American market had dwindled again just as it had in the late '20s.

The middle of the century was marked with the Festival of Britain in 1951. This was one of the most significant events of the post-war period, introducing a new design style known then as 'contemporary'. A new generation of young designers rejected the old ideas, developing new styles and shapes influenced by the latest American ceramic designs, best typified by W.R. Midwinter Ltd. with patterns by Jessie Tait.

The new decade saw advancements in superior printing machines that changed the industry forever. Indeed, many manufacturers adapted their production line to comply with the machines' capabilities, in order to use the new printing process to increase production. A typical example of this is the *Riviera* shape produced by James Broadhurst and Sons Ltd. The '60s also marked a period of takeovers with Josiah Wedgwood and Sons Ltd.

buying out a number of prominent manufacturers such as J.&G. Meakin and Johnson Brothers Ltd. The general financial difficulties and market slump in the '70s saw many factories closing down, resulting in hundreds of redundancies.

Innovative ideas and approaches were sought by manufacturers desperate to boost sales and increase business. Susan Williams-Ellis provided this for Portmeirion Potteries Ltd. with her *Totem* range, decorated with a brown glaze, that featured a very tall coffee pot. Initially derided as a passing whim, it soon proved popular, resulting in probably every other pottery manufacturer copying the style. Further changes in customer demand led to the production of associated items such as tea towels, pans and ceramic tiles to complement tableware; the popular *Botanic Garden* range, again by Portmeirion, led the way in this innovation.

At the lower end of the market exotic holiday destinations were adopted for new pattern names as more people were enjoying foreign holidays to Spain and France. Patterns such as *Monaco*, *San Tropez* and *San Marino* by Kathie Winkle for James Broadhurst Ltd. were typical.

The '80s saw a new demand for a much softer palette of pinks and light blues for pattern decoration and softer shapes in Britain. The biggest selling aspect of the early part of the decade was the introduction of co-ordinated accessories that included dishes, tablecloths, tiles, lamp bases etc. This was successfully exploited by several companies including Royal Doulton with its *Eternal Beau* pattern and *Botanic Garden* by Portmeirion Ltd., first issued in 1975.

During the latter part of the century the role of the resident designer decreased in favour of freelance designers, who could offer new ideas and inspirations for an ever-dwindling market. These designers might work for several different subsidiary companies. The end of the century saw an ever-increasing number of closures of once famous factories, alongside an increase in cheaper pottery imports.

Europe

Throughout Europe demands for good quality and attractive design were clearly acknowledged within the industry and amongst the many manufacturers operating during the 20th century. The contribution to design, and in particular pottery design, in Europe has been pinpointed to the 1925 Exposition Internationale des Arts Décoratifs et Industriels Modernes in Paris. This special event showcased the best of European design that went on to influence many aspects of industrial design.

One of the most important pottery companies in Europe must be Rosenthal, which has been a leading innovator in ceramic design since the '50s, always keen to push the boundaries and maintain a fashionable edge, and employing many artists and designers of international fame.

Whilst the French and Belgian pottery manu-

An interior view of a pavilion designed by Jacques-Emile Ruhlmann for the Exposition Internationale des Arts Décoratifs et Industriels Modernes, staged in Paris in 1925

The Cupola *shape, designed by Mario Bellini for Rosenthal, 1984*

Acapulco *pattern, designed by Christine Reuter for Villeroy and Boch, decorated on egg cups, 1967*

facturers created decorative and stylish patterns in the Art Deco style, the Scandinavian approach was very different: focussing on function rather than pattern, companies such as Gustavberg and Royal Copenhagen produced simple and practical ceramics, which are, nevertheless very aesthetically pleasing.

Unlike their counterparts in Britain, the Scandinavian pottery manufacturers were never reluctant to invest in design, and even set up art studios to develop new ideas free from production constraints. Some of these designs were then adapted for the commercial market. This innovative approach to design gained them international recognition and several important awards during the '30s. 1930 saw the launch of the important Swedish exhibition staged in Stockholm. The following year, the exhibition travelled to London, giving British designers an opportunity to see what Scandinavian design was all about. The Scandinavian approach to design was more democratic, producing good quality, affordable ceramics for everyone. The simple approach to both pattern and form proved very popular and inspired designers around the world.

By the '50s and '60s Scandinavian design had gained wide coverage in the pottery trade press and design books of the period, being held up by British design commentators as the best examples of ceramic design. The customers, however, were less convinced and the austere Scandinavian wares proved rather difficult to sell in a climate of bold colours and adventure being enjoyed by the buying public in Britain. Today some of the best examples of Scandanavian ceramics are considered to be design classics.

Colourful pottery made an impact in America following success of the Fiesta *range introduced by Homer Laughlin in 1936*

America

The American ceramics industry began with the development of art pottery created by a number of specialist companies such as Rookwood and Roseville, based in Ohio, at the end of the 19th century. At the same time many other manufacturers focused on the production of domestic pottery, ranging from toilet wares to mid-price tableware decorated with topical patterns. From the early part of the 20th century the American middle class preferred French porcelain rather than the cheaper American earthenware. However, that profitable market soon ended following the First World War. Some of the more prestigious British pottery manufacturers, such as Josiah Wedgwood and Sons Ltd. and Royal Doulton enjoyed good trade with the American dealers whose customers wanted the typically English pottery; exactly the sort of thing that many design commentators were trying to escape from in Britain during that period. Such was the success of these British firms that they set up offices and showrooms in New York.

American manufacturers responded negatively to the success of outside manufacturers, expressing concerns through serious debates about the quality of production and the issue of competing with foreign imports. In 1918 the Department of Education stated that if the country was going to compete with imports then it would have to improve the manufacturing methods to produce high-quality pottery. The issue of improved design came to a head following the 1925 Exposition Internationale des Arts Décoratifs et Industriels Modernes in Paris, at which it became apparent that the country did not have any modern design to exhibit at this important and prestigious event. Organisers put together a touring show of the highlights of the Paris Exposition, which travelled around America in 1926 in an attempt to raise awareness of good modern design. However, the American market was not that interested in Art Deco, preferring the machine age styling that developed on from the Deco style.

American companies took an early lead in recognising the important role of the designer, setting up design studios long before Europe and Britain. Designers such as Desmond Deskey, Russell Wright

Lenox China produced wares for the higher end of the market. A bone china plate decorated with the Florida *pattern, designed by Frank G. Holmes, 1922*

and Raymond Loewy made a significant contribution to industrial design throughout the century. Furthermore, many European designers who had fled Europe in the '20s and '30s, soon established themselves in the decorative arts in America.

By the early '30s there was already social change taking place: with families becoming smaller and women going out to work. This new market required dinner and tea sets with fewer place settings and that were well designed and affordable. One of the most important changes in style took place in the '30s with the introduction of coloured pottery, typified by the productions of Bauer and the *Fiesta* range introduced by Homer Laughlin in 1936. Many other manufacturers followed this concept and eventually this type of ware was sold in department stores such as F.W. Woolworth & Co. and Sears. These coloured wares fitted in perfectly with the modern American lifestyle and the new casual approach to dining and entertaining.

With the outbreak of WWII, British manufacturers were unable to supply the American market. This gave the American companies the impetus to develop and improve their own manufacturing industry and, at the same time, gave them the chance to experiment and devise new pottery both with regards to pattern and shape. It was at this time that the industrial designers in America, including Russell Wright and Eva Zeisel, made a significant contribution to ceramic design that went on to influence both Europe and Britain. These designers developed softer forms rejecting the angular Art Deco shapes.

New lines of pottery were introduced during the post-war period in response to the changes in everyday life in America. America was ahead of Europe with regards to new machinery and electrical goods for the home. New labour-saving devices, such as fridges and food processors, made cooking easier and gave families more time for leisure. Whilst the British people were still living under the austere restrictions of rationing, American families were enjoying eating outside in the garden, called a 'cook out' and, of course, sitting infront of the television. The latter resulted in the production of the TV tray, a large plate with a recess for a cup or glass,

The move towards softer forms in America during the late forties is typified by the shapes and patterns by Eva Zeisel such as Tomorrow's Classics *for Hall China, 1947*

A Lenox China trade advertisement

so that individuals could eat dinner whilst watching television rather than the family sitting together at the table; by 1955 over 65% of American households had a television.

As was the case in Britain, many American pottery manufacturers were unable to continue production after WWII for various reasons, not least the foreign and domestic competition in a dwindling market place. To keep their businesses going, many manufacturers turned to market research so they could produce exactly what the customer wanted, lessening the risk of investing in new lines.

A World of Shopping

Throughout the twentieth century social changes had a significant impact on how manufacturers responded to customer demand. The latter part of the nineteenth century saw the establishment of department stores across the world, including Bon Marché in Paris (est. 1852), Heal's and Liberty in London, KaDeWe in Berlin, Marshall Field & Co. in Chicago and Macy's and Bloomingdale's in New York. The stores were enormous – by 1924 Macy's alone claimed to have over a million square feet of retail space – and sold everything that a customer needed for the modern home. More than this, they allowed access to goods that often only the rich and well-heeled had even see before. Now the working classes, who would not have been welcomed in many of the smaller specialist shops, were free to browse and choose. The department stores, which also began to introduce credit payments, were able to keep prices low as they mostly bought in bulk direct from the manufacturer, sometimes even commissioning ranges exclusive to their store. The department store revolutionised shopping, making the customer king. For the first time it had become a customer-led market and manufacturers were forced to respond to the paying public's will.

Chain stores such as F.W. Woolworth & Co., which had hundreds of stores across America, also had a significant influence on the sort of product that was sold. Both department stores and chain stores often commissioned exclusive ranges that would be on sale for a number of years. Not only did this guarantee the pottery manufactures a steady income, but also made it possible to get decent quality design into the ordinary household.

Example of a typical TV set (known in America as a 'long plate' or 'snack plate'), and casserole dish with cover, produced by the Stetson China Company in Chicago. Both are in the Holiday *shape and decorated with the hand-painted* Sea Spray *pattern, diameter of casserole dish 9⅝in (24.4 cm), from 1954*

CHAPTER 1

BRITISH MANUFACTURERS

Earthenware teapot decorated with the Meadowlands *pattern (l.) and a coffee pot decorated with the* Inspiration *pattern (r). Designed by Susie Cooper for Adams Ltd., c.1983-84*

WILLIAM ADAMS LTD.

Over the 200 or so years of production the Adams family potteries have built a good reputation for well-designed, high-quality pottery, their most successful lines running for many years. The Adams family started manufacturing pottery as far back as 1779 and by the 19th century had introduced new ranges such as blue and white, basalts and ironstones. In 1896 the Greengates factory was purchased. In 1918 the Adams potteries in Tunstall became William Adams & Sons (Potters) Ltd.

Typical production in the early part of the twentieth century included a wide selection of toilet and domestic tablewares. The *Shakspere* [sic] series, comprising various jugs and plates featuring engraved scenes from the Bard's plays, was introduced in 1913. In 1921 the *British Pottery Manufacturers' Federation*

Standard Exporter illustrated a range of Adams products including its blue and white wares, Chinese inspired patterns on a solid black ground and a stylised bird pattern on various shapes including several different vases, tea wares, ginger jars and dinner wares.

During the early part of the 20th century Percy Adams came into the family business bringing with him news ideas allied with a thorough understanding of the tradition of the company. Importantly, he was aware of the latest tastes in pottery fashion and he responded by reproducing some of the earlier patterns from the eighteenth century, but this time hand painted in bright colours rather than printed. Simple shapes replaced the ornate period forms. He was also credited at the time for developing the distinctive warm ivory glaze called Titian, which was later used on a pattern range called *Titian Ware*, launched c.1910, which is a very popular collectable today.

Other revived patterns included *Lorraine* and *Old Chelsea* – the latter launched on the new *Classic* shape in 1933. The hand-painted Calyx Ware, from 1930, became a best seller and proved so popular that it was eventually printed rather than painted to meet the demand. Other popular patterns of the '30s included *Juliet*, *Old Bow* and *Mazara* as well as the series of earthenware plaques, *Cries of London*. The end of the decade saw an important commission from the prestigious and world-renowned department store Tiffany's of New York, which asked Adams to produce a souvenir plate for the New York World's Fair of 1939. Other importers of Adams wares included JonRoth, Fisher, Bruce & Co., and B. Altman.

Despite continuing to revive a number of 18th century patterns, the company was set back by a number of problems during the '50s. Both Percy Adams and his brother William died in 1952, then severe financial difficulties resulted in the closure of the Greengates factory. However, development was made with new shapes, such as *Claire*, which was introduced in 1961, and a new body called *Micratex* was perfected and unveiled in 1963.

In 1966 W. Adams Ltd. was bought out by Josiah Wedgwood and Sons Ltd. Various improvements to the small factory were made and Adams benefited from its parent company's resources. Within a year a new showroom was established in London for Adams, shared with Susie Cooper Ltd., which had also been taken over that same year. The best-selling patterns by Adams, such as *Baltic* and *Old Colonial*, were continued with the standard Adams backstamp and, for a short period, with the addition of 'Member of the Wedgwood Group'.

Robert Minkin, the prominent Wedgwood designer, was given special responsibilities with regards to design at Adams. One of his first contributions was the *Wayfarer* shape, an oven-to-tableware range,

introduced in the late '60s and decorated with patterns such as *Leda*, *Kempton*, *Greensleeves* and *Blue Mantle* – the latter two being designed by Susie Cooper. As the range was withdrawn after only a few years it is less well-known today. Robert Minkin also designed the *Toys* nurseryware set featuring silk-screened motifs in bright colours, whilst Peter Wall, Design Manager at Wedgwood, developed the new *Castella* range for Adams featuring embossed motifs with a warm brown glaze. Collectable mugs, in two sizes, were decorated with patterns such as *Sharon*, *Baltic* and *Minuet*, which were standard patterns also used on other wares.

By the early '70s the number of patterns in production decreased with the hotel ware range being discontinued. The '80s saw the introduction of a number of new patterns by Susie Cooper, who joined Adams following the closure of her own company. *Blue Daisy* on the *Hexagon* shape, *Meadowlands* for Boots Ltd. and *Inspiration* for Tesco were typical of the period.

In 1984 Adams utilised the *Micratex* body for a new cookware range decorated with patterns such as *Azalea*, *Blue Bell*, *Jazz* and *Florida*, the latter by Susie Cooper. At the same time the company launched the *Thomas the Tank Engine* range, which proved very popular.

- Adams produced a wide variety of tea, coffee and dinner wares that remain affordable for today's collector.
- The souvenir plate for the 1939 New York World's Fair for Tiffany's has become a popular collectable.
- Despite a strong collectors' market for Susie Cooper designs, her later wares such as *Meadowlands* are of less interest.

Further Reference

Casey, A. and Eatwell, A., (Eds.) *Susie Cooper: A Pioneer of Modern Design*. Antique Collectors' Club, 2002

Furniss, D.A., Wagner, J.R. and Wagner, J., *Adams Ceramics: Staffordshire Potters and Pots, 1779-1998*. Schiffer Publications Ltd., 1999

Example of the Adams backstamp, 1980s

98 EARTHENWARE, ETC., SECTION.
Section Poterie, Etc.
Sección Loza de Barro, Etc.

ORNAMENTAL EARTHENWARE, ETC.
Faïence Ornementale, Etc.
Loza Ornamental, Etc.

ISIK—PUOB

WILLIAM ADAMS & SONS,
TUNSTALL, STAFFORDSHIRE.
Reproducers of the original Adams Blue Printed Ware and Enamels.

1 (ABASE)   2 (ABODE)   3 (ACUTE)   4 (ADAGE)   5 (AGATE)

(AGLOW)   (AMITY)   6   7   (ANGRY)   15

(AMEER)   8   10 (AMOUR)

13 (ALOUD)   9 (APACE)

14 (ARRAY)   11 (APISH)   12 (ARROW)   16 (AVAIL)   17 (AXIOM)

(BELCH)   18   19 (BIPED)   21 (BLADE)   (BITTS)   22 (BLOTE)

23 (BEDEW)   (BENDY) 24   20   26 (BRIER)

25 (BLIND)

ADAMS
Established 1657.

27 (BUNCH)

29 (BREAM)   30 (BROIL)   28 (BOOTH)   31 (BRAID)

Selection of William Adams pottery illustrated in the British Pottery Manufacturers Federation Standard Exporter, *dated 1921*

A more detailed version of the Lion of Industry *figural piece. This version is impressed with 'GENOZO TOOTHPASTE BRITISH MADE', height 7½in (19cm), c.1924-26*

ASHTEAD POTTERS

The Ashtead Potters had a less than conventional beginning compared to other pottery manufacturers in Britain. It was originally set up in 1923 at the Victoria Works in Ashtead, Surrey by the philanthropist Sir Lawrence Weaver in association with the Rural Industries Board as a training centre for disabled ex-service men after WWI. They invested in the latest technology for the workers, who were assisted by trained potters from local industry. By the mid '20s, the number of workers had increased from 14 to over 20.

Ashtead pottery was either hand-thrown or moulded depending on the skills of the workforce. Breakfast, dinner, tea and coffee wares were available alongside various jugs such as *Liverpool* and *Dutch*. Coloured glazes were used to decorate the pottery alongside banded and simple decorative motifs and landscapes with some transfer-printed patterns being used. A number of examples were shown at the British Empire Exhibition in 1924

with two patterns, including a stylised cottage with trees depicted on a beaker, being illustrated in the trade press. Percy Metcalfe, a well-known sculptor and stamp designer, also produced figural pieces, including the *Lion of Industry* for the British Empire Exhibition, decorated with an orange glaze. A similar version was made to advertise toothpaste (see picture above); it is still sought after by collectors today. The majority of Ashtead's productions were marked with a backstamp depicting an ash tree.

The workforce increased alongside the growing popularity of the pottery that was, by the late '20s, being stocked in some of the most distinguished stores in London, such as Heal's. Over 300 patterns were recorded during this period and included a range of nursery wares designed by E.H. Shepard. He created a special set based on the *Winnie the Pooh* story for a nursery set for Princess Elizabeth in 1928. Ashtead also produced wares for outside organisations including souvenir pottery for the Portmeirion village in North Wales created by Sir

Collection of earthenwares with banded decoration, c.1929-30

Clough Williams-Ellis. These special items, much sought after today, were decorated with the name 'Port Merion' and the mermaid logo. The pottery's success was boosted by the number of notable artists and designers who provided designs, in particular Phoebe Stabler, an acknowledged sculptor and wife of Harold Stabler, a partner at Carter Stabler and Adams Ltd. The pottery closed five years after the death of Sir Lawrence Weaver in 1930.

* The limited period of production means collectors are very keen on all Ashtead pottery.
* Look out for less well-known pieces, such as the nurseryware, figural work and specially commissioned pieces.
* *Portmeirion* souvenir pottery, marked 'Port Merion' and the mermaid logo, and designs by Phoebe Stabler are popular with collectors.

Further Reference

Batkin, M., *Gifts for Good Children. The History of Children's China, Part II, 1890-1990*. Richard Dennis, 1991

Hallam, E., *Ashtead Potters Ltd. in Surrey 1923-1935*. Hallam Publishing, 1990

www.ashteadpottery.com

Example of the Ashtead backstamp

JOHN AYNSLEY & SONS LTD.

This prestigious pottery was known for its production of high-quality bone china cups and saucers, breakfast and dessert wares. Founded by John Aynsley in the late 18th century, over the years various family members took charge of the business, which was later based at the Portland Works in Longton. The family motto was 'Furth Fortune and Fill the Fettles'.

During the 20th century the company was one of the biggest manufacturers of bone china. Dinnerware decorated with traditionally-styled patterns on bone china coffee cups in an Edwardian style were introduced before the First World War. Important artists such as Frederick Micklewright, who had previously worked at Wileman and Co., and Richard J. Keeling joined the company during the early part of the century, contributing to the company's growing reputation for high-quality, hand-painted decoration. Some of the earliest creations included a series of outstanding lustre ware decorated with stylised butterflies, which were similar to the work of Daisy Makeig-Jones for Josiah Wedgwood and Sons Ltd., as were some of the shapes.

Besides using a number of standard bone china shapes, the company cautiously dipped into the Art Deco style but with a restraint that typified their main productions. The *Tulip* shape, from 1931, was an interesting response to the current fashion with the cup shape modelled to resemble the petals of a tulip with butterfly handles. An embossed shape called *Clyde* was introduced in the same year, then in 1932 an alternative version, known as the *Old Clyde* shape, with a newly modelled flower handle became available. The *Boston* shape, from 1934, was decorated with Art Deco style zig-zags and wavy lines alongside patterns such as *Arta*, *Plaza* and *Ascot*. According to the trade press, the simply decorated patterns such as *Blue Bird* and *Bluebell Time* were much in demand at the time.

In 1933 two patterns designed by George L. Maddox were shown at the important Exhibition of Industrial Art in Relation to the Home at Dorland Hall in London. In the same year, Aynsley's became a private company. The standard mark, with some small variations, featured a crown above the words 'AYNSLEY ENGLAND'.

Production was continued throughout the war with the management undertaking some modernisation and installing a new tunnel oven in order to increase production. Soon afterwards the British Pottery Manufacturers' Federation presented to the Princess Elizabeth several proposed patterns for an extensive dinnerware service that would be made on the occasion of her wedding in 1947. The Princess chose the design submitted by Aynsley that featured a stylish gold band with a royal cipher later called the *Windsor* pattern.

Like many manufacturers, Aynsley's saw the potential of introducing a contemporary line. Three years of development resulted in the bone china *Merit* shape in 1965. Initially produced as tea and coffee wares, reception to the new range was so good that dinnerware shapes were soon added. Nine patterns including *Sonnet*, *Trafalgar* and *Rembrandt* (the latter featuring a 17th century Adams style

Commemorative wares for the coronation of King George VI and Queen Elizabeth, 1937; and plate (centre, right) to commemorate their visit to Canada and the United States in 1939 Courtesy of the Study Collection at Southampton Solent University

border in blue) were created for this shape. Further modernisation of the factory was undertaken and in 1968 Aynsley's bought Denton China.

In 1970 the company was taken over by Waterford Crystal and renamed Aynsley China Ltd. Thereafter the company offered a wide range of goods from the *Aynsley Animal Kingdom* (a limited edition range of figures was produced in 1976), various new tableware patterns and bone china trophies. An outstanding pattern, *Cottage Garden* printed on the *Pembroke* shape, from 1972, was a best seller. During the early '80s the company commissioned Nick Holland to design for them. In 1986 Waterford took over the prestigious Josiah Wedgwood and Sons Ltd., and later, in 1997, Aynsley became part of the Belleek Pottery Group.

- Individual tea cups and saucers are very collectable, as are the small giftwares.
- Interest in Aynsley wares produced in the '50s and '60s is still very limited, making them affordable items for the new collector.

Further Reference

Ashworth, F., *Aynsley China*. Shire Publications, 2002

Selection of bone china displaying highly-skilled hand-painted pattern of fruit, 1940s and 1950s Private Collection

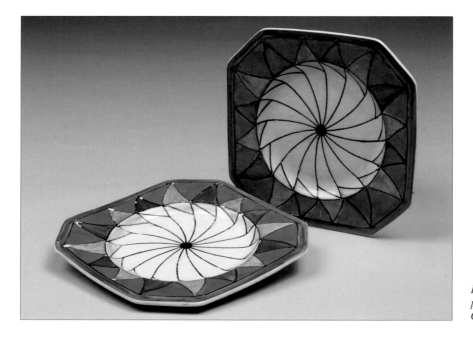

Hand-painted Arabesque *pattern designed by John Guildford, c.1929*

BARKER BROTHERS LTD.

A number of pottery manufacturers, established during the 19th century found it difficult to adapt to the demand for new styles and fashions during the early part of the 20th century. It didn't help that the market was also dwindling. Barker Brothers was able to succeed by concentrating production on its most popular styles. Operating from the Meir Works in Longton, Barker Brothers had set up in 1876 to produce both bone china and earthenware (*Royal Tudor Ware*). Little else is known about the company's early history.

During the early part of the 20th century Barker Brothers produced a wide range of products that included plain wares for the kitchen, toilet wares, fluted tea wares and some nursery wares. One such nursery set was the *Teddy Tail* pattern, a print and

Standard backstamp for Barker Bros. Ltd.

enamelled pattern based on the *Daily Mail* comic strip by Charles Folkard, which comprised teacups and saucers, mugs, tankards and beakers supplied in china, with porringers and plates in earthenware. New dinnerware patterns notably included *Bruges*, decorated under the glaze, which was later extended to include vases, flower pots and rose bowls.

The company's most prolific period was during the late '20s when it embraced the fashionable new styles. As well as improving the standard product and closing down the bone china department, Barker Bros. responded to the fashion for modern, brightly painted pottery. New patterns were created by John Guildford, previously decorating manager at A.E. Gray & Co. Ltd. Decorated on earthenware rather than bone china, these bold, hand-painted, geometric patterns such as *Arabesque*, *The Storm*, *Autocrat* and *Moulin Rouge* are evocative of the period; some were mentioned in the trade press in 1929, though no further information is available.

A new shape *Mentone* was introduced in 1929 and decorated with patterns such as *Tripoli*, a hand-painted bird motif, *Fantasie* and *Paradise*. The *Harvest* pattern, decorated under glaze, depicted stylised trees, whilst *Sandringham* was targeted at

Right:
Earthenware coffee pot and preserve pot (lid missing) decorated with hand-painted pattern, probably designed by John Guildford, c.1929

Below:
Chianti *pattern printed in black on an earthenware side plate, diameter 7in (17.8cm), mid '50s*

the more conservative market. The *Triumph* range was developed for hoteliers in 1928. Several other patterns of this period were clearly influenced by popular lines by other manufacturers, a version of *Titian Ware* by William Adams Ltd., for example. The '30s saw the introduction of the primrose glaze, which was used for several popular patterns; new shapes included *Modern* and *Eureka*. Typical patterns included *Pomona* decorated on embossed early morning sets.

Following WWII the company decided to offer a wide range of traditional and modern patterns, including a new shape range called *Mayfair*. This strategy was promoted in the company's trade advertisements, boasting that they could supply both "traditional or contemporary" pottery. *English County Crafts*, which featured various centre motifs and was similar to the *Tonquin* pattern by Clarice Cliff from the same period, sold well abroad. Further traditional patterns included *Century Rose* on the *Grosvenor* shape.

A more contemporary pattern, *Off Beat*, printed in blue, was probably created to attract the younger generation. In 1959 Barker Brothers was taken over by Alfred Clough, although production seems to have continued without any changes. The company was later sold to John Tams. Barker Brothers closed in 1981.

- ◆ Collectors now are particularly keen on the more contemporary patterns as typified by *Chianti*, which depicted stylised fruit surrounding a Spanish wine bottle decorated on the new *Manhattan* shape, c.1967.
- ◆ Look out for the hand-painted Art Deco wares especially those designed by John Guildford.

Further Reference
www.retroselect.com

29

Side plate, printed with Lavender Lady *pattern with a gold stamped border, diameter 9in (22.9cm), probably 1950s*

BARRATTS OF STAFFORDSHIRE LTD. / ROYAL STAFFORD TABLEWARE

Barratts is a relatively unknown pottery company despite its production of many popular lines during the '50s and '60s. In the early '90s Barratts took over Royal Stafford, later to be known as Royal Stafford Tableware, which is currently at the forefront of ceramic design.

Gater & Hall, established in Burslem in 1907, was renamed Barratts after its take over in 1943. The Chairman of the company was Mr. W.G. Barratt whilst Mr. Halsall, was appointed Managing Director in 1948. Over the previous thirty years the company had steadily been purchasing surrounding properties, these were then demolished to build a new factory. Following WWII the whole factory was modernised to increase capacity and to comply with new regulations for pottery manufacture. Many of the early wares from the new factory were rather traditional.

From the early '50s Barratts specialised in the manufacture of mid-quality general earthenware, sold under the name *Delphatic China*, a registered trade name deriving from the word delph, an old name for earthenware. During this period they produced affordable earthenware in carton packs selling to various catalogue companies including Great Universal Stores. This proved profitable: by the start of the '60s carton packs accounted for 50% of all orders. The popular printed *Blue Willow* and *Indian Tree* patterns sold for many years.

The early '60s saw sales increase over 30% with a production range of over 200 patterns. Though many of these patterns were printed border sprays, some under-glaze, banded and aerographed decoration techniques were also used. New patterns included *Arcadia* and *Symphony*, both decorated on the *Ribble* coupe shape, and the *Roslyn* pattern on the *Regal* fluted shape alongside a limited range of modern pastel patterns for contemporary tastes.

Earthenware dinner plate decorated with the Tanya *pattern, diameter 10in (25.4cm), 1970s*

Appointed as acting Managing Director in 1970, Tim Dyke steered the company towards a new image. The re-design of the carton packs in 1972 to include a cut away section to reveal the pattern enclosed were an instant success. In 1974 Barratts launched a new 18-piece box set by well-known freelance designer Jack Dadd; the *Revelation Collection* was available in a range of patterns including *Tapestry*, *Nottingham* and *Casanova*.

At this stage the company was sold to Great Universal Stores and was later purchased by a management team in 1986, who renamed the company Barratts of Staffs Ltd., however, soon going into receivership. The company was then bought by Queensway Securities, who brought in Norman Tempest as managing director. Eve Midwinter, who had gained a reputation for high-quality design whilst working at W.R. Midwinter Ltd., was drafted in to act as design consultant to develop new shapes and patterns in the hopes of taking the firm's image

and products more upmarket. Eve Midwinter found a set of old moulds dating from the '20s that she felt had potential and soon developed several shapes into a range called *Lincoln*, which was left undecorated to show the moulded border of fruit around the edges. This proved to be a best seller and is still sold in British Home Stores. This success prompted a whole new series of designs in the late '80s, including *Country Fayre*, *Ashford*, *Songbirds* and *Trellis* (on the *Regal* shape).

Angela Atkinson followed Eve Midwinter as

BARRATTS
Fine Tableware
ROYAL OVERHOUSE MANUFACTORY

Barratts backstamp used from 1988 onwards
© Royal Stafford

31

Selection of earthenware coffee and dinner wares from the Lincoln *range designed by Eve Midwinter for Barratts of Staffs. Ltd., c.1987*

design consultant in 1997 with the introduction in 1998 of designs such as *Daisy*, *Bluebell* and the highly popular *Gardener's Journal*.

In 1992 Barratts purchased a less well-known pottery firm Royal Stafford, which had gone into receivership. Royal Stafford, set up by Thomas Poole in Longton in 1840, produced a wide range of pottery goods including bone china sets decorated with typical patterns such as *Roses to Remember* on the *Trent* shape (from 1962). In 1993 the companies were amalgamated and became known as Royal Stafford Tableware from 1994. The new *Classique* shape, developed by Fred Hackney and Eve Midwinter, was used for a wide range of modern patterns including *Bordeaux* and *Geo Floral*, both designed by Julie Pople, one of several freelance designers employed by the company. The extensive range of well-designed and high-quality dinner services are very popular, many being exclusive to individual high-end stores such as Ralph Lauren.

Towards the end of the century, patterns such as *Fairfax*, *Newport* and *Sorbet* were typical.

In 2004 Norman Tempest, who bought the company following the retirement of Stanley S. Cohen OBE, met the legendary designer Eva Zeisel. She still had the original moulds to her *Tomorrow's Classic* (1952) and *Century* (1957) ranges originally produced by Hall China in the U.S.A. Royal Stafford used these moulds to produce a new range called *Classic Century*.

◆ Barratt's wares have yet to catch on with collectors, thereby remaining relatively inexpensive for even the more high-quality items.

Further Reference

Beckett, P., *A Victorian Pottery: The History of Royal Stafford and Gladstone China*. Peter Beckett, 2003

www.royalstafford.co.uk

Collection of Beswick horses including the Cantering Shire *(far right) designed by Arthur Gredington, launched in the mid '40s but produced in different colours over the years up to recent times*

JOHN BESWICK LTD.

James Wright Beswick founded his small pottery firm J.W. Beswick Ltd. in 1894. Initially he leased buildings but by about 1898 he had managed to acquire a small factory on Gold Street in Longton; he later moved the firm to the Britannia Works in Longton. In its early years, the company focused production on domestic and toilet wares decorated with transfer printed patterns alongside new shapes such as *Dresden* and *Leyden*.

On James' death in 1921, responsibility for running the factory passed to John Beswick. Not only did he discontinue some of the rather dated period-style wares, he also introduced an interesting range of modern wares, including vases decorated with many styles such exotic birds and Dutch scenes. It was noted in the trade press of 1928 that 80% of all Beswick production was now ornamental.

In the '30s Beswick launched many interesting novelty and embossed wares. One of the first of these ranges, *Gardena* (1931), included a teapot in the form of a large rose bud and a long celery dish in the form of a basket, lettuce wares, cucumber trays, beehive honey pots and dishes moulded to resemble pansies. The motifs were similar to those produced by Carlton Ware but were more expensive. The most popular of Beswick's lines at that time was *Cottage Wares*. Launched in 1934, the range featured items moulded in the shape of a thatched cottage, including teapots, preserve jars, and biscuit barrels; *Cottage Wares* remained in production

Two examples of Beswick fish designed by Arthur Gredington, Oceanic Bonito, *height 7½in (19cm), 1953-68, and* Trout, *6½in (16.5cm), 1945-75*

through to the '70s. Such success prompted similar ranges including *Sundial* from 1937.

Other novelty wares included a tea set (launched c.1931) comprising teapot, hot water jug and cream jug, all in the form of equilateral triangles, which fitted onto an irregular tray; an egg set of four eggcups on a tray with a duckling in the middle; and a brightly coloured Deco set called *Vortex* from about 1933. However, Beswick also continued to produce a number of standard lines such as *Tudor Times* and *A Bit of Old England* at the same time.

After the death of John Beswick, c.1936, a new management team, including John Ewart as Chairman and Gilbert Beswick as Managing Director, introduced new policies, shifting production from tableware to fancies. James Hayward, who had joined the company in 1926, was appointed Decorating Manager in 1934. To facilitate this change in direction, Arthur Gredington was brought

in as resident modeller in 1939. Beswick recruited several other modellers over the years with Jan Gramoska joining the company in the '50s.

Beswick is well known today for its range of high-quality animal models, in particular horses, which have been in production since the late '30s. These animal sculptures have not only given the company a very good reputation, they have also increased sales sharply.

Like many other companies during the late '30s, Beswick produced a set of 'flying duck' wall ornaments, these proved very popular and were available with either a matt or gloss glaze until the early '70s. Made of earthenware, the Beswick ducks were of a much higher quality than most of their competitors' ducks, which tended to be made of cheaper plaster that damaged easily. Lesser known Beswick flying birds included a pheasant, a seagull and a kingfisher, all from about 1939.

On a much smaller scale Beswick also introduced

Beatrix Potter figures and in 1947, under special licence from Walt Disney, some Disney characters such as *Donald Duck*, *Mickey Mouse*, and *Snow White and the Seven Dwarfs*. During the '60s the company launched its *Winnie the Pooh* range.

Following WWII, Beswick invited various artists to create new lines for them in contemporary styles. These included examples by Albert Hallam, who had joined the company in 1926 and had become head of the mould making department and a modeller. He developed a series of abstract shapes that were decorated with hand-painted designs, such as the stylised zebra pattern with coloured interiors, by Jim Hayward. Eric Owen, a freelance modeller, who had previously worked at Minton, also created several new ranges.

Of great interest to many Beswick collectors were the stylised animal figures created by Colin Melbourne: Series 1 ran from 1956 to 1962, and Series 2 (1962-66) included a bison, a horse, a fox and a peacock.

Popular tableware patterns of the '50s included the transfer printed *Circus*, *Mexican Madness* and *Ballet*. In 1969 Beswick was bought out by Royal Doulton. During the same year the company launched the new coffee set, *Zorba*, featuring a brown gloss glaze in line with other manufacturers. In 1994 the company enjoyed its centenary

- Beswick collectors have a wide variety of quality wares from which to choose: from flying ducks, to Deco face masks, from cottage-shaped teapots to '50s vases. Its figures of horses, however, are probably of greatest interest, and reach high prices at auction today.
- Collectors are particularly keen on the many interesting novelty and embossed wares that Beswick launched during the '30s, such as *Gardena*, the *Cottage Wares* and *Sundial*. Bear in mind that some of these wares were still being produced in the later part of the 20th century: just because it is a '30s design, does not mean it is necessarily an original '30s piece.
- Beswick's high-quality animal models are popular with collectors, in particular the work of Arthur Gredington. He produced a wide range of animals

but it was his detailed and authentic representation of horses, particular the famous Derby winning horse Bois Russell that he is most well known for. Collectors are particularly keen on horses with riders. Also popular are the stylised animal figures created by Colin Melbourne in the '50s.

- Following WWII, Beswick invited various artists to create new lines. These contemporary styles are highly sought after today on the collectors' market.

Further Reference

Baynton, V., *Beswick: A Catalogue*. UK International Ceramics Ltd., 1994

Callow, D., Callow, J., Sweet, M. and Sweet P., *The Charlton Standard Catalogue of Beswick Animals*. The Charlton Press, 1998

Jenkins, S., *Ceramics of the '50s and '60s: A Collectors Guide*. Miller's, 2001

www.collectingdoulton.com

www.retroselect.com

Novelty item, advertising Dulux paint, 1980s

Earthenware coffee pot decorated with a printed band, height 6⅞in (17.5cm), probably 1980s

BILTONS LTD.

Biltons is best known today for its wide selection of modern patterns on functional shapes. These competitively priced wares were sold in boxed sets during the '60s and '70s. The company began in 1901 when Joseph Tellwright purchased a small factory with two bottle ovens in Stoke; by 1912 the business was known as Biltons (1912) Ltd. As production grew a new tunnel oven was installed, with twenty people being employed by 1919. The factory produced a wide range of goods during the early part of the century including bulb bowls, flower holders, tea and coffee pots alongside *Jet*, *Rockingham* and *Samian* wares.

After WWI Biltons moved into the domestic earthenware market with the production of dinner, coffee and tea wares, alongside a small selection of nursery wares and some ornaments such as figures and 'grotesques'. Glazed fireplace tiles were introduced in the mid '30s; these proved such a commercial success that by the '60s they represented 50% of production. Complete fireplaces were also produced.

The factory was closed c.1941 until the end of WWII under the Government Concentration Scheme. After the war Biltons concentrated on the mass market, introducing cheaper ways of decoration including rubber-stamping. Woolworth's became an important customer, chiefly buying toy sets and, according to records, accounting for 40% of Biltons' sales. By the early 1960s, Biltons rationalised production to be more competitive in an ever-dwindling market. It had emerged that of the 160 items produced, 40 items represented 90% of the total sales; Biltons accordingly reduced the number of shapes it produced and halted production of tiles, a couple of years later it stopped producing nursery wares.

Biltons concentrated its whole business on the popular 'no frills' carry-home packs, selling to many countries abroad as well as hypermarkets and department stores. Improvements in transfer printed patterns were introduced and a once-fired oven was installed in 1964, thus enabling Biltons to sell good design to the mass market. Striking, modern patterns, which stood out from the other manu-facturers' wares, were decorated on a range of practical shapes. These were sold in different combinations such as a twelve-piece tea set or a thirty-piece dinner set. These early patterns were rubber-stamped onto the ware and then hand coloured, eventually two-colour rubber-stamping was introduced. During the same year Jim Parker was appointed to the position of Sales Director. John Blackhurst, the decorating manager, designed several patterns such as *Red Rose*, *Samoa* and *Summer Glory*, which were typical of the period. In 1965 the company launched the *Florentine* pattern available in two colourways alongside *Gold Rose*. One notable pattern was *Moonfleur*; launched in 1969, it was available in both blue and yellow and was advertised, alongside other patterns, in full-colour advertisements in the trade press.

The most important, and the most successful, design of the period was *Stonehaven*; introduced in 1973, it was created in response to the fashion for stoneware already successfully produced by manufacturers such as Denby. *Stonehaven* soon represented 30-40% of the total production, and by 1979 over 27 million pieces had been sold, prompting the company to introduce a range of co-ordinates such as saucepans, trays, glassware and household linen. Other best-selling patterns of the '70s included *Normandy*, *Blue Sierra*, *Basket Weave* and *Orleans*. Several patterns were created by Craig Sumner who, with Bob Rowlands, went on to establish an independent company called S.R. Design Associates, which created all the design work for Biltons.

During the 1980s Biltons started using a screen-printing technique that was ideal for the production of mugs, which were very much in demand during this period. Patterns such as *Lotus Blossoms*,

Earthenware plate decorated with a printed nursery-style pattern, diameter 7½in (19cm), 1980s

Priscilla, *Spring Bouquet* and *Rose Garden* were typical, with the latter two patterns also being used on a range of co-ordinated accessories. At about the same time the company introduced Victorian-style bone china tea wares, decorated with traditional patterns such as *Winchester* and *Glamis Rose*; these were possibly intended for the export market.

Following heavy financial losses during the early part of the '80s, Biltons was sold to the Coloroll Group in 1986, but continued to trade under its own name. Coloroll, known for home furnishings carpets and wallpapers, also purchased Denby pottery. Despite the take over, new patterns, using a range of pastel colours, such as *Mosaic*, *Saffron* and *Easter Bonnet*, were introduced. In 1990 Coloroll became part of the Staffordshire Tableware Group Ltd. following management buyout. Four years later the Group was put up for sale and, in 1998, it was puchased by the Dubelle Foundation.

♦ Biltons is not currently greatly sought after and, therefore, still inexpensive. Without a doubt some of the patterns from the late '60s and '70s, such as *Stonehaven*, will become collectables in the future.

Earthenware trio decorated with a hand-painted stylised floral design, possibly designed by Freda Beardmore, diameter 6½in (16.5cm), 1930s

E. BRAIN & CO.

The firm of E. Brain & Co. may not be well known today but, through the best part of the 20th century, it was associated with good taste and modernity. The company was formed in 1855 and based at the Foley Works in Fenton in Stoke-on-Trent, previously used by Robinson & Son Ltd. When the founder died, in 1910, his son William Henry Brain took over the business. He travelled to Australia and New Zealand to seek new business. William's son came into the business just before WWI.

The pottery established its reputation among the middle and upper classes for producing items of good taste with its bone china wares, exemplified by the most popular patterns *Checker Border*, *Torch* and *Tudor Green Edge*. During the '20s its products were often described in the trade press as being durable,

attractive with a simplicity and restraint. The company also understood the principles of modern design, using functional shapes and up-to-date patterns such as *Swansea*, which was introduced in 1922. In the same year the company opened a new showroom in Hatton Gardens, London.

E. Brain responded quickly to the fashion for brightly coloured patterns that came to the forefront during the late '20s. In 1928 it introduced two patterns, *Cubist Sunflower* and *Cubist Landscape*, both inspired by the Art Deco movement. The latter, illustrated in the trade press, featured a stylised border rather than an overall decoration and was applied to *Cube* teapots and other tea ware shapes. Interestingly it was also used to decorate a more traditional shape. A year later, further acknowledgments of the Art Deco style were evident in two new patterns, one featuring a stylised house and the other a tree landscape with clouds, a motif successfully used by Clarice Cliff at the same time.

E. Brain is better known by collectors today for its modernist patterns and, in particular, for its association with A.J. Wilkinson Ltd. during the mid '30s. This new development began c.1930 when the company introduced the *Pallas* shape, which had more in common with the modern European styles at the time rather than the usual Staffordshire view. The *Mayfair* range, launched in 1932, comprised twelve patterns featuring various graduated black lines complemented by a brightly-coloured circle, square or triangle; unusually this was decorated on white bone china rather than inexpensive earthenware. At about the same time, William Brain formed a close association with the designer Freda Beardmore, who worked as the company designer creating many hand-painted floral and stylised patterns and shapes. Her *Savoy* shape from 1932, decorated with modern stylised patterns, was typical. In 1932 Thomas Acland Fennemore was appointed Managing Director. As well as developing new patterns and shapes he invited a number of designers, including Milner Gray, to design for the company.

During the early '30s the many debates on uniting art and industry crystallised in a special ceramics project led by Thomas Acland Fennemore. A number of British fine artists were invited to submit pattern designs with the intention that the resulting examples would be shown in an exhibition. A.J. Wilkinson Ltd provided the earthenware *Bonjour* range, designed by Clarice Cliff, whilst Foley provided bone china wares to be decorated with the designs. The list of artists included Vanessa Bell, Duncan Grant, Graham Sutherland, Paul Nash, Ben Nicholson and Dame Laura Knight amongst others. In 1934 the display was mounted at Harrods in London. Many critics gave the display bad reviews and the project was a flop, probably because the artists had little experience of industrial design and the special sets would have been too costly to produce commercially.

Following WWII, the company continued to invest in contemporary design, recruiting new designers such as Hazel Thumpson, Peter Cave and Maureen Tanner. From 1956, Tanner produced

Example of The Gay Nineties *series designed by Maureen Tanner, height 5in (12.7cm), 1956*

several patterns depicting comical Victorian period characters by the seaside for a series of fancies called the *Gay Nineties*; a facsimile of the designer's signature was included on the backstamp. These are much sought after by collectors today.

In a period of fierce competition, E. Brain merged with Coalport China Ltd. in 1958, but continued to trade as E. Brain & Co. until 1963. In 1967 the company was taken over by Josiah Wedgwood and Sons Ltd. It closed in 1992.

♦ Look out for the small range of fancies, such as dishes, from the late '50s decorated with whimsical images by Maureen Tanner.

Further Reference

Spours, J., *Art Deco Tableware*. Ward Lock. 1988

www.retroselect.com

Standard backstamp for E Brain & Co.

Earthenware dinner plates decorated with (from left to right), Black Toast and Marmalade *(now called* Toast and Marmalade*),* Olives, *and* Sweet Pea

BRIDGEWATER

Though the Emma Bridgewater pottery company started as a very small concern in 1985, within a mere six years it had gained a first-rate reputation for good design and practicality; it is still well respected by the British pottery industry today.

Emma Bridgewater had no formal training in design or business management, but she had strong ideas. Her intention was to make pottery for the farmhouse kitchen using traditional methods of production rather than expensive machinery. Underpinning all the patterns and shapes was her passion for the family and English country life. She used the sponge form of decoration that had been used by the smaller factories from the late eighteenth century well into the 20th century. It was a simple and effective way of decorating plain ware without needing to buy expensive lithographic sheets that were not always of the best quality.

By 1985, more women were going out to work, which in turn had led to a change in family dining habits – casual dining was becoming more popular and acceptable; Bridgewater was at the forefront of this. Bridgewater used the traditional sponge decoration with a modern twist to great visual affect, which proved very popular amongst the British customer who wanted something a little different. Furthermore, the earthenware shapes, all designed by Emma Bridgewater herself, were simple and practical. As demand increased, new shapes and combinations were introduced to cater for practically all needs including tea sets, dinnerware, breakfast sets, mugs, nursery wares, a miniature doll's tea set and even, by popular demand, a decorated dog bowl.

One of the most popular pattern ranges was *Black Toast and Marmalade*, which, in the late '90s, became available in black or blue, and later in *Cambridge Blue*. Another popular line, *Kitchen Dresser*, encompassing six patterns including *Vine*, *Olives*, *Chintz* and *Farmyard*, was launched c.1989. The patterns were decorated on 22 shapes including dinnerware, jugs and two sizes of candlesticks. Other popular patterns were *Blue Hens* and *Sweet Pea*. New patterns were added to the range over the years.

The *Nursery Rhyme* range proved very popular, as did the bedroom and bathroom sets. Patterns for the latter included *Beach*, which depicted various shell motifs available in black or the new colourway of blue and green.

By the early '90s business was brisk and Bridgewater ranges were available in the leading British stores. New sponge ware patterns included *Circles*, *Bird and Flower*, and *Border and Flower*. The new *Waterfield* range, with the *Pink Plum* and *Purple Plum* designs, were entirely hand-painted.

Mugs were an important part of the business. With the new casual approach to living, mugs had come into their own – for day-to-day use at home and in the office they all but replaced the cup, they had even become suitable to give as presents. Bridgewater's most popular range of mugs were decorated with the *Fig* pattern and included the words, "FOR A FRIEND" or "THANK YOU". Further patterns included *Frogs*, *Dinosaurs*, *Planes* and *Diggers* whilst several patterns were only available on mugs.

In 1993 a wide range of new patterns was launched that included *Animals Parade*, a border of marching animals in printed black, and *Knives & Forks*. Two contrasting patterns, both hand-painted, were the striking *Black Salmon* and *Hawthorn*, a design reminiscent of early Wedgwood, for tea and dinnerware, which included a gravy boat – a new addition to the company's range of shapes.

In the mid '90s the company launched a range of fabric items manufactured under licence by Avlacco, later purchased by Ulster Weavers. Napkins, table-cloths and place mats were printed with the *Knives & Forks*, *Spongeware Stripe* and *Love* patterns; customers could also buy entire rolls of the printed heavy unbleached cotton. Some items were only available decorated with the *Toast and Marmalade* pattern, which also decorated *Hot Pot,* the new Cookware range made by Ulster Ceramics including a meat plate, round baking dish and casserole.

In 1996, due to the increase of business, the company moved to new premises at the Eastwood Works in Hanley, previously owned by Johnson Brothers since 1958. Shops in Fulham and London were also established.

During the latter part of the 20th century the company extended its range with new patterns and combinations including *Blackberry*, *Wild Strawberry*, *Working Elephants* and *Blue Stars*, the latter proving very popular. As the century came to a close the company launched new hand-painted patterns such as *Willow* and *Vetch* in contrast to the more formal *Egg and Dart* pattern available in either orange or blue.

The business has enjoyed continued success and in the first years of the 21st century new patterns such as *Love & Kisses* and *Polka Dots* have proved popular. Many of the new patterns are decorated with in-glaze litho prints, some designed by the founder's husband Matthew Rice.

◆ Recently the distinguished painter Mary Fedden RA was approached to design for the company. The resultant pattern, *Hellebore*, is without doubt a collectable of the future.

Further Reference
www.emmabridgewater.co.uk

Two earthenware mugs decorated with the Dog pattern introduced in 2000

Earthenware plate, decorated with the Viscount *pattern, printed with hand-painted decoration, designed by Kathie Winkle, diameter 7⅝in (19.4cm), c.1963*

JAMES BROADHURST AND SONS LTD
Churchill Group

James Broadhurst and Sons Ltd., was established in 1847. By 1854 the company had settled at the Crown Works in Longton and was manufacturing earthenware tea, dinner and general tableware at the lower end of the scale. By 1870 the company had moved again to the Portland Pottery in Fenton. The Managing Director of the firm, Peter Roper, who had joined the firm in 1928, gained experience by working in every department at the works. His two sons followed him into the business.

Broadhurst was well known for its practical earthenware lines including affordable printed dinner sets, tea sets, dishes pudding bowls, sets of jugs and toilet wares. Typical patterns included *Blue Willow* and a selection of border designs.

After WWII Broadhurst introduced a diverse range of contemporary patterns decorated by rubber-stamping by hand with emphasis on simple decoration. Margaret Turner was responsible for designing many of these patterns as was Reg Chilton, who had joined the company in 1952. Contemporary designs for the mid '50s included the popular *Wheat Rose*, *Tyne*, *Petula* and *Revel*. The *Harlem* pattern, created from open stock rubber stamps, was introduced following the success of patterns such as *Zambesi* by Midwinter. Although stylistically similar to Midwinter, the wares of Broadhurst were far cruder and cheaper. Broadhurst wares featured a simple mark with the words, "Broadhurst, Staffordshire England".

The '60s and early '70s were probably the most important period of the company's history, with Kathie Winkle coming to the forefront of its design.

Earthenware Kofti *pot, decorated with the* Rushtone *pattern, height 6⅛ in (15.5cm), c.1967*

Having started at Broadhurst as a decorator, she moved to design c.1958. Some of her first designs were similar to those previously issued by the company and collectors should be aware that patterns from the early '60s including *Calypso* (an earlier version by Reg Chilton), *Matador* and *Shanghai* were not by her. The majority of her patterns, including *Palma Nova*, *Safari* and *Viscount*, were decorated on the *Rim* shape and, later, the *Riviera* shape. The *Viscount* design was a

best seller throughout the '60s and '70s, prompting the company to incorporate Kathie Winkle's name into the backstamp from 1964.

As early as 1960 the firm initiated selling presentation packs direct to supermarkets and made profitable links with Littlewoods, Great Universal Stores and Grattan that lasted for several years. At the same time a large export market was developing through overseas agents to countries such as Australia and Canada. In 1965 Broadhurst

Earthenware cup, saucer, side plate and dinner plate decorated with the Compass *pattern, diameter 9½ in (24.1cm), 1968*

purchased hotel ware manufacturer Sampson Bridgwood and Sons Ltd., based at the Anchor Works in Longton. Broadhurst also developed its packaged goods range with the addition of the new *Kofti* pot, a combination of tea and coffee pot, designed by Kathie Winkle. The *Koftie* pot was ideal for the wide range of starter and combination sets decorated with patterns such as *Moselle*, *Acapulco*, *Calypso* and *Rushtone*. *Rushtone*, designed by Reg Chilton, was the most popular pattern produced by the company and 10 years later the 50 millionth piece had been fired!

During the early '70s Broadhurst and Sons maintained a stronghold on the market by producing a range of artistic and traditional designs; this was typified by the *Mexico* pattern, created to link in with the Olympic Games of 1970. Other sought after patterns by collectors include *Barbados*, *Roulette* and *Compass*. A studio range, *Sandstone*, which included patterns such as *Snowdon*, *Moorland* and *Country Lane*, was launched in about 1973.

In response to the rapid changes in taste, the company introduced *English Scenes* and *Constable Prints* based on the work of the famous artist John Constable, using new superior printing methods from 1976. Following Kathie Winkle's retirement, the company hired the John Russell Studio to develop patterns based on Winkle's style with the resultant designs including *Agincourt*, *Tashkent* and *Alicante* – all, incidentally, marked with the Kathie Winkle backstamp. In 1982 the company set up its own in-house design department to co-ordinate all of the group's design work.

In 1984 the combination of James Broadhurst, Sampson Bridgwood and Wessex Ceramics merged together under the name Churchill Group, registered as such in 1992, and based in Tunstall. The

Standard company backstamp, 1960s

Collection of earthenwares decorated with the printed Herat *pattern designed by Jeff Banks, c.1992*

company soon became one of the largest pottery companies in Britain.

During the same year the company commissioned the well-known fashion designer Jeff Banks to produce a range of patterns. Inspired by his global travels, these were sold under the brand name *Ports of Call*. The simple shapes and the subtle designs were an immediate success, in particular *Herat* and *Prague*.

- The main area of interest for collectors of Broadhurst today is the post-WWII period. The contemporary patterns, mostly by Margaret Turner or Reg Chilton, were decorated by rubber-stamping by hand.
- Recently there has been a demand for patterns designed by Kathie Winkle in the '60s and early '70s. Look out for the tea and coffee pots that are fairly rare but still affordable. Collectors should note that the company continued to use Winkle's name on later patterns that she did not actually design.

Further Reference

Casey. A., *Twentieth Century Ceramic Designers in Britain*. Antique Collectors' Club, 2001

Hampson, R., *Churchill China: Great British Potters since 1795*. University of Keele, 1994

Leith, P., *The Designs of Kathie Winkle*. Richard Dennis, 1999

BURGESS & LEIGH, LTD., Middleport Pottery, BURSLEM.

"Burleigh" Art Ware.

Illustration from the Burgess and Leigh Ltd. catalogue c.1927, showing a range of patterns including 3973, 4001, 4002 and 4016, which were designed by Charlotte Rhead

BURGESS AND LEIGH

Established by Frederick Rathbone Burgess and William Leigh in 1862, Burgess, Leigh and Co. was based at the Central Pottery in Stoke-on-Trent; in 1868 it moved to the Hill Pottery in Burslem. It was renamed Burgess and Leigh in 1877. By 1889 the business was expanding, and production was moved into a new, larger, modern factory in Middleport.

The company concentrated on producing functional wares such as earthenware dinner and tea sets, kitchen and toilet wares. By the end of the 19th century over 50% of the factory's output was dedicated to the production of toilet wares.

From the start of the 20th century the company enjoyed increased business partly due to the growing export market and a contract with Woolworth in America. The person responsible for design matters was known as 'Designer Leigh' (no

relation to William Leigh), who worked closely with the team of engravers, decorators and freelance designers. In 1909 a range of Art Nouveau patterns, such as *Florette* and *Tulipe*, were launched. A few years later, in total contrast to these artistic productions, Burgess and Leigh launched and found a ready market for a series of wares called *Ye Ballades of Olde Englande*, which was available in various shapes including a loving cup, flowers pots and a puzzle jug, the decoration depicted scenes that were individually named such as *Sally in Our Alley*,

From about 1906 the company traded under the name Burleigh, a contraction of the names of the two founders. In 1912 Richard Burgess, Frederick Burgess' son, died, and the Leigh family took on the whole business. In 1919 the firm became a limited company; William Leigh's son Edmund Leigh, who had joined the company in 1868, became a director alongside his three sons.

Burgess and Leigh had terrific success with the blue and white printed wares such as *Blue Willow*, which had already been in production for a number of years. During the mid '20s it launched a similar line, *Dillywn Willow*, which was decorated on an assortment of wares including the *Cranborne* shape teapot and *London* shape cheese dish.

Charlotte Rhead joined the company in 1926, and created several new patterns using the tube-line decorative style, many on shapes designed by the modeller Charles Wilkes, who had joined the company in 1889. Rhead's patterns used stylised flowers and fruit for inspiration with many detailed patterns created specifically for earthenware plaques, whilst simpler designs were used for ornamental and domestic wares. A popular pattern at the time was *Florentine*. *Arabesque*, painted in black, red and yellow, nodded to the Art Deco style fashionable during the period. Simple patterns such as *Garland* and *Sunshine* were designed for the less expensive lines such as suite wares and coffee sets.

Earthenware egg set decorated with the Sunshine *pattern, designed by Charlotte Rhead, c.1928-29.*

Whilst these are less well known today they are popular with collectors.

Harold Bennett, who had joined the company in 1929, also produced a number of tube-lined patterns. However, his style was noticeably different from Rhead's, being much less intricate and more stylised; therefore these should not pose any problems of identification for collectors.

Another important figure at the company, Ernest Bailey, joined in 1927. He was responsible for a wide range of moulded wares such as *The Runaway Marriage* and *The Stocks*, but his great success was the series of Art Deco vases during the '30s. Some of the first included *Squirrel* and *Parrot*, both featuring the subject moulded as the handle. Bailey also used the human figure for three designs: *Pied Piper*, *Dick Turpin* and *Guardsman*. His *Cricketer* jug was based on the popular Australian sportsman Don Bradman. New lines of decorative jugs were launched from 1936, including less intricate jugs decorated with

Example of the Cricketer *jug designed by Ernest Bailey, height 8in (20.3cm), c.1935*

simple patterns on shapes such as *Oxford* and *Cambridge* alongside Art Deco-style vases such as *Meridian*, *Luxor* and *Zenith*. These bore more than a passing resemblance to productions by Myott.

During the early '30s several practical and modern earthenware tea and dinnerware ranges were introduced decorated with simple hand-painted patterns such as *Tranquil*, *Golden Days*, *Blue Bell* and *Fragrance*, these proved very popular. The most successful were *Dawn* and *Pan*, the latter designed by Harold Bennett, both decorated on the *Zenith* shape.

Following WWII the company introduced a range of popular contemporary patterns many decorated on the new *Viscount* shape designed by Bailey. One of the best-known patterns of this period was designed by Bennett, *Fantasia* depicted stylised pottery printed on the flat ware. During the '60s design matters came under the direction of David Copeland, who joined the company in 1963. His *Cordon Bleu* pattern, from

1964, was very popular and he went on to create other successful patterns such as the striking *Orbit* pattern, decorated on his *Anglia* shape range, which embraced the fashions of the late '60s. The *Anglia* shape was also used for a wide selection of patterns such as *Coniston* and *Castile*.

In 1968 the company produced *Calico*, a blue and white printed pattern. A commercial success, *Calico* is still in production today, as is *Chinese Peacock* which has been in production since 1913.

The success of *Calico* prompted many similar patterns, often designed for specific stores such as Laura Ashley and Habitat. Typical patterns of the '90s included *Homefarm* and *Pictorial Britain* designed by Chris Nunn. Despite these successes the company endured several set backs and, in 1999, faced closure. However, the company was saved by Rosemary and Will Dorling who renamed it Burgess Dorling and Leigh.

Examples of the Dawn *pattern applied to Art Deco styled wares, 1960s*

- Blue and white printed ware *Dillywn Willow*, from the mid '20s, is sought after by collectors today as are the various colour variations issued over the subsequent years. Also popular is *Calico*, despite still being in production.
- Less well-known patterns such as *Garland* and *Sunshine*, from the '20s, are worth keeping an eye out for.
- *Arabesque*, painted in black, red and yellow, in Art Deco style and earthenware tea and dinner ranges *Dawn* and *Pan* from the '30s are currently popular with collectors.
- The Art Deco wares by Burleigh such as Ernest Bailey's moulded jugs, in particular the *Guardsman*, reach high prices at auction today. Collectors should note, however, that several moulded jugs, including *Rock Garden* from 1933, were in fact designed by Charles Wilkes.
- Art Deco vases from the '30s, such as *Meridian*,

Luxor and *Zenith*, are worth looking out for, but do remember that these bear more than a passing resemblance to products by Myott.
- Collectors should note that *Fantasia*, designed by Bennett in 1959, was later reproduced in the '90s for the Manchester City Art Gallery.

Further Reference
McKeown, J., *Burleigh, A Story of a Pottery*. Richard Dennis, 2003

www.burleigh.co.uk

Backstamp for the Calico *range*

CARLTON WARE LTD.

The earthenware company Wiltshaw and Robinson was founded in 1890 by James Frederick Wiltshaw and two brothers J. A. and W. H. Robinson at the Carlton Works. In 1911 Wiltshaw became sole proprietor and, on his death in 1918, his son F.C. (Cuthbert) Wiltshaw took over, running the company for the next forty-eight years.

Wiltshaw and Robinson's first products were similar to other manufacturers of the time: Blush Ware, white ware featuring floral decoration with gilding on ornate shapes and a series of blue transfer printed wares. As the company progressed, more patterns were introduced, such as floral designs decorated on a black background, which included the Japanese-inspired *Cloisonné Ware*. In 1928 the company purchased the bone china manufacturers Birks, Rawlins & Co., enabling them to introduce fine tea and coffee wares.

Like many of the pottery companies of the period Wiltshaw and Robinson developed new glazes for its luxury ranges, including a series of plain lustres from the early '20s. Their in-house designer Horace Wain used his great interest in the Orient to add chinoiserie patterns such as *Barge*, *Mikado* and *New Mikado*. In the latter years of the decade, inspired by Howard Carter's discovery, the *Tutankhamun* range was introduced. Various shapes were offered, including vases, plates and ginger jars. The *Armand* and *Chinaland* patterns were reminiscent of the design ranges *Ordinary Lustre* and *Fairyland Lustre* by Daisy Makeig-Jones for Josiah Wedgwood and Sons Ltd.

Tea set decorated with the Strawberry Tree pattern (No.4769), c.1930

Collection of embossed wares from the '20s and '30s

Today the company is best known for its dazzling and beautifully executed high-gloss, ornamental lustre patterns such as *Paradise Bird*, *Forest Tree*, and even *Chinese Bird* and *Cloud,* which were introduced during '20s and '30s, some of which were designed by Violet Elmer. The range of lustres, often available in various background colours, was not confined to decorative vases but also used on coffee wares, some on the *Melon* shape, the *Tree and Swallow* pattern being a good example. Clearly influenced by the Art Deco movement, patterns such as *Egyptian Fan*, *Bell*, *Scimitar* and *Fan* were introduced. From 1929 the company produced a series known as *Handcraft* wares with simple decoration on both matt and high glazes, and also an oven-to-tableware range decorated with silver wavy lines, which was in production until 1942.

Embossed ware, one of the company's most popular ranges, was introduced in the '20s. Two of the early patterns were *Oak* and *Rock Garden*. The more recognisable fruit and floral embossed range, known as *Salad Ware*, followed shortly after with dishes, toast racks, preserves pots, jugs and tea ware featuring moulded flowers or fruits (*Foxglove*, *Flower and Basket*, *Fruit Basket*, *Buttercup*, *Apple Blossom*, *Anemone*, *Cherries* and *Wild Rose*); some of these continued to sell well into the post-war era, with some new designs such as *Poppy*, *Poppy & Daisy* being introduced after the war.

Following WWII the factory was rationalised and new machinery installed to increase production in a competitive market. To keep up with changing tastes, several new lines were introduced and fresh lustre patterns, such as the striking *Mallards*, *Dragon Fly*, *Waterlily* and *Eastern Splendour* designs, were developed. The *Rouge Royal* range was also introduced in the post-war period. Through the '50s the company continued to build on its

Earthenware lidded preserve pot and stand, Modern *shape, decorated with lustre and gold, 1930s*

reputation for high-quality products, with demand in countries as far away as Australia, New Zealand, Canada and Norway.

In about 1957 the company was renamed Carlton Ware Ltd. A year later it launched a new range, *Windswept*, decorated on a free form shape called *Edinburgh* and produced in three sets of twin-tone colours: matt brown and cream, glossy pale green and bottle green, and dusky pink and pale blue. New versions of the *Salad Ware* range were launched including *Langouste* featuring lobsters as well as the floral *Magnolia* and *Convolvulus*.

Although not classed as *Salad Ware*, the new *Pinstripe* pattern was offered in shapes moulded as a leaf. Items offered in rust, green or cream ground included tea sets, television trays (an asymetrical saucer/ plate with the recess for the cup to one side leaving a space large enough to hold snacks), dishes and other small items.

From the '60s Carlton Ware also manufactured a popular range of Guinness advertising items such as

the Toucan lamp base, tableware, and giftware sets.

In 1966 the company was taken over by Arthur Wood and Sons Ltd. Rather than being a negative change it proved to be a period of artistic innovation, particularly following the appointment of Anthony F. Wood as Managing Director and Angela Fox as one of the in-house designers. The resultant products included Quartet dishes, cigarette lighters and other smokers' sundries available either in blue or orange raised enamel on a gold print and matt cream background or white raised enamel and gold on matt black. Martin Hunt designed a series of items for the younger generation such as a television tray, coffee mug, and three-way dish. Further fancies included dishes in the form of stylised birds, nursery wares, and the new *Persian* shape coffee ware.

In 1972 Carlton Ware introduced the *Walking Ware* novelty range designed by Roger Michell and Danka Napiorkowska, which proved extremely popular and continued in production until the factory closed.

Teapot decorated with the printed Windswept *pattern on the* Edinburgh *shape, length (spout to handle) 8in (20.3cm), 1959*

Carlton Ware was purchased in 1987 by County Potteries; production ceased in 1989. Between 1989 and 1997 the Carlton name was the property of John McCluskey, owner of Grosvenor Ceramics. McCluskey had some success re-issuing a few of the Carlton lustre items and novelty teapots from 1992 to 1994. After a dormant period, the Carlton Ware name was acquired in 1997 by the publisher Frank Salmon, along with the remaining moulds. Salmon initiated a new era of Carlton, at first concentrating production mainly, though not exclusively, on figures, later introducing a new range of gollies and tea ware.

- Carlton Ware is well-known today for its high-gloss lustre patterns introduced in the '20s and '30s. A particularly striking example of this is the Art Deco-style *Jazz* pattern, featuring stylised lightning strikes on either a mottled orange lustre, blue or red ground. Currently the most sought after designs are those featuring the *Red Devil*.
- Another popular and more affordable area for collectors today is the range of *Salad* wares that were produced from the late '20s to well after WWII. *Apple Blossom* and *Foxglove* were longest in production and are popular on today's collecting market; *Cherries* was only in production for a short period and is therefore less well-known.
- Look out for Carlton Ware Guinness advertising items such as the *Toucan* lamp base, tableware, and giftware sets. Be careful though – given the popularity of these items it is not surprising that there are many fakes on the market.
- *Walking Ware*, designed by Roger Michell and Danka Napiorkowska in 1972, continued in production for many years. and is now sought after by collectors – but, again, watch out for reproductions.

Further Reference

Serpell, D., *The Carlton Ware Collectors' Handbook*. Francis Joseph Publications, 2003

www.carltonware.co.uk

www.carltonwareworldwide.com

One of the better-known standard back-stamps for Carlton Ware

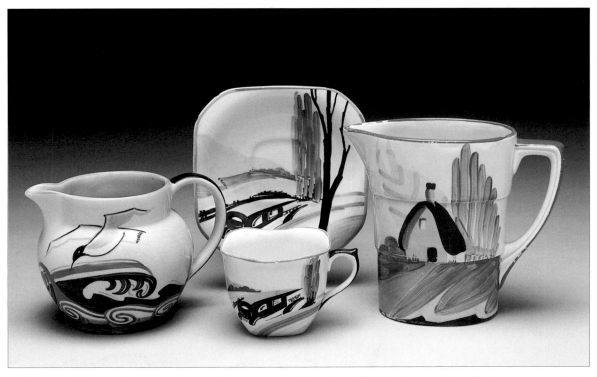

Collection of hand-painted early Susie Cooper wares all dated to 1931-32. Left to right: Earthenware Dutch jug decorated with The Seagull *pattern; cube-shaped cup and saucer decorated with the* Panorama *pattern; stepped jug decorated with* The Homestead *pattern, height 5½in (14cm)*

SUSIE COOPER LTD.

The small pottery firm Susie Cooper Pottery Ltd. was established in 1929 by Susie Cooper with the backing of her family and her brother-in-law. Initially based at the George Street Pottery, after moving to the Chelsea Works in Burslem, it soon built a reputation for good modern design at a reasonable price and, despite the international financial depression, the company blossomed during the early '30s. Sadly little information is available on the items from that short-lived period, although they can be identified by the backstamp, 'A SUSIE COOPER PRODUCTION TUNSTALL.'

Susie Cooper had left A.E. Gray and Co. Ltd. in 1929 having become increasingly frustrated with the fact that blank wares were being bought in from other factories. She was unhappy working with different shapes that, having been bought from different suppliers, often didn't match.

By April 1930 Susie Cooper Pottery Ltd. had taken its first order from the Nottingham store Griffin and Spalding. A year later Harry Wood of Wood and Sons Ltd. offered her the empty Crown Pottery, which had been used by Charlotte Rhead during the '20s. Significantly, Wood also offered to produce shapes based on her designs thus providing the breakthrough she needed to be in complete control of both pattern and shape. With the move came a new backstamp featuring a leaping deer motif.

Her most important shape, *Kestrel*, was unveiled in 1932; both practical and functional, it could take all manner of decoration. The following year the range was expanded to include a tureen, the lid from which could cleverly also be used as a separate serving dish. Her consideration for the practicalities

Collection of earthenware shapes, including the less well-known Curlew *tureen, decorated with* Wedding Ring *pattern from about 1933-34, height of tureen 6⅞ in (17.5cm)*

of shapes and not just decoration gave her a lead over other manufacturers. However, *Curlew* shape, launched in 1933, was not in production for long as it did not give the designer the same flexibility as her other shapes.

A series of studio wares, both hand thrown and moulded, was produced during this period, incised with stylized animals such as squirrels as well as abstract motifs. Alongside this came a limited range of face masks, in 1933, and figural table centres including a leaping deer (reissued by Wedgwood in 2002) and *Angel Fish*, both from the late '30s.

Her new banded decorations, using a subtle combination of colours, soon became known as *Wedding Ring* and proved very popular. Similarly simple patterns included *Polka Dot* and *Exclamation Mark*. As hand-painted decoration started to prove too expensive, her pioneering

approach to transfer-printed designs put Susie Cooper at the forefront of the international market. Insisting on maintaining the highest quality, she unusually submitted her own artwork to the manufacturers of lithographic sheets. *Dresden Spray*, a printed centre motif with a shaded band,

The 'Leaping Deer' mark used 1932 to the mid '50s

Rare bone china trio decorated with the lion and unicorn pattern for the Royal Society of Arts, diameter of plate 6⁵⁄₁₆ in (16cm), 1950

was an instant hit with the buying public; *Nosegay, Swansea Spray, April, Cactus* and *Patricia Rose* followed. From about 1936, she also used this method for a series of nursery ware patterns featuring ducks, pigs and hens and, for the older customer, *Cowboy, Skier* and *Golfer*. New shapes including *Falcon* and *Spiral*, from 1937 and 1938 respectively, were popular, especially in the U.S.A. and Canada.

Following WWII, the factory returned to hand-painted decoration as the stock of lithograph sheets had been damaged. A range of patterns, such as *Tree of Life* and *Chinese Fern*, many shown at the Britain Can Make It exhibition in London in 1946, were exported during this period and only seconds were allowed on the British market.

Rare bone china vase aerographed with sgraffito decoration of stylised leaves, height 9½in. (22.8cm), c.1956

Earthenware Kestrel-shaped teapot, height 4¾in (12 cm), and jug decorated with variations of the Patricia Rose *pattern with a cup and saucer decorated with a stylised floral printed pattern, c.1952-53*

At this point Susie Cooper Ltd. moved into the bone china market purchasing Jason China, based in Longton in 1950. Within months she had received her first, and important, commission: a set of sixty cups and saucers for a reception to be held in honour of Princess Elizabeth in 1950 by the Royal Society of Arts. She used the topical lion and the unicorn theme, later also used for the Festival of Britain, to maximum effect. The same motifs were used for a set of plates for the Royal Faculty at the Festival of Britain.

For the commercial bone china patterns simple floral motifs, ferns, and scrolls and spot patterns decorated the new *Quail* shape, which encompassed tea, coffee, dinnerware and some fancies, all sporting a new backstamp including the words 'BONE CHINA'. Patterns such as *Gardenia*, *Clematis*, *Raised*, *Wild Strawberry*, and *Parrot Tulip* were bestsellers. As demand for bone china patterns increased, earthenware was eventually withdrawn.

In 1958 the company merged with Tuscan Holdings Group Ltd. Towards the late '50s Susie Cooper introduced the *Can* shape, which was decorated with a selection of popular patterns such as *Katina*, *Venetia* and *Assyrian Motif*. One of the most outstanding patterns of the decade was *Black Fruits*, featuring harlequin interiors to the cups

In March 1966 Josiah Wedgwood and Sons took over both Tuscan and Susie Cooper Ltd. Artistically there was no change in her production, in fact Wedgwood continued to manufacture her most popular patterns. In line with current fashions she produced patterns such as *Carnaby Daisy*, *Nebula*, *Harlequinade* and *Pennant*.

During the '70s Susie Cooper produced one of her most outstanding patterns, *Cornpoppy*. In 1977 she brought out a series of silver lustre patterns for the Silver Jubilee. Produced in a limited edition of 2,000, this was one of the best-selling commemorative wares for the Wedgwood firm. Wedgwood closed

Bone china coffee pot, height 8in (20.3cm), and milk jug decorated with the Black Fruit *pattern, 1958*

down the Crown Works in 1980. Susie Cooper went on to work at W. Adams for a short period of time.

- Unlike many of her shapes, *Curlew*, launched in 1933, was not in production for long as it did not give the designer the same flexibility as her other shapes. As a result, it is much sought after by collectors.
- Look out for the modern Art Deco shapes from the early '30s, with the simple geometric patterns and lesser-known patterns such as *The Seagull*, *Panorama* and *The Homestead*.
- The limited range of face masks, from 1933, and the figural table centres such as *Leaping Deer* and

Angel Fish, both from the late '30s, are rare and therefore highly desirable. *Leaping Deer* was also reissued by Wedgwood in 2002.

- From about 1936 Susie Cooper started using printed patterns for nursery wares. However, the earlier hand-painted nursery wares, with many not listed in the pattern books, are more sought after.
- Post WWII hand-painted wares, with patterns such as *Tree of Life* and *Chinese Fern*, were mainly exported and only seconds allowed on the British market, with the result that these rare exported designs are now sought after by a number of dedicated collectors in Britain.
- Most of the 60 Lion and the Unicorn cups and

Set of bone china cups and saucers decorated with the Pennant *pattern with the original box, diameter of saucer 5½in (14cm), c.1969*

saucers made for Royal Society of Arts in 1950 were given away. A few have come on to the market and are highy collectable.

• Patterns produced during the late '60s, such as *Carnaby Daisy*, *Nebula*, *Harlequinade* and *Pennant* are all of growing interest to collectors.

Further Reference

Casey, A. and Eatwell A., (Eds.) *Susie Cooper, A Pioneer of Modern Design*. Antique Collectors' Club, 2002

Casey, A., *Susie Cooper Ceramics – A Collector's Guide*. Jazz Publications, 1992

Eatwell, A., *Susie Cooper Productions*. Victoria and Albert Museum, 1987

www.susiecooper.net

Bone china Can *shape coffee pot decorated with the* Pimento *pattern, c.1968*

Earthenware part tea set decorated with a hand-painted geometric pattern, 1930s

CROWN DEVON
S. Fieldings & Co.

Over the last century S. Fieldings & Co., better known today as Crown Devon, produced a wide range of high-class pottery that was both attractive and innovative. The pottery was founded by Simon Fielding in 1878 at the Railway Pottery, Sutherland Street in Stoke-on-Trent. The main production included Majolica ware, which was popular at the time, on a range of shapes such as jugs, cheese dishes and umbrella stands. Simon Fielding's son Abraham joined the company in 1878.

In 1897 a trade advertisement illustrated a range of ornamental, domestic and toilet wares as well as some tea wares ornately decorated with stylised floral subjects. Dinnerware inspired by the Far East was added to the range alongside patterns such as *Cedric* and *Ascot* both featuring black vellum grounds.

In 1905 Fieldings & Co. became a limited company with £13,000 capital. Six years later the factory name was changed from the Railway to the Devon Pottery and from that point on the company was known as Crown Devon. Recognising the changes in public taste, the company withdrew its Majolica and Vellum ranges and replaced them with a selection of 'fancy' wares, which would prove popular for both the home and the export markets. In 1917 an important new range was introduced; *Lustrine*, a collection of ornamental wares, was decorated with ten different patterns, which included mermaids, leopards and lizards. Examples of Crown Devon ware were shown at the British Empire Exhibition in 1924.

The extensive range of salad wares, including cheese dishes, salad bowls and dishes modelled as lettuce leaves in primrose green and tomatoes in red, were introduced in the late '20s and proved very

Crown Devon lustre decorated ginger jar depicting The Royal George, *1930s*

Earthenware jug, from the Mattajade *range, decorated with the* Fairy Castles *pattern, 9½ in (24cm), 1932*

popular. Another good seller was the *Garden Ware* range, which featured a crazy paving surface with embossed flowers hand-painted in bright colours. Particularly popular in the U.S.A. and Canada were musical novelties, such as half-pint and pint mugs, whisky flagons and cigarette boxes, all of which would play a tune when lifted off the table. These were decorated with a variety of patterns, such as *John Peel*, *Widdiecombe Fair* and *Auld Lang Syne*.

During the Art Deco period Crown Devon was competing directly with several other well-known pottery manufacturers such as Carlton Ware. Much credit must be given to both the sales director George Barker and the decorating manager Enoch Boulton, both of whom had defected to Crown Devon from Carlton Ware in 1930; their contribution to the success of the company was invaluable. Together they produced a stunning range of new patterns and shapes such as *Vogue* and *Modane*. Their stylised *Orient* pattern for coffee and ornamental wares was typically Art Deco in style. They also enjoyed success with a range of lustre wares and matt glazed wares that included

Mattajade, *Chinese Dragon* and *Fairy Castles*. A wide range of hand-painted patterns, both floral and geometric were introduced with some similar to the designs by Susie Cooper for the Gray's Pottery. When Abraham Fielding died in 1932, his son, Arthur Ross Fielding, joined the company as Chairman, remaining in tenure until 1947. His son, Reginald, became Managing Director in 1947, retiring in 1967.

Major redevelopment of the factory commenced in 1938 and was completed after WWII. A disastrous fire in May 1951 caused extensive damage to the building and production remained limited for several months. Despite this setback, Crown Devon soon had a wide range of contemporary lines in production including the commercially successful *Stockholm* design by William Kemp, depicting a stag motif, and a variation called *Greenland*.

During the early '60s Crown Devon produced its first modern shape range. Consultant designer Colin

Range of '50s shapes, tallest item 7in (17.8cm), decorated with the Stockholm *pattern designed by William Kemp, 1956*

Melbourne's *Coronel* shape was decorated with nine silk-screened patterns including *Green Canberra*, *Stardust* and *Everglade*. In 1963 he created a range of ten modern decorative vases called the *Memphis* range but these were not commercially successful. In 1964 the company took over Shorter and Sons Ltd. Further shapes were developed including *Allegro* in 1966, *Form 500* in 1969 and *Omega* in 1972.

In 1967 the family sold the Fielding Group of companies to accountants in Liverpool, ending its long family connection. The company closed down in December 1982.

* Crown Devon is well known amongst today's collectors through the staggering range of novelty items, such as wall ornaments, novelty cruets, grotesque animals and figural pieces that were produced during the '20s and '30s.
* Crown Devon is also closely associated with the Art Deco style and it is these examples that appear in specialist auctions.

Further Reference

Hill, S., *Crown Devon. The History of S. Fielding & Co.* Jazz Publications, 1993

Roberts, A.H., *Crown Devon Musical Novelties, Collectors' Hand Books*. Fairview Promotions, 1998

www.fieldingscrowndevclub.com

Detail showing Greenland, *a colour variation of the* Stockholm *pattern*

Opposite:
Crown Devon figure Rio Rita *by Kathleen Parsons, height 11in (28cm), 1930s*

Collection of earthenware shapes decorated with the printed and painted Red Tree *pattern (now known as* Orange Tree*), height of coffee pot 7½in (19cm), 1925*

CROWN DUCAL

Albert Goodwin Richardson established this successful company in 1915, at the Gordon Pottery in Tunstall, Stoke-on-Trent, trading under the name Crown Ducal. It soon became a well-known factory, producing attractive decorated tea and coffee sets for the higher end of the market alongside flower-pots, octagonal bowls and trinket sets.

In 1917 W.B. Johnson was appointed as Art Director. Typical of the company's production at that time were toilet wares decorated with trellis and rose motifs on black backgrounds as illustrated in a 1918 trade advertisement. Also shown in the same advertisement were Crown Ducal's two speciality lines: Victorian silver ware and ivory vellum decoration.

The founder of the company left after only four years; the two remaining directors, John Rushton and Joseph Harrison, thereby becoming sole directors.

Crown Ducal was most prolific during the '20s and '30s with production undergoing a distinctive change. This was possibly due to the appointment of Norman Keats as designer in 1922. Whilst some of his first patterns, such as *Carnival* and *Cairo*, proved popular, it was his tableware patterns that were most successful for the company. In 1925 the *Red Tree* pattern, depicting a line of trees printed in black and finished with hand-painted decoration of oranges was launched. This outstanding design decorated on simple shapes sold in the high-class department stores in London and proved so popular that it was extended to incorporate fancies and glassware. Today it has become known by collectors as *Orange Tree*. This pattern, alongside other lines,

Examples of the printed and hand-painted Sunburst *pattern from the early '30s, height of teapot 5½in (14cm)*

was exhibited at the Exposition Internationale des Arts Décoratifs et Industriels Modernes held in Paris in 1925. The success of *Red Tree* prompted the introduction of similar lines such as *Sunburst*, which was also an outstanding success. These wares can be found with various different backstamps.

Towards the end of the '20s the company introduced a range of lustre wares, *Radiance Lustre*, created by Roland Heath, the patterns included *Lotus*, *Fish*, and *Seaweed*. Early patterns, such as *Cairo*, were also given the lustre treatment to extend customer choice. At the same time a number of Chintz patterns were introduced, including *Ascot*, *Blue Chintz*, *Delhi* and *Festival*, which proved popular in North America. Later Chintz patterns from the '30s, such as *Primrose* and *Pansy*, did not achieve the same level of popularity.

In contrast to the highly decorated wares, Crown

Ducal also produced self-coloured wares that were aerographed in various colours such as blue, lilac, yellow, pink, and lined in black. The success of domestic tableware prompted a wide range of new shapes and patterns being issued, starting with the *Regent* shape in 1928 and soon followed by *Cotswold* and *Victory* in 1933. Typical patterns from this period included *Acacia*, 1929, *Red Poppy* on the *Ionic* shape, 1931, and *Wild Rose*, 1933.

In order to meet the increasing demands of the international market Crown Ducal purchased a second factory, the Britannia Works in Cobridge, in 1933. They also targeted the higher end of the British market by placing advertisements in magazines such as *The Sphere* to promote new lines, both traditional and modern. Examples included the embossed *Embassy* and *Gordon* on traditional

Range of self-coloured wares, height of coffee pot 7½in (19cm), 1930s

Earthenware one-handled jug decorated with the tube-lined Ankara *pattern by Charlotte Rhead, height 10¼in (26 cm). This pattern was launched in 1939 with other colour variations of this pattern being introduced in the post-war period*

shapes alongside various examples of art pottery such as the *Simplicity* sets available in blue, yellow, pink and apple green. Crown Ducal also produced specific ranges for the export market, including the *Queen Anne* shape decorated with typical patterns such as *Havanna*, *Virginia* and *Mayfair*.

Having introduced some of the company's best-selling ranges, Norman Keats decided to leave the company in 1930. Harold Bennett, who had joined the company in about 1929, began developing new patterns but little information is known about him. Probably the most important contribution alongside that of Norman Keats was the work of Charlotte Rhead, who joined Crown Ducal in about 1931, after some years at Burgess and Leigh Ltd. She brought with her the great skill of tube lining, which had been developed many years earlier and been successfully exploited by her father at Wood and Sons Ltd. Over a ten-year period she produced a wide range of domestic wares and decorative items with stylised fruits and flowers for the luxury end of the market. *Byzantine* was launched in 1933 and was soon followed by *Persian Rose*, *Rhodian*, *Golden Leaves*,

Typical backstamp from the inter-war period

Earthenware plaque decorated with the Granada *pattern, diameter 10⁷⁄₁₆ in (26.5 cm), introduced in 1933*

Foxglove, Manchu and *Wisteria*. Rhead's work was marked with a Crown Ducal backstamp and, on occasion, her signature "C Rhead", this is usually only seen on more expensive items and would have been tube-lined, though applied by a decorator rather than the designer herself. Rhead, who also designed a range of simple patterns for tableware such as *Stitch*, left Crown Ducal in about 1942.

The Gordon Pottery was not reopened after WWII and production was concentrated at the Britannia Works. During the '50s a wide range of patterns that required hand-applied decoration were introduced, such as *Gay Meadow*, *Chinese Garden* and *Chatsworth*; these proved popular for the export market. The printed method was used for the modern patterns such as *Skandia* and *Zambia* on the *Europa* shape. In the '60s the bottle ovens were demolished and replaced with new kilns alongside a general reorganisation of the factory.

During the late '60s Crown Ducal produced a new range of shapes and patterns that looked very similar to products by other manufacturers such as Wood and Sons Ltd. The *Berkeley* shape, new in 1968, was decorated with patterns such as *Esquire*, *County* and *Concept*, possibly by the new designer Tina Davenport. As well as continuing production of hotel and catering wares, Crown Ducal developed an oven-to-tableware range, *Concorde*, with a repeat embossed surface, decorated in plain *Aztec* (gold), *Inca* (brown) and *Mayan* (green). In 1974 Enoch Wedgwood Ltd. purchased the pottery.

- The *Red Tree* (or *Orange Tree*, as it is now known) is probably one of the best known and collectable designs. Standard wares such as tea and coffee wares are still affordable. Serious collectors should search out the rare shapes, sets and glass ware, which are, however, more expensive.
- There is great interest in the work of Charlotte Rhead, particularly with tube-lined decoration.

Further Reference

Bumpus, B., *Collecting Rhead Pottery*. Francis Joseph, 1999

www.rhead-crownducal.info

The Byngo *dog, height 6½in (16.5cm), from the 1930s*

DENBY POTTERY

Joseph Bourne and the Bourne family established the famous Denby pottery, known today for its distinctive and stylish tablewares, in Denby, Derbyshire in 1809. The earliest productions were salt-glazed stoneware pottery, during the later part of the 19th century they added majolica, sgraffito wares and butterfly ware. In 1916 it became a limited company.

During the first part of the 20th century Denby began to develop a new look, having rejected some of the outmoded shapes and production lines that were no longer selling. A decorating department was set up under the direction of Albert Colledge in 1923, with some of the first results being shown at the British Empire Exhibition a year later. Modernisation of the works took place under the direction of Joseph Wood and later his son, Norman Wood, who between them made production more efficient as the emphasis moved away from industrial to domestic wares.

In about 1930 the sculptor Donald Gilbert joined the company and developed a new series of domestic kitchenwares decorated with a blue glaze, called *Cottage Blue*. The range, which included casserole dishes and roasting trays, proved so popular that it was soon followed by *Manor Green*. Donald Gilbert also designed the *Manor Green* and *Epic* oven-to-tableware ranges, with the latter featuring three moulded wavy lines on a green glaze. In the 1930s the company produced novelty wares that included all sorts of birds, fishes and elephants as bookends and several vases.

Following WWII the company made great artistic contributions to the pottery industry by commissioning various artists and designers but it was the work of Glyn Colledge that set the tone for the new decade. He had trained with his father, Albert, at Denby before the war and was then given the opportunity to experiment and develop new ideas with the intention that the resultant trial pieces may be developed into standard lines for the company. One such result was a hand-thrown stone-ware range called *Glyn Ware*, featuring hand-painted motifs such as leaves, animals and abstract designs on a selection of handled jugs, vases and decorative plaques. A notable example, illustrated in the trade press in 1949, was a vase decorated with a stylised sea horse painted in greens with slip trail decoration. On the whole, the general colour range was soft browns and greens with some banded decoration.

Hungarian designer Tibor Reich worked at Denby for a short time during the '50s. His modern range called *Tigo* ware, which included wall plaques depicting stylised faces of *The Knight*, *The Three Sisters* and *Rendezvous*, were outstanding artistic productions.

Launched in 1955 and designed by Albert Colledge, *Greenwheat*, depicting a hand-painted wheat motif on a white ground, was one of the most important patterns of this period, becoming one of the company's best sellers and remaining in production until the mid '70s. Another ground-breaking design, *Arabesque* by Gill Pemberton, was launched c.1964. These successes helped establish Denby as a progressive company known for its artistic patterns and shapes.

Gill Pemberton went on to create further out-

Examples of the Electric Blue *range, c.1930*

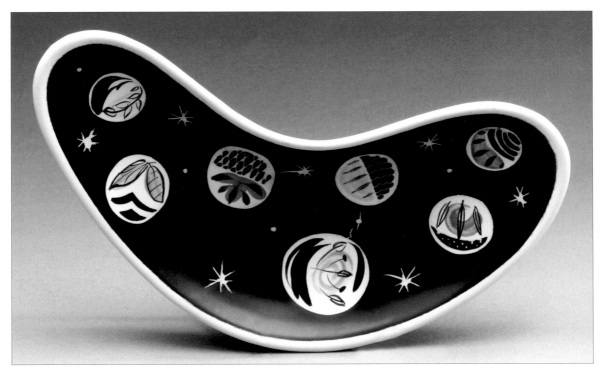

Example from the Cheviot *range, designed by Glyn Colledge, mid-1950s*

Right:
Stoneware mug, decorated with the Greenwheat *pattern, height 4½in (11.4cm), c.1956*

Below:
Typical Denby backstamp from the '50s

standing patterns and shapes in the '70s, including the *Renaissance* shape decorated with patterns such as *Castile* (blue) and *Seville* (beige) from about 1975, these are probably still in use in many homes across the country today.

Denby Pottery was floated on the Stock Exchange in 1970; six years later the company was renamed Denby Tableware Ltd. Throughout the '70s and '80s the company introduced a wide range of tableware collections including *Chateau*, *Artisan* and *Sherwood*, 1983; and by the early '90s examples included *Shiraz* and *Marrakesh*. In 1981 the company was taken over by Crown House and then by Coloroll in 1987.

- ◆ Look out for kitchen wares, *Cottage Blue* and *Manor Green*, designed by Donald Gilbert in the '30s. Collectors should note, however, that cups and saucers were not introduced to these ranges until after the WWII.
- ◆ Collectors are particularly keen on the rare designs and patterns such as the *Cheviot Wares* from 1956.

Further Reference

Hopwood, I. and Hopwood, G., *Denby Pottery 1809-1997*. Richard Dennis, 1997

Key, G. and Key, A., *Denby Stonewares*. Ems & Ens Ltd., 1995

www.denby.co.uk

Earthenware coffee pot decorated with the Arabesque *pattern, 1964*

Group of Gloria Lustre *wares designed by Susie Cooper, diameter of bowl 9⅞in (25cm), c.1925*

A.E. GRAY AND CO. LTD.

The pottery firm A. E. Gray & Co. Ltd. (well known today as Gray's Pottery) was acknowledged during the early part of the 20th century for its progressive approach to all matters of design and modernity. The founder Albert Edward Gray had previously worked in retail as a sales man for a pottery and glass business in Manchester. Aware of the poor quality of pottery design, he decided to set up his own company. With financial support from Alfred Royle and John Wilkinson, who later became directors of the company in 1907, a small works in Back Glebe Street in Stoke-upon-Trent was purchased. In 1912 the business moved to a new site in Hanley, which was named the Glebe Works.

After the disruption of the WWI, production increased during the early '20s under the direction of designer John Guildford, who left the company in 1922 to join Barker Brothers Ltd. Rather than manufacture its own white wares, Gray's bought them in from suppliers such as Johnson Brothers and Lancaster & Sons Ltd. Typical production of the early period included *Hardwicke*, a Jacobean style pattern, and *Old Bristol*, from 1915. The first Gray's advertisement boasted that it produced, "tea, dinner and toilet services, vases and general sundries in choice decorations".

During the '20s and '30s Gray's came to the forefront of British pottery design, as the founder was a great exponent of good design and modernism, as well as having a keenness for hand-painted decoration. An association and friendship with Gordon Forsyth, recently appointed Superintendent of Art Education Instruction in Stoke-on-Trent in 1920, led to the development of a new range *Gloria Lustre*. Gordon Forsyth, who had previously designed for Pilkingtons, created several patterns for decorative ginger jars, plaques and large bowls hand-painted with heraldic beasts. Susie Cooper, who had joined the company in 1922, assisted him, eventually producing her own designs for this range; it is difficult to determine who designed which patterns although some Cooper designs do feature her monogram "S.V.C.". Examples were shown at both the British Empire Exhibition in 1924 and the

Group of earthenwares decorated with geometric patterns including Cubist, *designed by Susie Cooper, applied to the coffee pot, small dish and cigarette box and cover. Height of coffee pot 8in (20.3cm), 1928-1932*

Exposition Internationale des Arts Décoratifs et Industriels Modernes in Paris a year later.

When Susie Cooper became chief designer she developed a wide range of hand-painted floral patterns that emphasised the brush strokes in bright colours as well as more detailed examples, such as *Golden Catkin*, *Crocus* and a nursery pattern called *Quadrupeds*, that were printed and enamelled. She also developed the use of banded decoration for decorative and kitchen wares, including the popular *Harmony* range, a best seller for many years. Susie Cooper was given her own individual back stamp depicting a liner with the words, "DESIGNED BY SUSIE COOPER".

Probably the most sought after of Gray's items are the range of geometric patterns boldly decorated in the bright colours of the Art Deco style. Whilst most of the designs by Susie Cooper (such as *Cubist* and *Moon and Mountains*) are well known, many others were probably actually created by other designers.

When Susie Cooper left to set up on her own, the task of creating new patterns passed to Dorothy Toomes, who is thought to have been responsible for a series of large, decorative, hand-painted, floral patterns and the attractive *Hampton* pattern, all of which are often wrongly attributed to Susie Cooper. At about the same time another designer, signing her name as "Nita" on the pattern itself, created several floral and leaf patterns.

The most important designer at Gray's in the '30s was Sam Talbot, who had joined the company in 1925. Talbot was responsible for leading the change in artistic direction at Gray's, creating an extensive range of popular patterns, including the restrained *Stella*, a ground laid design with spots, c.1938. Unlike Susie Cooper, his name was not included on the backstamps. In 1933 Gray's moved to a larger factory space in Whieldon Road in Stoke. At about the same time a new hand-painted "A" was added as a prefix to the number code and on the backstamp. The company began to offer a wider range of products, including stoneware lemonade sets with matt glazes, wall ornaments and animal figures. Some of these were created by Nancy Catford, who worked for the company, on a freelance basis, as a figure modeller from 1934 to the late '30s. During

Typical examples of abstract floral designs from the early thirties

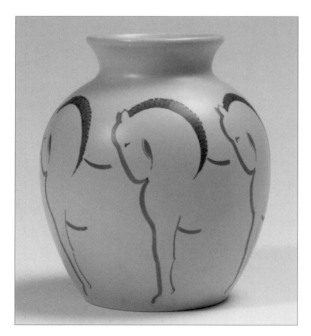

her short period at Gray's she created the popular *Budgerigar* wall pocket.

Edward Gray retired after WWII. Examples of Gray's pottery was exhibited at the Festival of Britain in 1951. The use of lustre finish continued but was limited to simple patterns on gift wares rather than the elaborate designs associated with the company from the '20s. One particular lustre decoration introduced before WWII was *Sunderland Splatter*, a combination of black and white prints of various subjects including sailing ships. Sam Talbot continued to develop new patterns, which were often illustrated in the trade press and *Decorative Art Studio Year Books* including the *Carnation* pattern, a hand-painted resist decoration on a green lustre ground, and *Tudor*, a stylised

Stoneware vase, decorated with a hand-painted pattern of stylised horses, height 6½ in (16.5cm), c.1937

Earthenware jug in Paris *shape, decorated with a banded pattern, height 5in (12.7cm)*

floral border design for dinnerware, both from 1951; and in 1956 several patterns including *Tree*, *Magnolia*, and *Ludlow* were illustrated. At the same time the range of giftwares was extended, the souvenir wares proving very popular.

During the late '50s Gray's manufactured a range of wares for Portmeirion village in North Wales.

Standard Gray Pottery mark from the '30s onwards

Designed by Susan Williams-Ellis, daughter of the architect Sir Clough Williams-Ellis, these small giftwares became so popular that Portmeirion eventually bought the company in 1960. The Gray's name continued in use until the start of 1962. *(Please see also entry for Portmeirion Potteries Ltd)*

- The hand-painted patterns are the most sought after by collectors today, particularly *Cubist* by Susie Cooper in the '20s.
- Keep an eye out for Art Deco items from the early '30s, including a range of floral plaques.

Further Reference

Casey, A. and Eatwell, A. (Eds.), *Susie Cooper: A Pioneer of Modern Design*. Antique Collectors' Club, 2002

Niblett, P., *Hand Painted Gray's Pottery*. City Museum and Art Gallery, Stoke-on-Trent, 1982

Examples of Cornish Ware *items*

T. G. GREEN & CO. LTD.
Cornish Kitchen Ware

Functional domestic kitchen ware becoming a favourite amongst design commentators at the time, let alone collectors today, probably seemed completely unlikely to the owners of T.G. Green Ltd. during the '30s. However *Cornish Ware* proved an outstanding success, placing the company at the forefront of British ceramics industry, a fact confirmed by the several manufacturers who copied the style then and by the buoyant collectors' market today.

This popular pottery company was established by Thomas Goodwin Green in Church Gresley in Derbyshire in 1864. By the mid 1880s the range included various glazed wares, kitchen and hospital ware and nursery wares.

The 20th century began with a disaster for the company when a fire devastated the works, though the factory was soon rebuilt with some modernisation. Thomas Goodwin Green died in 1905, prompting his two sons to join the family business. The range of products on offer during this period was

extensive and included toilet and appliqué ware, vases, cube teapots and various domestic wares. In 1910 the company launched the *Ivanhoe* range followed two years later by a rose pattern.

In the early '20s the company introduced what was to become its most significant range: *Cornish Kitchen Ware*, which featured bold bands of blue and white in a traditional ware that was dipped in blue slip and then turned on the lathe to reveal the white body. The range was available in a wide range of kitchen shapes including lipped bowls, fruit sets, muffin dishes, tea sets, pudding bowls, household jars, flour dredgers and graduated milk jugs. The range, successfully publicised as being 'for the modern housewife', was exported across the world.

During the '30s the design commentators praised T.G. Green's utilitarian products, in particular the *Cornish Kitchen Ware* that "set a new standard in kitchen wares". Examples were shown at the Britain Can Make It exhibition in London in 1946.

To complement the *Cornish Ware*, T.G. Green introduced the *Blue Domino* range c.1933, followed by *Polka Dot* three years later. Throughout the '20s and '30s, whilst the *Cornish Ware* was selling well, the company continued to introduce new shapes and patterns, including simple hand-painted patterns on earthenware like *Pomona* in 1933, *Grasmere* and *Crocus*. Some more Art Deco influenced patterns were launched c.1930, including *Pharos* and *Alpha*, hand-painted onto the earthenware *Obliqué* shape.

After the war T.G. Green demonstrated its awareness of contemporary design and during the '50s it launched the square shaped *Patio Modern* range, reminiscent of both the work of Eva Zeisel and the Midwinter Pottery. Contemporary patterns for this range included *Samba*, *Safari* and *Central Park* designed by Colin Haxby c.1956. In the '60s Audrey Levy created patterns such as *Harlequin*, *Quatro* and *Trio*. Tom Arnold, a well-known consultant designer, created several patterns for the company including country style print *Rutland* in 1962, *Bountiful*, a border design of stylised fruit, and *Overleaf*, depicting stylised leaves, in 1964. Hand-painted patterns *Roulette* and *Gingham* were decorated on all sorts of wares including ceramic wall clocks.

During the '60s the *Cornish Ware* range was rationalised and some of the shapes were redesigned by Judith Onions.

Despite these successes the company struggled during the '60s, going into receivership in 1965. Following various buyouts and takeovers, the pottery was bought by a London-based finance group. In 1987 T.G. Green became part of the Cloverleaf group, later merging with Mason Cash. When Mason Cash folded, T.G. Green was bought by the Tabletop Company, which extensively revised and expanded Cornish Ware.

• Collectors are really keen on *Cornish Kitchen Ware*. Unfortunately, as with anything this popular, fakes abound, so be cautious when buying.
• Look out for other patterns by T.G. Green, especially from the early '60s.
• Popular with collectors today are the *Lily* and the *Rosebud* embossed wares first produced in the late 1930s. Occasionally pieces of embossed ware appeared covered in chintz and these are perhaps the most sought-after pieces by collectors around the world.

Further Reference

Atterbury, P., *Cornish Ware and Domestic Pottery by T.G. Green*. Richard Dennis, 2001

www.cornishware.biz

Part tea set decorated with the Grasmere *pattern, height of teapot 5½in (14cm), 1930s*

Examples of chintz patterns

GRIMWADES LTD.

The Royal Winton trade name is well known today for the wide range of highly attractive and commercially successful chintz patterns produced from the late '20s until the mid '50s. Like so many Staffordshire factories Grimwades produced a surprising variety of goods for the middle-class market, ranging from the lustre *Byzanta* line of the 1920s and hand-painted Art Deco patterns of the 1930s to the musical and character jugs of the late '30s.

Leonard Lumsden Grimwade and his brother set up in 1886 as the Grimwade Bros., based at the Winton Pottery in Stoke-on-Trent. They soon made an impact on the market and within a few years became a limited company. 1900 was a time of change: production was extended, J. Plant & Co.'s Stoke Pottery was acquired and the company became known as Grimwades Ltd. In 1913 it also purchased the Rubian Art Pottery, soon followed by the Atlas China Company Ltd., giving the company the opportunity to expand its domestic tableware range and meet the demands from the international market. The earliest products were chiefly toilet, dinner and tea wares, hotel and invalid ware. New rose bowls were illustrated in the trade

press in 1916 whilst new patterns, such as *Jacobean*, decorated on the new *Octavius* shape for toilet wares from 1919. The *Peter Rabbit* tea set for children was launched three years later.

At the British Industries Fair, Grimwades introduced an array of new patterns and shapes, which by the late 1920s included the *Rustic* and the *Bungalow* patterns decorated on the new *Octron* shape. The company responded to the fashion for Art Deco styled wares with a new line of brightly coloured wares, including *Delhi* depicting a stylised sunset, as well as a new lustre range called *Byzanta Ware*, designed earlier but expanded to include a variety of exotic patterns. In total contrast to these rather sophisticated patterns the company also introduced the *Cosy Cottage Ware* series in the mid '30s.

The *Chintz* range by Grimwades started in a small

Typical backstamp

way in 1915 but blossomed during the late '20s and early '30s with some of the first patterns including *Marguerite*, *Springtime* and *Summertime*. Launched in 1932, *Summertime* was very popular and remained in production for many years. This decorative treatment was applied to a wide range of wares, including tea wares, cake stands, toast racks and butter dishes. Grimwades also produced a range of embossed wares in line with the popular trends such as the *Regina* range, a moulded water-lily shape available in various colours, in 1933 and *Gera*, moulded in the form of geraniums. This was followed by the *Chanticleer* range, in 1936 with each item of the set modelled as a cockerel.

Occasionally pieces of embossed ware appeared covered in chintz. Following WWII, several chintz patterns were continued in production. By the early '60s the company had moved to a new site on Norfolk Street in Shelton. The company became part of the Howard Pottery Group in 1979 before being taken over by Coloroll in 1986. In 1995 Taylor Tunnicliffe bought Royal Winton from the liquidators and moved the works to Chadwick Street, Longton. Within a few years Royal Winton was once again producing chintz ware to be sold around the world.

- Grimwades is very well known today for its range of chintz designs that it has produced over the years. Collectors should keep an eye out for rare shapes and patterns, which can reach high prices at auction.
- Some of the most sought after patterns include *Royalty*, *Evesham*, *Welbeck*, *Hazel*, *Julia* and *Sweet Pea*.

Further Reference

Miller, M., *The Royal Winton Collectors' Handbook From 1925*. Francis Joseph, London, 1996

Scott, S., *The Charlton Standard Catalogue of Chintz*. The Charlton Press, 1999

www.royalwinton.co.uk

www.royalwinton.com

A 1920s catalogue for the overseas trade illustrating the range of toilet wares. Patterns listed include a wide range of decorations from flying birds on the Struma *shape to simple border patterns on the* Cordeila *shape*

Teapot moulded in the form of a half-timbered building, 'Ye Olde Swan', height 5in (12.6cm), c.1930

Earthenware shell, height 3½in (8.9cm), 1953

HORNSEA POTTERY

The Hornsea pottery rose from a small family concern to international status during the '60s and '70s. This was mostly due to the innovative designs of John Clappison, who played an important part in the shift from the whimsical fauna wares and other fancies of the early years of production to cutting-edge modernity as typified by *Home Décor*. These two areas of production today attract two very different groups of collectors.

The Hornsea Pottery was established in 1949 by Desmond Rawson, Colin Bentley Rawson and Caesar Philip Clappison in Hornsea, East Yorkshire. Within a few years business was going so well that they were forced to seek larger premises at Old Hall, and later moved to Edenfield Estate. In 1954 the Hornsea Pottery officially became the town's biggest employer. Some of the first examples of Hornsea pottery included character jugs, vases, boots and clogs, impressed with the word "Hornsea" or a simple "H". Marion Campbell created a range of modelled animals, such as giraffes, panthers and dogs.

Hornsea came to the forefront of the British pottery industry during the late '50s when Caesar Philip Clappison's son, John Clappison, began developing shapes and patterns, starting with the *Honeymoon* range, launched in 1955, and soon followed by the commercially successful *Elegance*, a set of small vases, bowls and jugs decorated with a vertical white line on a black ground in the contemporary style. Clappison was sent to the Royal College of Art to study for one year, on his return his *Tricorn* range was put into production. The limitations of machinery and skilled workers made it difficult and too costly for the company to use hand-painted decoration. Instead, it was decided to create an individual style, different from other manufacturers of the time; this became known as the 'Hornsea Look'. The *Summit* range, from 1960, featured vertical indentations on the body, which was sprayed with colour and then wiped off, leaving the colour inlaid to create a distinctive utilitarian look. *Summit* was available on an extensive range of practical wares such as condiment sets, preserve pots, jugs and cheese dishes.

Probably the most sought after Hornsea items are from the *Home Décor* range, which Clappison designed. These matt-glazed shapes, including *White Thorn*, *White Bud* and *White Frost*, gave the company a leading edge in the industry. A follow-on range, *Studio Craft*, was a combination of some shapes from *Home Décor* and the decorative process used for *Summit*. The *Studio Craft* range included large vases, jardinières, plant potholders, bulb bowls and bulb troughs. Brand new lines included *Summertime*, probably one of the most extensive collection of items, which incorporated spice jars, eggcups and oil and vinegar bottles. Alongside these practical wares Hornsea also produced *Fish Light* by Clappison and a vase with stylized decoration by Ronald Mitchell.

The most significant breakthrough for the

Home Décor *vase decorated with the* Lattice *pattern, designed by John Clappison, 1960*

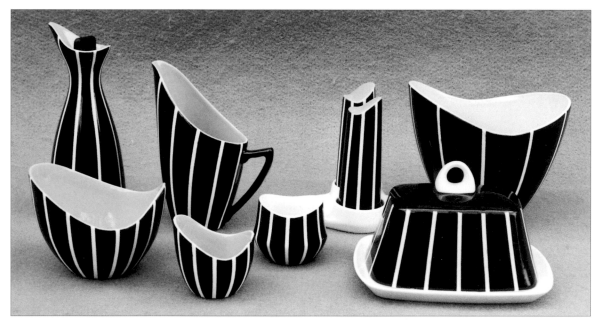

Selection of earthenware giftwares decorated with the Elegance *pattern. Designed by John Clappison, c.1955-59*

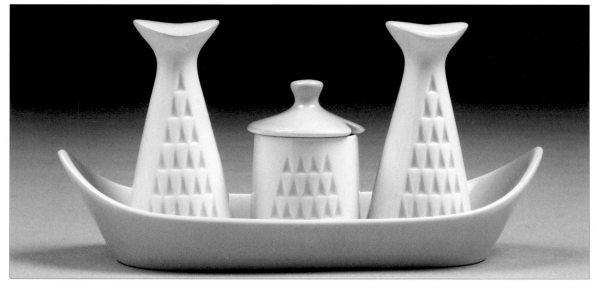

Earthenware cruet decorated with the Alpine *pattern, 1960-63*

company was when it developed a unique way of printing directly onto pottery. The resulting pattern, *Heirloom*, featured a contrasting semi-matt area of colour complemented by matt, glazed areas and was decorated on a new shape, also named *Heirloom*, which was much admired by other manufacturers. The *Heirloom* pattern was such a massive success that it prompted other patterns such as *Saffron* (1970) and *Bronté* (1972), whilst the *Fauna* range of plant pots and vases were withdrawn.

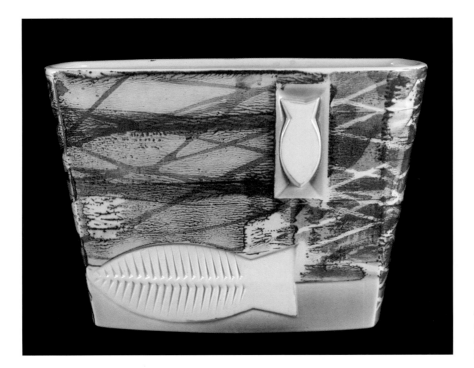

Abstract styled vase, designed by Ronald Mitchell, height 6in (15.5cm), c.1961

Earthenware coffee pot, milk jug, and cup and saucer decorated with the Heirloom *pattern, designed by John Clappison, 1967-1986*

Examples of the Concept *range decorated with the* Image *pattern, c.1977*

By 1970 Hornsea was so successful that it had to further expand its production facilities, a 36-acre factory site in Lancaster was acquired. An important part of the business was the continuous release of mugs and beakers decorated with a whole range of images, slogans and messages designed by Clappison with notable examples from the mid '70s including half pint mugs decorated with patterns such as *Uncle Tom Cobleigh*, *Golfers*, and G*eorge and the Dragon*. Clappison resigned from the company in 1972. Subsequently, Hornsea contracted the Queensbury/ Hunt Design Group to design shape ranges, resulting in the very successful *Contrast* and *Concept*; the latter featured swan knobs with patterns such as *Cirrus*, decorated in turquoise blue with clouds. Clappison returned to Hornsea as 'House Designer' in 1976, creating the *Sequel* and *Midas* designs. After changes in direction for the Hornsea Company and the subsequent buyouts, Hornsea was put in the hands of the receivers and closed in 2000.

- Look out for the collectable range of rare animals by Marion Campbell.
- The contemporary designs by John Clappison, especially the *Home Décor* range, are probably the most sought after Hornsea items today.
- There is also a strong demand for Hornsea's earlier flora and fauna giftwares.
- Later wares such as *Heirloom*, may become collectables in the future.
- Collectors should note that *Elegance*, the contemporary set of small vases, bowls and jugs decorated with a vertical white line on a black ground was later copied by Burt and Edwards (Hull) Ltd.

Further Reference
Casey. A., *Twentieth Century Ceramic Designers in Britain*. Antique Collectors' Club, 2001.

www.retroselect.com

Earthenware printed and painted plate decorated with the Friendly Village *pattern, diameter 10in (25.4cm)*

JOHNSON BROTHERS

The story of Johnson Brothers begins in 1883, when the two sons of Robert Johnson, Frederick and Alfred, decided to form a partnership to manufacture durable earthenware. They soon became famous for their *White Granite* ware, which was produced at the Charles Street Works in Hanley, Stoke-on-Trent. They were quick to maximise on the demand for high-quality pottery in North America after the Civil War. At the same time they extended the product range to include under-glaze printed ware to increase their market share. By 1888 it was clear that larger premises were required resulting in the erection of new works situated on Eastwood Road,

Hanley alongside subsequent purchases such as the Imperial Pottery in 1891 and the Trent Sanitary Works in 1896.

The early part of the new century was spent consolidating the rapid increase in business. After WWI new shapes and patterns, such as *Lytton*, *Matlock* and *Cremona*, were developed and a high-quality range of coloured bodies called *Dawn* was introduced. These coloured bodies were praised by those design commentators of the period who rejected the overly decorated, brash Art Deco patterns. They were used by a number of other pottery firms including the Gray's pottery. The company issued new improved printed patterns alongside its very popular banded wares.

Earthenware teapot with banded decoration. The backstamp includes the word "MODERNE", which could refer to the pattern name or a range of designs, width of teapot 10in (25.4cm), possibly 1930s

Following the recession of the late '20s the company rationalised the sites, demolishing the Charles Street Works. Other than its latest patterns, such as *Satsuma* and *Mayfair* from 1930, being noted in the trade press, on the whole the Johnson Brothers did not receive much press coverage, possibly due to their concentration on the export market during the '30s. Typical patterns that were sold in America included *Old Britain Castles*, 1930, and *Historic America*, 1936, which was based on 18th and 19th century engravings. One of the most popular patterns was *Friendly Village*, a multi-motif pattern that was printed and painted; it remained in production for many years.

In the late '40s the factories underwent modernisation, starting with new tunnel kilns. Johnson Brothers also purchased the Sovereign Potteries, based in Hamilton in Ontario, Canada. However this new venture did not prove profitable. In 1957 the company built a factory for manufacturing earthenware near Melbourne, in Australia; in 1960 it purchased the Eastwood Works from J. & G. Meakin and five years later the British Aluminium Company. This latter site was used for the bulk manufacture of cups and saucers and as a centralised packing department.

During the '60s the company launched the new shape range called *Contempo*, available for purchase decorated in several different patterns such as *Persian Rose*, *Marakeesh* and *Bramble*. In 1968 Josiah Wedgwood and Sons Ltd. purchased Johnson Brothers, alongside J. & G. Meakin. At the start of the '70s Johnson Brothers decided to break away from traditional design and produce modern shapes and patterns with one of the first being the *Chelsea Collection* in 1974, developed by Jessie Tait featuring

Earthenware dinner plate, bowl, and cup and saucer decorated with the Eternal Beau *pattern designed by Sarina Mascheroni, mid-1980s. Diameter of plate 10in (25.4cm)*

four patterns: *Pimlico, Cheyne Walk, Kings Road* and *Sloane Square*. Other patterns included *Windrush, Corn on the Cob*, from 1975, and *Alpine*, on the *Tivoli* shape.

One of the best-selling patterns of all time for the company was *Eternal Beau*, a simple pastel design of ribbons by Sarina Mascheroni. This proved so popular that several kitchen and dining accessories were introduced to complement the range.

During the early '80s the design team, which included Julie Holland, Colette Bishop and Susan Kennedy, developed numerous patterns for the company. The *Sweet Briar* and *Floral Dance* patterns were both designed by Jessie Tait for the modern white-bodied *Regency* shape, one of her last patterns was *Lugano* from 1992. That same year Wedgwood closed the Johnson Brothers buildings and the design team was moved to the Barlaston site.

♦ Johnson Brothers produced a very wide range of styles and shapes over the century, in particular look out for patterns such as *Friendly Village* and *Eternal Beau*. These are both popular on the American market but remain relatively affordable.

Johnson Brothers' backstamp

Two earthenware dishes decorated with lustre colours, 1960s

C.T. MALING & SONS LTD.

In 1853 Christopher Thompson Maling succeeded his father to run the family's pottery works, which had been founded in 1762. By 1859 business was brisk enough to warrant building a larger factory, known as Ford (A), which reputedly produced over 800,000 pieces a year. Continued good business necessitated more production space so a further factory, Ford (B), was built in 1878. Covering over 14 acres, the new factory enabled new types of production, which included kitchen and dairy equipment, sanitary ware, chemical apparatus as well as toilet and tableware. Christopher Thompson Maling's three sons joined the business in 1889 and within a year were managing both sites.

During the late 19th century Maling manufactured a wide selection of products, including bowls, teapots, jam jars and preserves pots with typical patterns including *Kilda* and *Jesmond*.

In 1906 Maling launched the *Cetem* range, a semi-porcelain body, of domestic and toilet wares targeted at the middle classes. At the same time a new designer Harry Clifford Toft joined the company direct from Staffordshire. Initially he was responsible for the development of the *Cetem* range, which was extended to include table and toilet wares. The backstamp on *Cetem Ware* showed a three-towered castle, a sunburst logo and the words "CETEM WARE".

The '20s was a most prolific decade for Maling, with expansion of the overseas market, popular

A typical Maling backstamp

87

Art Deco vase from the Ripple *range, 1930s*

new patterns such as *Wylam* and *Belsay*, on the new *Raeburn* shape that encompassed coffee, tea and dinner wares. Maling also offered decorated electric lamp stands, umbrella stands, imposing flowerpots and smokers' sundries, with the *Sefton* floating bowl, from 1922, proving very popular. The company was credited by the trade press as being one of the first manufacturers to introduce all-over black back-grounds decorated with fruit or flower patterns on items including the *Stanley* shape.

From 1924 until the early '60s, Maling's products were marked with a backstamp showing a castle within a circle with the words "MALING NEWCASTLE-ON-TYNE, ENGLAND".

On Harry Clifford Toft's death in 1922, Charles Newboult Wright, who had previously worked at Royal Doulton and Josiah Wedgwood and Sons Ltd., became Maling's designer. When Wright left the company in 1926, his place was taken by Lucien

Emile Boullemeir, the son of the famous Minton painter Antonin Boullemeir.

Maling is best known today for its lustre decorations, which it launched in 1923. Patterns include *May Bloom*, *Anemone* (1935) and *Rosine* (1961).

During the late '20s Maling suffered financially following the loss of orders after the Great Strike in 1926 and, with increasing competition from abroad, Maling decided to close Ford (A). Fortunately this proved a temporary set-back, in 1928 Maling was commissioned by famous tea merchants Ringtons Ltd. to produce blue and white transfer-printed earthenware tea caddies, which were designed by Lucien Boullemeir. This association, which would last until the early '60s, provided Maling with much important business. In 1929 Maling registered as a limited company with a capital of £25,000.

In response to the fashion for Art Deco styled pottery, Maling introduced a number of brightly painted patterns such as *Anzac*, applied to the new angular shape *Jazz* in 1931. *Jazz* may have looked thoroughly modern but it was not very functional, so was phased out in favour of the softer lines of *Empress*, introduced in 1932.

During the same period examples of hand-painted embossed wares were introduced, with notable patterns including *Windmill* c.1935, as well as a practical range of kitchenware shapes called *Cobblestone*, launched in 1931 and available in brown and green.

Modeller Norman Carling, who had previously worked at A.J. Wilkinson Ltd., joined the company in 1936. He developed an extensive range of shapes for the new *Blossom Time*, from 1936, alongside *Bambola* and *Flight*.

Maling's successes of the '30s were soon diminished by the devastation of WWII. Despite producing some utility ware during the war the company found it difficult to re-establish itself without the skilled workers who had enlisted for the war.

In August 1946 Maling was sold to Hoults, an expanding furniture removal company. The new owners, keen to develop the product, invested in new pottery machinery. During the '50s further commissions were forthcoming from Ringtons for a number of special lines including an order in 1955 for 44,000 *Jesmond* shape teapots decorated with the *Blossom Bough* pattern. Well over forty new patterns were developed and introduced between the '50s and '60s. Patterns such as *Peony Rose*, *Rosalind*, *Dahlia* and *Golden Spray* were typical. The *Voluta* shape, launched in 1960, was decorated with a range of aerographed plain colours. With the furniture business doing so well little time was left for production development at Maling. This was compounded by losing the contract to supply crockery to the London and North Eastern Railway Company. In 1962, after 40 years of doing business together, Ringtons pulled out of their contract. In June 1963 the factory was closed.

♦ Maling is best known today for its lustre decorations first launched in 1923. Patterns included *Anemone*, *Rosine* and *May Bloom*.
♦ A collectable pattern from the late '20s is *Chintz Blue*. This printed pattern was marketed as having been inspired by old French tapestries; an eight cup tea pot retailed at 6/-.

Further Reference
Moore, S., *Maling, The Trademark of Excellence*. Tyne and Wear Museum Services, 1989

www.geocities.com/RodeoDrive/6544

Lustre plate decorated with the Clematis *pattern, 1940s*

Earthenware plate decorated with the printed pattern, Montmartre, *with silver line to the edge, diameter 7in (17.8cm), c.1955*

ALFRED MEAKIN (TUNSTALL) LTD.

The Meakin name has become synonymous with the British pottery industry for many years. The fact that there were two companies bearing the name and operating during the 20th century has often confused collectors. Alfred Meakin first set up his pottery works in 1874; his brothers James and George had taken over the running of their father's company in 1851 and traded as J. and G. Meakin Ltd. (*please see separate entry*).

Alfred traded as Alfred Meakin (Tunstall) Ltd., based at the Royal Albert Works in Tunstall. He produced Ironstone and earthenware for export to America from 1913. During the '30s he offered a wide range of goods decorated with assorted patterns such as *The Homestead*, which depicted a cottage with delphiniums, *Garden Scenes* on the *Vesta* shape and a nursery set called *Peter Pan* in 1932. Two years later the company promoted its new *Marigold* body, which was used for several patterns including a litho border called *Yvonne* on the *Astoria* shape.

The '50s were a very busy time for the company: it introduced a number of best-selling patterns, including a series of overtly contemporary patterns, such as *Jivers* and *Seine*, in the late '50s. Meakin also produced a black and white printed pattern called *Poodles*, probably inspired by the commercial success of the *Homemaker* and *Parisienne* patterns by Ridgway. The most popular was *Hedgerow*, a

Above:
Earthenware teapot decorated with the Hedgerow *pattern, 1960s*

Left:
Typical backstamp

transfer-printed pattern featuring a stylised centre spray of grasses finished with a band at the edge, on simple earthenware shapes. This outstanding design was available on many sets and dinnerwares. In 1957 the company built the Victoria and Highgate Works.

Following the popularity of the Bill and Ben children's television programme, a new design called *Bill and Ben* was launched in the early '60s. It was also during the '60s that Alfred Meakin introduced its new glo-white earthenware body, which was used for the majority of the subsequent ranges, such as the *Cranbrooke* pattern on the *Princess* shape, and the *Fenland* pattern on the *Doric* shape.

In 1976 the company merged with Myott Son & Co.

◆ Look out for Alfred Meakin's contemporary patterns, such as *Parisienne*, from the '50s.

Further Reference
Jenkins, S., *Ceramics of the '50s and '60s: A Collectors Guide.* Miller's, 2001.

www.retroselect.com

Habitant earthenware jug, decorated with a hand-painted plaid pattern, height 7½in (19cm), 1950s

J. & G. MEAKIN LTD.

James Meakin formed the Meakin company in about 1845, his two sons James and George Meakin taking over in 1851. (A third son, Alfred, set up his own company, Alfred Meakin Ltd., in 1874. *Please see separate entry.*) The company chiefly designed and produced pottery for the North American market with its tableware being standard equipment on the wagon trains carrying settlers westward across America. Demand was so high that a brand new factory, the Eagle Works, was built in 1859, this was later supplemented with the purchase of the Eastwood Pottery in Hanley. J. & G. Meakin became a limited company in 1890.

Throughout the 20th century J. & G. Meakin produced a wide range of domestic tablewares, often transfer-printed motifs, with a large portion for export particularly to the American market. One of its most important lines was the *Sol* range produced between 1912 and 1963 for both home and hotel use. It was so popular that by the '50s over one million pieces were being manufactured per week!

In 1933 the new *Moderna* shape, decorated with a range of contemporary patterns including *Grantham*, was launched and also exhibited at the British Industrial Art in Relation to the Home exhibition at Dorland Hall in London. Several Art Deco patterns, many created by the Art Director J.G. Slater, were used for this range. Other popular patterns and shapes included *Nevada* on the *Sunshine* shape and *Grace and Beauty* on the *Basket* shape.

Earthenware Studio
*shape coffee pot
decorated with the*
Impact *pattern, designed
by Jessie Tait, height
9¼in (23.5cm), c.1972*

Following WWII the works were modernised and extended; the family's involvement decreased towards the latter part of the '50s, thus requiring a new team of executives to run the company. Meakin came to the forefront of modern design during the early '50s following an important visit by a member of the design research department to Canada and the United States in 1949. In 1953 Meakin launched the organic *Studio* ware in response to designs by Russell Wright at the time. The *Studio* range, modelled by Frank Potts, included the *Habitant* teapot, tea, coffee and dinnerwares and a coupe shape plate. The initial patterns, designed by Frank Trigger, included the hand-painted *Almond Blossom*, *Spring Ballet* and *Abstract*; later Robert Williams designed *Sea Horses* and *Perspective*. By the early

1950s about 80% of production was allocated for the export market, including Scandinavia, Australia, New Zealand and the Far East. In order to keep ahead of the market Meakin produced a wide range of new shapes including *Horizon* in 1955.

Probably the most important achievement of J. & G. Meakin was the introduction of a new shape in 1964, again called *Studio*. This modern approach to pottery design made a strong impact on the market. The *Studio* range was designed under the direction of Frank Trigger and Tom Arnold and launched with eight printed patterns including *Symphony*, *Allegro*, *Riverside* and *Garden Party* with further patterns such as *Topic*, *Cadiz* and *Bali* dating from 1967, the latter two were designed by Alan Rogers. Further patterns included *Elite* and *Tulip Time*, which featured in a

Studio *shape coffee set decorated with the* Maidstone *pattern, designed by Eve Midwinter, c.1972*

special promotional campaign with *Woman's Own* magazine in 1972 and *Impact*, a blue abstract motif.

By the late '60s Meakin was employing over 1,400 people with over 60% of production being exported, mainly to North America.

In 1968 J. & G. Meakin took over W.R. Midwinter Ltd. and subsequently used several Midwinter patterns, such as *Inca* and *Manderley* designed by Jessie Tait, on the *Studio* range. Meakin also made a modified version of the Midwinter *MQ2* shape and called it *Apollo*, which was shown to the trade in 1970 bearing a lesser-known pattern by Jessie Tait. During the same year both companies were taken over by Josiah Wedgwood and Sons Ltd. Under the new trade name 'Bull in the China Shop', Meakin

extended production of tablewares during the early '70s. From 1974 Jessie Tait was transferred from Midwinter to work for Meakin and Johnson Brothers Ltd. She created many successful patterns whilst Eve Midwinter created the *Poppy* pattern, in 1972, and *Bianca* for the Maidstone range.

◆ Generally speaking, collectors of the '60s *Studio* range are keen on the more abstract patterns such as *Impact* and *Amulet*. In particular, it is worth looking out for designs by Jessie Tait.

Further Reference
Jenkins, S., *Ceramics of the '50s and '60s: A Collectors' Guide.* Miller's, 2001

Earthenware meat plate, decorated with the hand-painted Primavera *pattern for the Stylecraft range designed by Jessie Tait, height 13¾in (35cm), 1954*

W.R. MIDWINTER LTD.

The W.R. Midwinter factory was associated with progressive design and innovation from the mid part of the 20th century onwards, gaining a reputation for bright modern ceramics that completely captured the mood of the day.

William Robinson Midwinter established the company in 1910, at Bournes Bank in Burslem, Stoke-on-Trent, moving to larger premises in 1914. During the early part of the century the company produced ornamental wares, toilet sets and dinnerwares decorated in traditional styles similar to other manufacturers, a typical example being an underglaze banded pattern of blue with gold lines. A more traditional printed design based on engravings from the late 19th century, *Roger*, was a best seller for many years. Midwinter also issued a popular line

Earthenware Salad Ware *plate, designed by Terence Conran, diameter 8in (20.3cm), 1955*

95

Selection of Fine *shape coffee pots decorated, from left to right:* Mexicana *from 1966,* Sienna *from 1962, and* Spanish Garden *from 1968. Height of tallest coffee pot 8¼in (21cm)*

of all-over silver lustre ware teapots, sugars and creams on the *Georgian* shape, with a black handle.

During the '20s Midwinter manufactured several different lines in order to appeal to a much wider market. At the same time the company had a change in artistic direction, issuing new shapes such as *Avon*, *Doric* and *Belle*, decorated with simple and improved lithographs. William Heath Robinson designed the *Fairyland on China* set c.1928. In response to the fashion for Art Deco style, several stylised patterns including a windmill design in orange and silver were produced. Midwinter also introduced a selection of chintz patterns, such as *Springtime*.

Roy Midwinter, son of the founder, joined the company during the 1940s. He introduced a range of handcraft patterns decorated with coloured crayons. These depicted stylised floral subjects were painted by decorators who were given a free hand rather than having to work from a set pattern guide and were made for the home market, in particular Boots.

MQ2 *shape earthenware coffee pot, decorated with the printed* Columbine *pattern designed by Jessie Tait, height 8¼in (21cm), 1967*

Earthenware meat plate decorated with the printed and painted Gay Gobbler *pattern, 13¾in (35cm), 1955*

Robert Lamont, a relation of the owner, had his own art studio for designing new patterns but very little is known about his work other than that his name was included on the backstamp.

The most important period for Midwinter was the '50s when Roy Midwinter achieved great artistic and commercial success with his new contemporary patterns and shapes. The breakthrough happened when Roy Midwinter took a selection of trial patterns to show the important North American buyers. These samples were rejected for not being contemporary enough for their market and he was advised to go to the West Coast of America to look at the work of leading designers such as Raymond Loewy, Russell Wright and Eva Zeisel, who were developing softer more organic shapes. Inspired by what he saw he returned to the factory to develop a new range of shapes and patterns ready for a pottery trade fair in 1953. Jessie Tait, who worked closely with Roy Midwinter, was one of a new breed of contemporary designers to emerge during the immediate post-war period and played a significant role in the success of the company with her innovative and colourful patterns that complemented the new *Stylecraft* range, launched in 1953. Using both printed and hand-painted treatments she created, amongst others, patterns such as *Fiesta* and *Primavera*, which were introduced in 1954.

In order to keep ahead in such a competitive market, Midwinter introduced new lines created by freelance artists and designers such as Hugh Casson,

Typical backstamp from the '50s

Two earthenware plates decorated with the Sun *and* Earth *patterns designed by Eve Midwinter, 1973*

who created the popular *Riveria* pattern for the *Stylecraft* range, and Terence Conran, who created the *Chequers*, *Nature Study*, *Plant Life* and *Salad Ware* patterns for the *Fashion* shape launched in 1955. Jessie Tait also created patterns for the *Fashion* shape, such as *Zambesi* and *Festival*.

In the early '60s hand-painted decoration was phased out. In 1961 the new *Fine* shape, for dinner, tea and coffee ware, was launched decorated with a number of printed patterns, including *Sienna*, *Country Garden* and *Spanish Garden*. This new shape was very successful and profitable for the company. It is at this point that Eve Midwinter, Roy's wife, began to make an important contribution to pattern designs for the company, including *Roselle*. Eve had moved in to design informally, starting by designing room settings for the company at trade shows.

In 1964 Midwinter purchased A.J. Wilkinson Ltd. and Newport Pottery Ltd. to cope with demand. However, new shapes, including *Portobello*, *Trend* and *MQ2*, were not popular with customers and soon had to be withdrawn. As a result, Midwinter suffered financial losses that eventually led to the company being taken over by J. & G. Meakin Ltd.

in 1968. Two years later Josiah Wedgwood and Sons Ltd. took over both companies.

During the '70s Midwinter developed the new *Stonehenge* range that set a new standard in both shape and pattern. Eve Midwinter developed a new glaze called *Creation* for outstanding patterns such as *Sun*, *Earth* and *Moon*. Best-selling patterns included *Wild Oats* and *Rangoon*. A similar range, called *Stoneware*, was introduced in 1979 with patterns designed by a team of freelance designers: *Denim*, *Hopsack* and *Blueprint* are typical examples.

By the '80s it was clear that a new fashion was emerging. In order to capitalise on this, Eve Midwinter, with her group of young designers, developed a new shape called *Style*. To complement the white body and delicate shape, simple pastel colours were used for patterns such as *Confetti*, *Coral Mist* and *Crystal*. Unfortunately, a number of items in the *Style* range were not very practical and it was soon withdrawn. Midwinter's next shape, *Reflex*, was altogether more functional. Introduced in 1986, *Reflex* was decorated with a series of patterns, including *Enchantment*, *Rhapsody* and *Monmartre*, banded in yellow and blue. *Reflex* was followed by the popular

Group of Style *wares including a tureen decorated with the* Confetti *pattern designed by Eve Midwinter and a teapot, cup, saucer and covered preserve jar decorated with* Rainbow *designed by Carol Lovatt, 1983-85*

Roland Rat giftware range. A year later Wedgwood ceased using the Midwinter name, although the best-selling patterns continued in production.

- Of particular interest to collectors is the work of both Peggy Gibbons, who designed nursery patterns such as *Jack and Jill* and *Three Little Pigs* during the late 1940s, and Nancy Great-Rex, who created a range of modelled animals including *Larry the Lamb* and *Peggy the Calf*.
- The 1950s were the most important and creative years for Midwinter. Look out for the hand-painted patterns by Jessie Tait, such as *Primavera*, *Zambesi* and *Festival*.
- Patterns by Terence Conran are much sought after.
- Launched in the 1960s, *Portobello*, *Trend* and

MQ2, were not popular shapes with customers at the time and soon had to be withdrawn. These items are, therefore, rare – resulting in them being collectable items today.

Further Reference

Casey, A., *Twentieth Century Ceramic Designers in Britain*. Antique Collectors' Club, 2001

Jenkins, S., *Midwinter Modern: A Revolution in British Tableware*. Richard Dennis, 1997

Peat, A., *Midwinter, A Collectors' Guide*. Cameron & Hollis, 1991

www.retroselect.com

Pair of Secessionist Ware *vases, c.1902*

MINTON

Minton has a history of excellence in ceramic production over two centuries with its outstanding tablewares, both in bone china and earthenware, alongside decorative wares, tiles, art wares and figures. In particular, Minton made an outstanding contribution to the industry, particularly from the 1840s to the 1880s.

In 1793, the company Minton & Poulson was formed by a partnership between Thomas Minton and Joseph Poulson. Financial backing came from William Pownall, whose name was later added to the company name. Land was purchased in Stoke during the same year and a small factory was built. In 1858 Colin Minton Campbell, nephew of Thomas Minton, became Managing Director of the company and his interest in Middle Eastern design influenced the company's patterns and shapes. Another important figure in the success of the company was Thomas's son, Herbert. In 1873 the company became known as Minton, and was registered as a limited company in 1892. Colin Minton Campbell died in 1885. By the latter part of the century the company had suffered some financial losses.

Towards the end of the 19th century Louis Solon developed a range of ceramics using the *pâte-sur-*

pâte process. His son Léon V. Solon worked closely with John Wadsworth to develop the new *Secessionist Ware* based on the Art Nouveau styles of Austria; the range included toilet wares, jardinières and plates, and was launched in 1902. John Wadsworth became Art Director in 1909 but left after six years to work for Royal Worcester.

Alongside these new wares the company continued many of its successful lines that dated back many years. In 1915 the new art director Walter Stanley Woodman re-introduced a selection of older traditional patterns, such as *Clive Japan*, *Willow* and *Poonah*, but in new colour ways. In 1924 he designed a number of lustre patterns, with contrasting coloured interiors. The following year patterns such as *Babes in the Wood*, *Parrot* and *Duck* were decorated on a wide selection of shapes including jars, vases, tazzas and bowls.

Following the 1925 Exposition Internationale des Arts Décoratifs et Industriels Modernes in Paris and subsequent financial problems after the Wall Street Crash in 1929 the company recognised that it had lost its way artistically and subsequently decided to concentrate on mass-produced wares. Walter Stanley

Woodman left the company to join Grindleys in 1930 and was replaced by Reginald Haggar. Haggar's contemporary ideas resulted in an exceptional range of patterns and shapes that boosted the company's profile. He was fully aware of the importance of French design and in particular Art Deco. This is evident in the dinnerware pattern *Modern Art*, which depicts a women set against a landscape inspired by the French designer Jean Dupas. Haggar also produced some geometric vases called *Les Vases Modernes*. Haggar designed several shapes, including *Ionic*, *Empire*, *Clare*, *Doric* and *Hollywood*, the latter featuring an angular handle complemented by several modern tableware patterns with a hint of Art Deco, such as *Landscape* and *Mexican* in 1932; *Landscape* was shown at the British Art in Industry exhibition at the Royal Academy in London in 1935. At the same time Doris Lindner, a freelance modeller, created *The Bather* alongside Eric Owen's *The Hikers*.

In about 1934 John Wadsworth returned to his position at Minton after the resignation of Reginald Haggar, following some artistic disagreements with the company. In 1937 Wadsworth introduced *Solano*

Earthenware tureen, decorated with a printed and painted Art Deco pattern, designed by Reginald Haggar, height 8½in (21.5cm), c.1932-35

Period illustration showing a range of Solano Ware, *1937*

Ware, with patterns for this range including *Tulippa*; he also designed several new shapes such as *Isis*, *Duchess*, *Titania* and *Una* and a range of commemoratives for the coronation of George VI. Ten years later he designed a bone china goblet, in a limited edition of one hundred, for the wedding of Princess Elizabeth and Prince Philip.

Before WWII the production of earthenware was halted, as demand for traditionally-styled bone china patterns increased, especially for the export market. In 1949 Wadsworth created by far one of the most popular Minton patterns, *Haddon Hall*, which is still in production today. He also created a special vase, which was presented to the Queen by the British Pottery Manufacturers Federation to mark the Coronation in 1953. John Wadsworth died in 1955 and was eventually replaced by Douglas Henson in 1957.

In 1968 Minton was taken over by Royal Doulton but production continued largely as normal in to the early '90s. Several artists and sculptors, such as Robert Jefferson and Eric Griffiths, worked for the company during the late '70s and early '80s. Eric Griffiths created the figure *Sea Breeze* in 1980. In

1987 Jean Muir designed a collection of boxes decorated with strong bands of colour.

In 1992 all production ceased at the Minton factory, though the most popular lines continued to be manufactured in other factories. In 2005 Royal Doulton ceased production.

+ Minton offers the collector a range of high-quality and expensive ceramics; notable examples are the *Seccessionist Wares* and the *Solano Wares* from the '30s.
+ One of the most popular of Minton's patterns is *Haddon Hall*, first introduced in 1947 and still in production today.

Further Reference

Atterbury, P. and Batkin, M., *The Dictionary of Minton*. Antique Collectors' Club, 1999

Jones, J., *Minton, The First Two Hundred Years of Design and Production*. Swan Hill Press, 1993

www.royaldoulton.com

MOORCROFT

Moorcroft Pottery is one of the most influential and important British pottery companies of the 20th century. Its uniquely styled products stand out above many of the rest and transcend the various trends and fashions in British pottery over the century.

In 1897 William Moorcroft, whose family had been associated with the production of pottery for many years, joined James Macintyre & Co. Ltd. (an influential manufacturer producing a varied range of products from architectural fittings to commercial pottery in both china and earthenware) as manager of ornamental ware, giving him complete control of production. Over the following few years he created new patterns and several shapes including tablewares.

William Moorcroft is best known for his decorative art wares such as *Florian Ware*, which used slip trailing to create a range of different patterns in the fluid Art Nouveau style, using butterflies, flowers, peacock feathers, fish, daffodils, cornflowers and other British native plant species for inspiration. *Florian* was introduced in 1901 and was sold in Liberty's of London and Tiffany's in New York, inspiring several other similar designs, such as stylised floral motifs and landscape patterns including *Claremont*, *Hisperian* and *Hazledene* in 1902. James Macintyre & Co. enjoyed international acclaim and recognition at the important world expositions including the St. Louis World's Fair in 1904 where the company won a gold medal. During that year it launched the *Flamminian* range which was exclusive to Liberty; both *Pansy* and the pomegranate pattern were launched in 1910.

Surprisingly, despite this success the company decided to close down the ornamental department and concentrate on other production. Having built up good contacts through the international trade, William Moorcroft decided to set up on his own. Despite some

Earthenware vase decorated with the Hazledene *landscape pattern designed by William Moorcroft, first introduced in 1903 by James Macintyre & Co. with a colour variation introduced in 1912*

Earthenware jar and cover decorated with a later version of the pomegranate pattern, which was originally designed by William Moorcroft at James Macintyre & Co. in 1910. This colour variation dates from c.1913

Salt-glaze vase decorated with the Cornflower *pattern, height 6⅝in (17cm), c.1925-1930*

set backs, he built a new factory at Cobridge that he moved into in 1913, paid for by Liberty and Co. Some of the staff and equipment from James Macintyre & Co. joined this new venture and Moorcroft also took with him some of his designs. In 1913, on advice from Liberty, Moorcroft introduced a cheaper range of tablewares; *Powder Blue* was finished with a blue speckled pattern and sold through the prestigious Liberty store. It was such a critical and commercial success that it remained in production until the early '60s.

During the early '20s, Moorcroft developed his flambé glazes, which he used on new patterns, such as *Orchid* and *Freesia*. In response to demand he also produced several of his earlier patterns from his time at Macintyre & Co., such as *Claremont*, featuring toadstool motifs, and *Hazledene*. In 1928 Moorcroft was granted an honorary title, Potter to H.M. The Queen, and in 1930 the company was awarded the Grand Prix at Antwerp. The '30s brought economic setbacks following the Wall Street Crash in 1929, but it was also a time of adventurous and experimental design and production.

William Moorcroft died in 1945 leaving his son

Right:
Earthenware vase decorated with a stylised carp, designed by Sally Tuffin, 1991

Below:
Earthenware powder bowl and cover decorated with the Pansy Nouveau *pattern, designed by Walter Moorcroft, 1972*

Walter Moorcroft, straight out of army service, to run the business. Walter, who had very limited experience (he had worked briefly at the pottery before the war), initially used and adapted pre-war patterns, but by the '50s was introducing distinctive new styles and colours. Walter Moorcroft created several new patterns based on flowers, such as *Arum Lily, Campanula* and *Tulip*. Walter broke away from his father's work by using a lighter background as is typified by the *Clematis* pattern from 1954; his most popular pattern was *Anemone. Pansy Nouveau* was made for the American market c.1972.

On Walter Moorcroft's retirement in 1987, Sally Tuffin becoming chief designer. Tuffin created outstanding new patterns that were modern but maintained the distinctive Moorcroft tradition, including *Finches, Tulip, Violet* and *Carp*. Rachel Bishop joined the company in 1993 and went on to create over 300 designs, the first of which was *Tigris*. Many of her designs were made in limited editions.

Moorcroft is still active.

- The earliest Moorcroft wares are the most sought after; however, there is a growing interest in the later wares, particularly the designs by Sally Tuffin from the '80s and '90s.
- Look out for limited editions by Rachel Bishop.

Further Reference
Atterbury, P., *Moorcroft, A Guide to Moorcroft Pottery 1897-1993*. Richard Dennis, 1996

www.moorcroft.com

105

Earthenware trio decorated with a hand-painted floral design, 1930s

MYOTT

The Myott story began with James Myott, of Newcastle-under-Lyme, who had a commercial business as a linen draper, which by 1900 had expanded to incorporate a warehouse for china and glass and earthenware manufacture in Wolfe Street, Stoke-on-Trent, known as Myott Son & Co. One of his sons, Ashley Myott, became an apprentice potter to George Thomas Mountford in 1895 whilst an older son, Sydney, worked with his father in the drapery business. When the owner of the pottery died James Myott purchased the factory and gave Ashley Myott the responsibility of managing it. His brother Sydney helped him, and together they built up the business, eventually moving to larger premises in Cobridge in 1902.

From the start, the company enjoyed success and installed new machinery to meet the many orders for dinnerware, toilet sets, jugs and flowerpots. In 1903 an agent was established in Canada for the much needed export market with new showrooms in Liverpool and Manchester. By 1921 the company had representatives in many countries including Australia, America and South Africa.

By the early '20s Myott was noted in the trade press as producing "semi-porcelain of the first grade" for domestic wares with many items featuring smart distinctive borders or simple maroon bands, alongside new patterns such as *Indian Tree*. During the '30s the company developed a range of Chintz wares, including *Bermuda*, available in both blue and brown, *Spring Flower* and *Summer Flower*. It also produced plain white tablewares for the Cunard shipping line.

Myott embraced the Art Deco style bringing out a variety of vases and jugs and patterns in the first few years of the '30s. These bold and striking shapes were decorated with a diverse range of patterns often covered in blocks of colours, the predominant colours being orange, yellow and brown; patterns very often featured stylised flowers. The *Dante* jug, which seems to have been the most popular during the period, was offered in around 50 different patterns. In total contrast to anything the company had produced before, these contemporary items were clearly introduced to compete in the new fashionable market of hand-painted pottery pioneered so successfully by Clarice Cliff. A company advertisement from this period illustrates the *Fan* and *Moderne* vases that are very similar with clear reference to both the Aztec and Egyptian styles. Shapes such as *Evert Wavy Rim*, *Beaky* and *Torpedo* simply ignore any of the concerns for practicality or function that was being discussed at the time. Notable examples of the more practical shapes include *Bow Tie* and *Trumpet*.

Alongside the Art Deco ranges, Myott also continued production of its more traditional lines, such as the *Georgian* shape, featuring an embossed edge, the *Conway* tea for two set, both from 1933, and patterns such as *Chelsea Bird* and *Bouquet*. Myott opened a larger showroom in 1933; two years later over 500 hundred patterns were registered. In 1937 the company launched the *Queens* shape alongside some rustic ware, matt glaze wares and a new hand-painted pattern called *Iris*.

Myott's collaboration with Austrian Marcel

Right:
Earthenware Moderne *vase decorated with a stylised tree pattern, 1933.*
Courtesy of the Myott Collectors' Club

Far right:
Extremely rare hand-painted owl bookend, height 6½ in (16.5 cm), 1930s.
Courtesy of the Myott Collectors' Club

Goldscheider was an interesting point in the company's history. Myott gave Goldscheider space to develop his famous figure work and he created a range of ceramic figures and face masks for the company. This special arrangement ended in 1950 when Goldscheider set up locally on his own. Very little is known about this association or the products that resulted from it. By the late '30s Myott seems to have reverted back to its patterns and shapes from the '20s.

During WWII Myott continued production for the export market. It was at this time that Myott became a private limited company. In 1949 a fire caused extensive damage to the factory.

By the '50s and '60s a wide selection of traditionally styled patterns aimed at the conventional market were introduced alongside patterns such as *Blue Rosanna* and *Heritage*, which proved popular in the U.S.A. In 1963 Myott launched the new *Viking* range decorated with ten different patterns including *Zodiac Black*, *Malaga Blue* and *Concorde*, which was a best seller in Canada. In 1969 the company was bought out by Interpace, an American corporation based in New Jersey, and, at that time the largest manufacturer of tableware in North America. In 1976 the company merged with Alfred Meakin Ltd. to become Myott-

Meakin Ltd., which, in turn, was taken over by the Churchill Group in June 1991.

♦ The brightly painted patterns on Deco shapes are the most sought after of Myott's wares. At the moment prices are relatively low, though rare pieces still command up to £3,000.

♦ Sadly, there is little archive material available for Myott from the '30s, so information has been gathered by many of the dedicated Myott collectors who have recently given names to the many different shapes and patterns. The trade press reviews, although limited, do give some indication to the range and dates. For instance in 1933 they noted the new *Egyptian* flower jug and the *Persian* jug that featured a 'pinched' top.

♦ Look out for the ceramic figures and face masks created by Marcel Goldscheider

Further Reference

Myott, A. and Pollitt, P., *The Mystery of Myott: A History of the Myott Pottery Stoke-on-Trent 1898-1991*. Published privately, (2003)

www.myottcollectorsclub.com

Bone china trio decorated with a printed stylised floral border, diameter of plate 6¼in (16cm), c.1935.

PARAGON CHINA CO. LTD.

In 1897 William Illingworth started up a pottery at the St. Gregory's Works, to be joined a year later by Herbert James Aynsley. By 1903 they had formed Star China Co. and moved the operation to the Atlas Works in Sutherland Road, advertising the wares as 'The Paragon of Excellence'. When Illingworth retired in 1910, Aynsley's son-in-law Hugh Irving became a partner. It was under Irving's control, in 1919, that the company name was changed to Paragon China Co. Ltd., to suggest a quality product.

Paragon specialised in high-quality bone china tea and breakfast sets for export to South Africa, New Zealand and Australia; this later expanded to include Canada and North America. Paragon also enjoyed Royal patronage from about 1926, when it was commissioned to produce nursery wares for the Royal family; in 1933 the company was granted a Royal Warrant of Appointment by Queen Mary, followed five years later with another by Queen Elizabeth, the wife of George VI.

Paragon was swift to respond to the latest changes in taste. In 1929 Thomas Acland Fennemore was brought in to work closely with the owner to develop the marketing side of the business. The company also employed several designers to create modern new patterns and shapes, including J.A. Robinson, who was engaged as a full-time designer from the late '20s and who was credited for his Royal Commemoratives and the *Modern* shape introduced c.1931. This new shape featured an open round top with the sides sloping sharply to the foot, it could be purchased with either a normal handle or one of an embossed flower. The range was decorated with floral patterns such as *Iceland Poppy*, *Jasmine*, *Lily of the Valley* and *Wisteria*.

Reginald Johnson joined the company in the 1930s, eventually becoming Art Director. Other designers included Ceri Clayton and Agnes Pinder Davis, who created the *As You Like It* pattern in 1935.

Typical patterns of the late '20s included simple landscape scenes, such as *Lugano* depicting a floral scene on the banks of a winding river, and

Bone china teapot decorated with a floral pattern, height 6in (15cm), 1930s

Gainsborough, showing an island in a lake with flowers and fairies in the foreground. These patterns and others, such as *Foxglove* decorated on the *Windsor* shape, and *Tulip* hand-painted on the new *Modern* shape.

Paragon was also well known for its nursery wares having produced in 1929 the dainty china nursery ware depicting a young curly-haired Princess Elizabeth, printed in blue, and called *Princess Elizabeth* nursery china. In 1930 Paragon secured the exclusive rights to introduce a pattern range featuring *Mickey Mouse* from Walt Disney, with twelve motifs. In the late '20s and early '30s Paragon introduced a number of nursery ware patterns, including *Animal Alphabet* by Constance Grace and *Two for Joy* by Beatrice Mallett in 1927.

Following WWII, the company continued in production, later extending its range of products to include breakfast sets, ashtrays and animal figures.

It also introduced a range of figures modelled by Reginald Johnson. In 1960 Paragon was taken over by T.C. Wild & Sons; four years later it merged with the Lawley Group to form Allied English Potteries Ltd. In 1968 the company was taken over by the Doulton Group, although the company name was retained as a separate identity. The trade press reported that in 1969 six new tea set patterns were being introduced including *Elegance, Cadenza* and *Nocturne*, which were designed by Reginald Johnson.

◆ The exquisite and delicately painted tea wares by Paragon continue to be favoured by collectors. In particular, examples of the Art Deco designs are much sought after.

Further Reference

www.paragonpottery.com

Earthenware dish, decorated with hand-painted Persian Deer *pattern designed by Truda Adams (Carter) in 1924, painted by Gertie Warren 1924-27, diameter 14¾in (37.5cm), c.1924-27*

POOLE POTTERY

The Poole Pottery, originally known as Carter, Stabler and Adams, has become one of the most important and innovative pottery manufacturers operating outside the Staffordshire area during the 20th century. During this time the company has produced striking Art Deco wares, free-form vases in the '50s, bold coloured experimental plaques in the '60s and, at the end of the century, a new 'living' glaze.

In 1873 Jesse Carter bought the Poole Pottery, a near derelict tile works on the East Quay in Poole. The business expanded when he introduced the making of glazed architectural faïence and decorative tiling used in hotels and public houses. In 1901

Carter's sons, Owen and Charles, took over the running of the business; in 1908 they renamed it Carter & Co. Ltd. They quickly introduced a wide range of domestic wares including lustre decorations. Many of these were designed by James Radley Young, who was responsible for the patterns exhibited at the British Industries Fair c.1920.

Following Owen Carter's death in 1919, Charles was assisted in running the company by his son Cyril. In 1921, in order to expand the art pottery side of the business, Cyril Carter, John Adams and Harold Stabler set up a subsidiary company known as Carter, Stabler and Adams. Initially the new company produced high-quality decorative pottery using a grey semi-stoneware body, hand-painted on a grey glaze. In 1922 a red earthenware body was introduced, and two years later later this was matched with a white slip ground and semi-matt clear glaze. Throughout the '20s the company produced vases, plates, fancies and other useful wares decorated with geometric motifs, banding, stylised birds and floral motifs. The company was an immediate success, selling in all the important retail outlets such as Heal's in London and exhibiting at the British Empire Exhibition in 1924 and the Exposition Internationale des Arts Décoratifs et Industriels Modernes in Paris a year later.

During this period, John Adams' wife, Truda Adams (later Truda Carter), was an important figure in the company. She created an outstanding range of colourful, stylised and abstract hand-painted patterns such as *Persian Deer,* in 1924, as well as several bird and fish motifs. From the early '30s Truda Adams embraced the Art Deco movement, her patterns featuring lightning strikes and bold flower heads. Decorated mainly on vases and ornamental plaques, her work was both distinctive and original.

In contrast to the highly decorative wares, the company also introduced a popular range of giftwares including the famous *Springbok* bookends, table centres and giftwares created by John Adams. He also concentrated on the production of tablewares including the *Streamline* shape, which was introduced in 1936, and available in various two-tone finishes. Both nursery wares and decorative tiles were also produced and decorated by many freelance designers, such as Edward Bawden and Cecil Aldin.

During the immediate post-WWII period and subsequent reconstruction, the company needed a new designer to give new impetus. Alfred B. Read took the position and over the next few years introduced a series of free-form 'Contemporary' shapes, such as vases decorated with simple vertical coloured bands, stylised ferns and circular motifs, in various colours, which were first introduced in 1953. He also created several stylised patterns for tablewares that included *Ripple, Feather Drift* and *Constellation,* for the *Streamline* shape. Read left the company in 1957.

In 1963 the company was purchased by Pilkingtons Tiles and renamed Poole Pottery Limited.

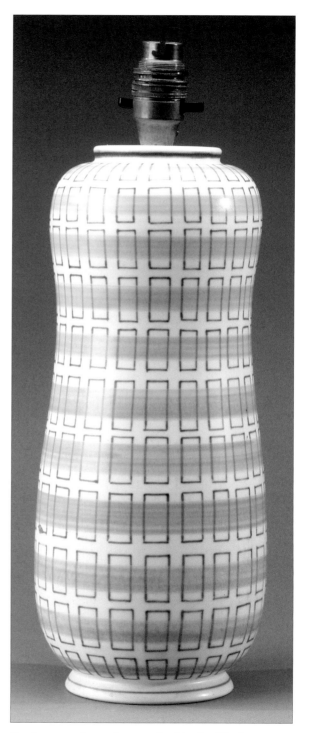

Earthenware lamp decorated with the PJ. L *pattern, designed by Alfred B. Read, 1953*

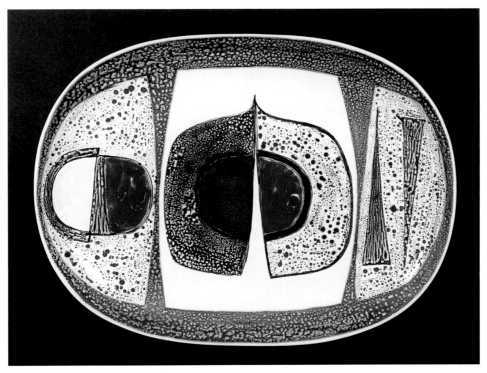

Earthenware plaque, decorated with stylised apple motif designed by Robert Jeffferson, length 16in (40.5cm), 1962-63

Earthenware plate decorated with stylised owl, possibly designed by Robert Jefferson, c.1962-1963

In the '60s Robert Jefferson made an important contribution to Poole. His oven-to-tableware range was launched in 1961, finished in either Blue Moon, Celadon Green or Heather Rose and later decorated with screen-printed patterns such as *Herb Garden*. This was followed by *Contour* tableware from 1963-64 and a year later by *Compact*, a multi-purpose set initially decorated with transparent glazes.

However, Jefferson's biggest success was his *Delphis* studio range (1962-64), which was developed through experimentation using all sorts of sources including landscapes and animals. These boldly-coloured patterns were decorated on earthenware plaques, vases and bowls and initially marked with a Dolphin and the words 'POOLE STUDIO'. In 1964 the range was modified for commercial production and renamed *The Delphis Collection*, the backstamp was also changed to include the words, 'POOLE STUDIO ENGLAND'.

The success of *Delphis* inspired other new lines

such as the *Aegean* range, which was decorated with stylised fish, landscapes and other similar motifs, and introduced in 1970. From the '70s, Poole's products were very diverse, from a new series of calendar plates designed by Tony Morris in 1973 to stoneware sculptures by Barbara Linley Adams. In 1979 Poole launched an interesting range of gift wares called *The Beardsley Collection,* which used the drawings of Aubrey Beardsley for the decoration. New tableware shapes from the '80s included *Style, Concert* and *Flair.*

In 1984, the *Calypso* range was developed through a partnership with the Queensbury Hunt. The early '90s saw Poole developing several ranges decorated with sponge motifs by Anita Harris.

Having been under the control of the Thomas Tilling and later BTR (British Tyre and Rubber) groups since 1971, Poole Pottery became an independent company again in 1992; it continues trading and is still developing new and innovative patterns that will surely become collectables in the future.

◆ Poole Pottery offers the collector a diverse range of collectables from Art Deco vases to *Delphis* studio wares from the '60s. Collectors should look

Earthenware casserole dish decorated with the Lucullus *pattern, designed by Robert Jefferson, height 6⅛in (5.6cm), 1962*

out for some of the less well-known patterns and shapes from the '60s and '70s.

◆ Look out for the colourful abstract designs by Truda Adams (Carter), such as *Persian Deer.*

◆ Robert Jefferson's *Delphis Studio* range, from 1962-64, is highly collectable. Collectors should note the difference between the backstamps on the *Delphis Studio* range ('POOLE STUDIO') and the later *Delphis Collection* ('POOLE STUDIO ENGLAND'), which is less sought after.

◆ Launched in 1979, *The Beardsley Collection,* using the drawings of the famous artist Aubrey Beardsley for the decoration, has proved to be popular with collectors.

Further Reference
Atterbury, P., *Poole in the 1950s.* Dennis, R. and Clark, J. at the Richard Dennis Gallery, 1997

Hayward, L., *Poole Pottery: Carter and Company and Their Successors, 1873-2002.* Richard Dennis. 3rd Edition

www.retroselect.com

Earthenware vase decorated with the BN pattern first introduced in the '30s and adapted in the '50s

Two earthenware apothecary jars and covers decorated with the Portmeirion Dolphin *pattern designed by Susan Williams-Ellis, c.1961*

The Totem *range decorated with various flow glazes, 1963*

PORTMEIRION POTTERIES LTD.

The story of Portmeirion Pottery began during the 1920s, when the architect Sir Clough Williams-Ellis created the Portmeirion village in North Wales. This tourist attraction, built in Italian style, boasted a hotel and several shops. During the '20s the Ashtead Pottery made a number of souvenirs, featuring the mermaid logo, to be sold in the village.

When Susan Williams-Ellis, Sir Clough's daughter, left art college during the mid '40s she moved to North Wales and undertook various tasks for the village, such as painting murals. Asked by her father to design a range of giftwares for the village, she approached the Stoke-on-Trent based pottery, A.E. Gray & Co. Ltd. The resulting wares, designed by Susan Williams-Ellis, were finished with the 'Sunderland Splatter' decorative technique; one of the earliest of her patterns was *Going to Wales* c.1957. Unsurprisingly these giftwares were

very successful, ultimately leading to Portmeirion making an approach to buy the company in 1960. For the first two years the Gray's mark was continued but with the words 'PORTMEIRION WARE' added.

This new company gave Williams-Ellis an unparalleled opportunity to create new patterns such as *Malachite* and *Moss Agate*. As a designer trained in the fine arts rather than the manufacture of pottery, she was not used to designing with commercial restrictions in mind and these first sets proved too expensive to produce. As a result, the company focused on more affordable domestic wares, such as *Tigerlily* and *Portmeirion Rose*, which combined transfer-printed motifs and banded decoration. In order to economise on transfer sheets, Williams-Ellis designed patterns that could be wrapped around the ware and the spare pieces used on other parts. Notable examples include *Talisman* and *Variations*.

The fact that Gray's bought in white wares rather than manufacturing its own shapes frustrated Susan Williams-Ellis, so she decided to purchase white ware manufacturer, Kirkhams Pottery in 1961, thereby giving her the opportunity to design modern shapes to match her innovative designs.

Williams-Ellis experimented with alternative forms of decoration as hand-painting was proving too costly during the post-war period. The breakthrough came with her *Totem* pattern, launched in 1963, featuring embossed abstract symbols on the body of the shape and finished with coloured glazes, including brown and green; a less well-known white version was produced a few years later. The combination of pattern and the extremely tall *Cylinder* shape coffee pot caused a sensation within the pottery industry.

The company had moved to the Kirkhams Pottery site and, from January 1962, the company became known as Portmeirion Potteries Ltd.; the original site was sold to Royal Doulton. With the increasing popularity of coffee sets, particularly as gifts, Portmeirion decided to introduce a number of new patterns for coffee sets, including *Magic City* in 1966, *Magic Garden*, in 1970, and the less well-known *Gold Six,* which encompassed different designs such as *Gold Sign* and *Gold Rule*. Portmeirion also enjoyed commercial success with a series of *Zodiac* mugs and *A Year to Remember* tankards.

Previously concerned with the quality of transfer-printed patterns, Susan Williams-Ellis was inspired by the high-quality printed reproductions offered by a German company. This enabled her to reproduce the delicate studies of flowers and plants

Original leaflet for the Variations *pattern, 1964*

from her collection of antiquarian books. The resulting range, *Botanic Garden*, which was launched in 1972, featured different floral motifs on each piece; this was very unusual for the time. Initially reproduced on a few items, it was soon extended to incorporate other shapes and special items; by the early '80s it could be found on various matching pans, tea towels, clocks and furnishing materials. By 1997, the *Botanic Garden* range amounted to a large part of the company's business. Further patterns included *Birds of Britain* in 1978 and *The Compleat Angler* in 1981.

In 1998 Portmeirion was floated on the stock exchange and in 1990 became known as Portmeirion Pottery Holdings, PLC. At this point the company decided to move into the bone china market with its *Moonstone* range of shapes and patterns such as *Ladies Flower Garden* and *Welsh Wild Flowers*.

Earliest backstamp for The Botanic Garden *range, 1972*

Two earthenware plates from the Botanic Garden *range*

The company continues to create innovative patterns and shapes, though sales are still dominated by *Botanic Garden*.

- The most popular range with Portmeirion collectors is *Botanic Garden*. Through the years a number of the original patterns were replaced and these are now sought after by collectors.
- The strikingly tall *Cylinder* coffee pot decorated with the *Totem* pattern caused a sensation on its launch. *Totem* was produced in large quantities, making it an easy to find collectable, and still relatively cheap. Follow up ranges included *Cypher* and *Jupiter*.
- A small number of dedicated Portmeirion collectors are interested in the wares from the early '60s. The sophisticated *Portmeirion Dolphin* design is popular, both with *Sunderland Splatter* and single colour glaze finishes. Collectors should look out for the less well-known patterns, such as *Gold Six*, as well as the more unusual patterns developed from old engravings and other materials, such as *Corsets*, *Idols of the Stage*, *Chemist Prints*, *Velocipedes* and *Reddington's New Foot Soldiers*.
- It is worth noting that Portmeirion's early ranges of affordable domestic wares, such as *Tigerlily*, which combined transfer-printed motifs and banded decoration, are not particularly sought after by collectors.

Further Reference

Casey, A., *Twentieth Century Ceramic Designers in Britain*. Antique Collectors' Club, 2001

Jenkins, S. and McKay S., *Portmeirion Pottery*. Richard Dennis, 2000

www.portmeirion.co.uk

Opposite:
Dinnerware shapes decorated with the printed The Compleat Angler *pattern, 1981*

Earthenware dish decorated with a Wemyss-style pattern, c.1910

POUNTNEY'S

According to the trade press, a pottery works was first established in the Bristol area in 1652 by Robert Collins. In 1813, John Decimus Pountney gained employment at the works, becoming the owner from 1830 until 1850. Despite subsequent changes of ownership, the company kept its new name of Pountney's.

The company was bought in 1878 by a London solicitor, Patrick Johnston, who amalgamated it with the Victoria Pottery, founded in 1865, later building a new modern pottery works at Fishponds in 1904. His nephew, T.B. Johnston, joined the company in 1905.

During the early part of the 20th century Pountney's produced a wide variety of pottery including pearl ware; over the subsequent years it introduced earthenware and semi-porcelain dinner sets with typical patterns for toilet wares including hand-painted roses on a black border with many decorated on the *Champion* shape. Interestingly, at about this time Pountney's produced a range of wares in the Wemyss style under licence. Pountney's kept costs low by using inexpensive transfer-printed designs and also some chintz patterns in about 1917. The company exported across Europe, North America, South Africa and Australia.

In 1910 Cecil Garland joined the company and after WWI was appointed Artistic and Decorating Manager under Mr. Brunt. On Mr. Brunt's death, Cecil Garland took charge of all the decorating departments. Aware of the interest in the new Art Deco style and the push towards mass production, he employed a new designer, Jack F. Price. This partnership was a success, with Price designing a number of long-lasting shapes, including *Dorland* c.1933 and *Academy* in 1937, alongside a number of kitchenwares, which were later used for the *Long Line* range in the early '60s. The well-known artist and designer Agnes Pinder Davies also worked with Cecil Garland on a number of ideas, with some put into production during the late '40s. Examples of the company's latest wares, many designed by Garland, were shown at the Paris Exposition in 1937; in 1941 Queen Mary visited the company and was presented with a reproduction of a Champion bowl, painted by Garland, and a unique plaque to commemorate the visit. Following T.B. Johnston's death in 1938, his son, Patrick, took control of the company.

After WWII Kenneth Clark headed the design team, producing a number of contemporary and traditional patterns in the '50s and '60s based on Victorian designs. Contemporary patterns included *Lilybell*, *Golden Days* and *Seed Cress* (designed by Clark), which were used on shapes such as *Burlington* (designed by Jack Price), *Mooncurve* (similar to the Holiday shape by J. & G. Meakin) and *Boston*. In 1959 the company issued the *Bristol Scenes* patterns on the *Gadroon* shape, a new interpretation of a 120-year-old pattern.

In 1961 a new modern kitchenware range designed by Honor Elliot, was introduced. *Long Line,* available in three different colours, depicted cutlery around each item, including pudding bowls, jars, mixing bowls and flour dredgers. She also created *Desert Mist*, which was commended by the Council of Industrial Design.

Pat Chewter, a lecturer from Liverpool College of Art, succeeded Kenneth Clark as consultant designer; she created a number of patterns including *Kudu*, in 1965,

Earthenware plate decorated with the Blue Scroll *pattern, 1930s*

decorated on the *Clifton* shape. In 1967 the company launched the *Bristol Garden* patterns, which included the variations *June Garden*, *Autumn Garden* and *Winter Garden*. The same year saw the *Blue Scroll* pattern, originally designed in the '30s, displayed by the Council of Industrial Design in London.

In 1962 Pountney's purchased Royal Cauldon Pottery; in 1969 the company was renamed Cauldon Bristol Potteries Ltd.; within two years the company had been bought out by A.G. Richardson Ltd. Production ceased in 1971.

♦ Although Pountney's wares are still relatively unknown on the collectors' market, they will, no doubt, in time become collectable. Look out for hand-painted patterns, such as *Blue Scroll*.

Further Reference

Batkin, M., *Gifts for Good Children. The History of Children's China, Part II, 1890-1990*. Richard Dennis, 1991

Levitt, S., *The Bristol Pottery*. Redcliffe Press, 1990

Collection of hand-thrown vases, height of tallest item 7in (17.8cm), decorated with various tree patterns

EDWARD RADFORD

The relatively unknown artist potter Edward Thomas Brown Radford (b.1882) came from a long line of pottery artists. His father was apprenticed at Josiah Wedgwood and Sons Ltd. and worked at Linthorpe Pottery, Burmantofts in Leeds, Doulton & Co., and Pilkington's Tile & Pottery Co., Manchester where he worked alongside Gordon Forsyth, Gladys Rogers and Richard Joyce; he retired in 1936. Edward learned his trade from his father at Pilkington's, where he was taught all the important aspects of pottery production and of running a business. Following time in the army – he was awarded the Military Cross for bravery at Passchendaele during WWI – he moved to Burslem, Stoke-on-Trent. From about 1920 he was advertising his services as a pottery agent in the trade press and attending trade fairs demonstrating the art of throwing.

By the late twenties, possibly early thirties, he had established the Radford Handcraft Pottery based at H.J. Woods Ltd at the Alexander Works, on Amicable Street, Burslem, owned by Wood and Sons Ltd. As a skilled potter he was able to develop a whole series of shapes both traditional and modern that included bowls, vases and jugs. These shapes were decorated with bold and artistic patterns, such as a series of abstract tree patterns in the Art Deco style, a range of sgraffito patterns as well as many stylised floral patterns in bold colours. In contrast, he also produced a series of naturalistic tree and landscape patterns painted by James Harrison. There is limited information about this period or exactly what Radford was designing, although it is known that a number of patterns featured a sponged or mottled ground under a matt glaze and painted with stylised flowers. These early examples of pottery were usually marked with 'E RADFORD BURSELM'.

Radford spent time each year travelling to gain new orders, leaving the pattern designing to Mabel Hadgkiss. Furthermore, it has been suggested that some patterns were designed by the paintresses themselves. His wares from this period were called 'Radford Handcraft Pottery'.

Notable lines included simple floral motifs, such as *Anemones*, often featuring stippled grounds. Not a confident pattern designer, Radford would apparently give his decorators packets of seeds so that they could be inspired by the pictures and then interpret the image to develop a pattern. It is also possible that he may have used some of the standard Woods shapes.

In 1948 Edward Radford retired and became a

Above:
Hand-thrown wares decorated with various patterns by Edward Radford, height of tallest item 6in (15.2cm)

Right:
Two hand-thrown vases by Edward Radford

teacher of pottery, living first in Derbyshire then moving to Manchester in 1954. His work was featured over several pages in the Radford Handcraft and Bursley Ware catalogue produced by H.J. Wood in about 1954. Whilst this catalogue illustrated several known patterns and shapes by him, there were also a number of undecorated vases, jugs, ginger jars, flower baskets, and candlesticks with his trademark that were clearly not actually his.

H.J. Wood continued to produce his work into the 1960s, alongside Charlotte Rhead's work.

- Radford Pottery is much sought after today by collectors who are willing to pay high prices for the less well-known designs: hand-painted wares from the early '30s being the most popular.
- The most common backstamp was 'E RADFORD BURSLEM', although other marks were used, including 'RADFORD HANDCRAFT WARE'. 'E RADFORD MADE IN GREAT BRITAIN' is believed to have been used for export pieces, possible during WWII.

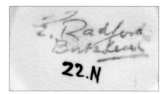

Example of the earliest backstamp

Further Reference
www.sdawe.freeserve.co.uk

Earthenware trio decorated with the printed Homemaker *pattern on the* Metro *shape, 1950s*

RIDGWAY POTTERIES LTD.

Ridgway, a Shelton-based pottery, was founded by Edward John Ridgway c.1866. Within a few years he was joined by his two sons, who continued the business when he retired in 1872. In 1873 Joseph Sparks joined the business as a partner, from then on the company traded as Ridgway, Sparks and Ridgway. Early wares produced by the company included stoneware, terracotta and jasper ware. Following the departure of Joseph Sparks the pottery was known simply as Ridgways, from 1920 the company traded as Ridgways (Bedford Works) Ltd.

The earliest productions of this factory were, for the most part, traditionally styled and Japanese and Chinese-inspired patterns that were transfer printed. By the early '30s several hand-painted patterns were issued including *Somerset*. Ridgways bought the Cauldon Potteries in 1929, at the same time moving into the production of modern wares. A new shape called *Ramsdell* was launched in 1937.

In 1955 the company was renamed Ridgway Potteries Ltd., incorporating several smaller pottery manufacturers such as Booths Ltd., H.J. Colclough and Adderleys. Soon after, the company introduced a new modern shape, *Atlantic*, designed by A.M.Turner, which was decorated with several stylish patterns and virtually led the market in contemporary decoration alongside the *Stylecraft* and *Fashion* lines by Midwinter.

Tom Arnold, a prominent designer who had worked for Ridgways since 1953, developed the bone china *Sapphire* range with coupe plates following his visit to the United States in 1956. A year later he was appointed Art Director for Ridgway Potteries, with a new design studio in Cobridge. *Metro*, an earthenware version of the *Sapphire* shape, was now produced exclusively for the influential department store Altman's in New York. At the same time the company invested in new machinery for faster application of transfer-printed decoration to blank wares.

Enid Seeney, a young designer, joined Booths & Colcloughs at the start of the '50s; her earliest patterns included *English Garden*, *Samoa* and *Bamboo*. One of the most important and popular patterns of the 20th century was *Homemaker*, featuring contemporary furniture with a black linear background. Woolworth commissioned Ridgways each year for a new pattern exclusive to them. By chance, the Woolworth buyer saw Seeney's trial designs on her desk and selected it as their new line. The pattern was decorated on the *Metro* shape; it was an outstanding success and was copied by several manufacturers. It is now considered to be a design classic.

In some respects the success of *Homemaker* and the interest in it by collectors today has overshadowed the patterns and shapes by the other designers working at the time including *Thistledown* and *Allegro* – the latter by Margaret Simpson. In 1960 Eddie Sambrook was appointed Art Director, following the departure of Tom Arnold. Sambrook had worked for several years at Wood and Sons and, during the late '40s, with Charlotte Rhead. By the mid '60s the *Metro* shape was looking rather dated so, with the help of Margaret Simpson, Sambrook developed the new *Cadenza* shape, which was decorated with several patterns including *Valencia*, *Contessa* and *Argosy*. From about 1966 the *Homemaker* pattern was reproduced onto this new shape as well.

Earthenware plate printed with the Parisienne *pattern, 1950s*

In about 1964 the company was taken over by Allied English Potteries and later became part of the Royal Doulton Tableware Group although the company continued to trade as Ridgway Potteries. In 1965 Gerald Benney designed the *Ondine* pattern on the *Albion* shape and a three years later a new shape range called *Atlanta* was launched. The *Indian Summer* tableware range was introduced in 1973. Ten years later the trade name was dropped by the parent company.

- The *Homemaker* pattern is, without a doubt, the best-known design of '50s ceramics and is considered a design classic.
- Designed by A.M. Turner in the mid '50s, the *Atlantic* shape, decorated with contemporary patterns, was a fashion leader and is popular with collectors today.
- Look out for *Homemaker* reproduced on the *Cadenza* shape coffee and teapots, which are quite rare.

Further Reference

Moss, S., *Homemaker, A 1950s Design Classic*. Cameron and Hollis, 1997

Bone china coffee pot, decorated with an over-glaze printed pattern of stylised flowers, height 7⅝in (19.3cm), c.1934

ROYAL ALBERT
Thomas C. Wild & Co.

The story of Royal Albert goes back as far as the late 19th century when it was founded in the 1890s as Thomas C. Wild & Co., at the Albert Works in Longton, by Thomas Clark Wild and his father; later Thomas Clark's two sons joined him with both becoming directors in 1914.

The firm traded under the name Royal Albert, which was included in the backstamp from around 1905. From the early days of production its high-quality bone china wares enabled Royal Albert to build up strong export sales in countries such as Africa, New Zealand and Australia. This was aided by the company buying out and incorporating several smaller manufacturers.

One of the earliest and best-selling patterns was *Longton Derby*, under-glaze printed in claret brown, panelled in blue, enamelled in red and illuminated in gold. For most of the 20th century Royal Albert was associated with simple pleasant floral patterns decorated on delicate bone china in the traditional manner such as *Albert*. During the late '20s, patterns such as *June*, which depicted a printed hawthorn motif with blue border and was decorated on the

Cecil shape, or another depicting a crinoline lady amongst hollyhocks, were typical. In 1934 Harold Holdcroft joined the company as Design Director and under his direction shapes became more rococo in style and patterns much bolder, in line with current taste. As well as a number of nursery patterns, Holdcroft created a mixture of traditional patterns, such as the hand-painted *Dog Rose* and printed *Chelsea Bird*. He also designed many contemporary patterns such as one featuring a central abstract floral motif in white and gold on a black background from the mid '30s. Other patterns, noted in the trade press included *Hydrangea*, *Harmony* and *Embassy*. The transfer-printed pattern *Sampler* had the effect of decorated fabric, which was achievable due to the improved quality of prints, which were exclusive to Royal Albert.

During WWII production continued mostly for the export market. New processes were developed to improve the quality of the bone china, as well as to improve working conditions.

Launched in 1962, *Old Country Roses*, designed by Harold Holdcroft, was Royal Albert's best-selling pattern. Decorated on the *Montrose* shape, this has out sold any other bone china pattern, with 100 million pieces having been bought on the international market to date.

In 1964 Royal Albert merged with Pearson & Co., becoming a member of the Allied English Potteries, which subsequently merged with Royal Doulton

Despite the change of ownership, Royal Albert continued to develop new patterns and shapes including small giftwares. In 1983 it introduced the *For All Seasons* range, but this proved rather too traditional for customers; conversely, five years later the *Horizon* shape was deemed too "way out".

In the early '90s a new shape range, *Encore*, was developed by John Clappison, Royal Doulton chief shape designer, formerly of the Hornsea Pottery in East Yorkshire. Modern, yet not so modern as to detract from Royal Doulton's house style, for which they were justly famous, this new shape was available undecorated and with three introductory patterns, *Marguerite*, *Fonteyn* and *Ophelia*, the latter designed by Bronwen Kerrigan. In recognition of the modern

Above:
Bone china coffee pot decorated with the Old Country Roses *pattern, 1960s*

Left:
Modern Royal Albert backstamp

needs of the kitchen the range was introduced without gold lining to make it suitable for microwaves.

Royal Albert is still in production, but current product ranges are unlikely to become collectables for some time.

* The earlies wares, often hand-painted, are the most sought after.
* Although the *Old Country Roses* is the best known and most popular pattern, it is not sought after by collectors of 20th century ceramics.

Further Reference
www.royaldoulton.com

The Classic Ladies, *from left to right:* Persephone, Penelope, Dione *and* Athena, *height 8⅝in (22cm), introduced 1986, withdrawn 1994.* Courtesy of the Royal Crown Derby Museum

ROYAL CROWN DERBY

Based in Derby, Royal Crown Derby has enjoyed a reputation of producing finely painted patterns on high-quality pottery and figures for the higher end of the market for over 100 years.

Set up in 1876 as Derby Crown Porcelain Co., the firm produced expensive and richly gilded decorative wares similar to those by Sèvres and continued the popular Derby styles and many Japanese inspired designs. Over the years the company produced a wide range of new lines, with many special items given to the British Royal Family. In 1882 the company appointed a new Art Director, Richard Lunn. Typical examples of the product range included plates decorated with realistic hand-painted scenes such as *Rhuddlan Castle*, which was finished with an ornate embossed border (1875) and decorative plates painted with fruit by James Rouse (1879). In 1890 the achievements of the company were recognised when Queen Victoria gave them a Royal Warrant, the company thereafter being known as the Royal Crown Derby Company.

The new art director T. Reed replaced Lunn in 1889; at about the same time, the company was joined by Désiré Leroy, who had previously worked at Sèvres and brought with him a strong French influence.

Royal Crown Derby continued to produce wares in the style of the 19th century well into the 20th century. This is seen clearly in the company's 1934-35 catalogue, which showed tea, coffee and dinner wares, vases, snuff boxes, figures such as *French Sheperd*, and *The Gardener*. During the late '30s the company, like many others, suffered financial problems and, as a result, production focused on plain domestic wares.

After WWII, rather than introducing contemporary styles to meet the new markets in the post-war period, the company chose to expand its successful lines with new bird figures modelled by Arnold Mikelson.

In 1960 Mr A.T. Inch took over the company as Managing Director and initiated modernisation alongside a new approach to marketing and some rationalisation of the product line. Modern

Shell shaped dish, decorated with landscapes attributed to the painter William Corden, c.1820-1825.
Courtesy of the Royal Crown Derby Museum

tableware was produced alongside the well-known traditional lines. Tom Arnold, recently appointed consultant designer, created a new range of china tableware in the modern style in 1964. During that year the company became part of the Allied English Potteries Ltd., a subsidiary of S. Pearson and Co. Ltd. Despite the takeover, many new product lines were introduced in the following decades especially those by Brian Branscombe, Chief Designer, who created the new *Gadroon* shape, which was decorated with several patterns including *Brocade*, *Prince Consort* and *Imperia* c.1973. In the early

'70s the company became part of the Royal Doulton Tableware Group.

Robert Jefferson, who had previously worked at Poole Pottery, joined Royal Doulton in 1972 and undertook some special projects with Design Director Jo Ledger for Royal Crown Derby; the first result of this creative partnership was the *Quail* tea set. In 1981 Jefferson produced several animal and bird paperweights. Decorated with traditional company patterns, these proved very popular and prompted further wares such as *Royal Cats*, the first four of which being *Abyssinian*, *Siamese*, *Egyptian*

127

Blue Tit paperweight, modelled by Robert Jefferson, designed by Avis Garton, height 2¾in (7cm), introduced 1994, still in production.
Courtesy of the Royal Crown Derby Museum

Cat paperweight, modelled by Robert Jefferson, designed by Brian Branscombe, height 5⁵⁄₁₆in (13.5cm), introduced 1985, still in production. Courtesy of the Royal Crown Derby Museum

and *Persian*. During the '80s a number of new simple border patterns keeping the distinctive Royal Crown Derby look, were introduced, including *Grenville* on the *Surrey* shape, and *Kedleston* on the *Duesbury* shape from 1986-87.

- ◆ Royal Crown Derby created its high-quality wares for a very specialist and limited market. Accordingly many of the company's products are quite expensive and out of reach to the more modest collector.
- ◆ Today's collectors especially like the skilfully painted scenes by artists such as Albert Gregory and Cuthbert Gresley. These are usually signed.

Further Reference
Twitchett, J. and Bailey, B., *Royal Crown Derby*. Antique Collectors' Club, 1988

www.royal-crown-derby.co.uk

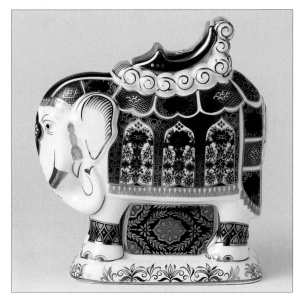

Large Elephant paperweight, modelled by Robert Tabbenor, designed by Jo Ledger, height 8¼in (21cm), introduced 1990, still in production. Courtesy of the Royal Crown Derby Museum

Collection of Bunnykin *figures, designed by Barbara Vernon, introduced in 1934*

ROYAL DOULTON

Royal Doulton is one of the best-known pottery manufacturers in the world. The company was founded by John Doulton in southeast London in 1815. Initially known as Doulton & Watts, it soon became the foremost manufacturer of drainpipes and sanitary wares. In the 1860s the company established an art studio called the Lambeth Art Pottery, which employed several designers including Hannah Barlow.

In order to expand into the production of earthenware, a partnership was formed with Pinder, Bourne and & Co., in Burlsem in 1877. Shadford Pinder managed the Burslem factory but retired in 1882 following some disagreements. From that point the works became known as Doulton & Co.

Henry Doulton was keen to establish a good reputation for the new Burslem factory and employed many artists and designers to develop the product range. The number of Doulton employees at Burslem increased dramatically: from about 160 before the take over to around 500 in 1884. John Slater, Art

Director of Pinder, Bourne & Co., was retained; he developed new decorative techniques, such as a new photographic process for transfer-printed designs. In 1897 Sir Henry Doulton died. In 1901 the company was granted a Royal Warrant by King Edward VII, thereafter becoming known as Royal Doulton.

Although the artistic achievements of the Lambeth Art Pottery lay chiefly in the 19th century, a number of important contributions were made during the early part of the 20th century, despite severe economic problems, which particularly hit the market for expensive art wares, as well as changes in customer taste.

A key figure at the Burslem factory was Charles Noke, who had joined in 1889, initially as a modeller but soon becoming an accomplished designer and, in 1914, Art Director. He created several popular lines, including the successful *Series Ware*, from c.1900, which included *Shakespeare* and *Dickens*, the latter was introduced in 1908 and remained in production for several decades. From about 1913 Noke introduced a whole new series of ceramic figures including *Shy Anne*, *The Little Land*

The Marietta *figure, designed by Leslie Harradine, height 8¼in (21cm), 1930s*

and *A Child's Grace*. He also revived the traditional *Character* and *Toby* jugs in 1934.

Important to the success of the company was the early development of special glazes that were created through intense experiments by John Slater and artist-potter Bernard Moore, who acted as a consultant to the company. The resultant glaze was used on the Chinese inspired *Flambé* wares, which were much admired when exhibited first at St. Louis in 1904 and later, with other experimental glazes, at the Exposition Internationale des Arts Décoratifs et Industriels Modernes in Paris in 1925. These items were praised in the official review of the British exhibits written by Gordon Forsyth. Examples of the *Rouge Flambé* wares were also displayed in Royal Doulton's London showrooms with variations marketed as *Sung* from 1919.

Following WWI, the '20s saw the development of more typical figures many of which were created by Leslie Harradine, who was employed as a freelance designer. His figures included *Chorus Girl* from 1930 and *Old Balloon Seller* from 1929; many are still in production today. He also made a series of flapper girl figures.

Noke, as Art Director, commissioned several designers, such as Charles Vyse and Peggy Davies, to create new lines. Frank Brangwyn, who had previously worked with William Morris, was invited to design a range of pottery that included coffee and tea wares, lamp bases, and plaques and biscuit barrels;

the most popular of his designs was *Harvest* from 1930. In total contrast was the *Bunnykins* nursery ware range, which had started life as a series of figures, designed by Barbara Vernon in about 1934.

At Lambeth during the '30s, both Richard Garbe and Reco Capey were producing designs. Gilbert Bayes created the stoneware relief frieze *Pottery through the Ages*, which decorated the main entrance to the company's headquarters in London from 1939, and is now in the Victoria and Albert Museum.

During the '30s Charles Noke worked closely with his son Cecil Jack Noke, who became Art Director in 1936. Cecil was very aware of the new feeling in the industry for modernity and went on to develop a series of stylish and functional shapes and patterns. The streamlined *Casino* shape, launched in c.1932, was decorated with simple banded patterns, such as *Radiance*, *Lynn* and *Marquis*, which complemented and successfully accentuated its contemporary lines. Towards the end of the decade, as customers' tastes changed Doulton launched the *Saville* shape.

For a limited period after WWII Agnete Hoy produced a series of incised and hand-painted stonewares. In 1956, the Lambeth site was closed. In 1960 Royal Doulton China Ltd. launched one of its most significant developments, English Translucent China, a new durable and practical body used for many of the new shapes such as *Tempo* in 1966. Four new patterns were designed for use on *Tempo*: *Tapestry*, *Westwood*, *Morning*

Earthenware tureen decorated with the Marquis *pattern on the* Casino *shape, 1932*

Earthenware vase decorated with a stylised bird design and a Flambè *glaze, c.1920s*

Star and *Moonstone*. The company also showed for the first time eleven new figurines and several display plates, including *Tower of London, Clovelly* and *Anne Hathaway's Cottage*.

During the '60s and '70s the company took over several well-known pottery manufacturers, including Royal Crown Derby, Minton and Paragon. During the '80s the company enjoyed great commercial success with the *Snowman* figures, based on the story by Raymond Briggs, and *Winnie the Pooh*, from A.A. Milne's famous books. In 1993 Royal Doulton registered as a limited company.

♦ With such a prestigious output over so many years of production, Royal Doulton offers a vast choice of wares to collect. In particular, the collector should look out for early wares, examples of Art Deco tablewares and the figures such as *Old Balloon Seller*.

Further Reference

Atterbury, P. and Irvine, L., *The Doulton Story*. Royal Doulton, 1979 catalogue

Eyles, D., *The Doulton Burslem Wares*. Barrie & Jenkins, 1980

McKeown, J., *Royal Doulton*. Shire Publications, 1998

Spours, J., *Art Deco Tablewares*. Ward Lock, 1988

www.royaldoulton.com

ROYAL WORCESTER LTD.

Royal Worcester is one of the most important names in the history of British ceramics. Over the many years of production, the company has, through innovation, remained at the forefront of high-class, expensive bone china and porcelain. Royal Worcester's decorative wares have been hand painted by some of the best artists in the industry.

Before the start of the 20th century, the company enjoyed great success at the Exposition Universelle in Paris in 1878, where it showed an extensive range of vases and services. From 1890 Royal Worcester produced a more affordable range of pottery decorated with printed patterns; these were also used on some commemorative wares. During the 1890s it developed coloured glazes such as *Coral Ware*, in 1894, and *Sabrina Ware* a year later. William Moore Binns became the company's Art Director in 1897 with Charles William Dyson Perrins appointed as Chairman in 1901. A year later the company bought out Grainger and Co., one of its competitors.

From the start of the 20th century greater emphasis was placed on the production of domestic tablewares, such as those decorated with simple border patterns, coffee services in neo-classic styles, and brighter wares. In 1915 John Wadsworth joined the company as Art Director, having been at Minton for a number of years. Like many factories, Royal Worcester found that expensive goods were not in demand in the difficult economic climate. As early as 1930 the company was put in the hands of the receivers, but was saved by Charles William Dyson Perrins who purchased it in 1934.

During the '30s Worcester introduced a wide range of figures both historical and military. In particular the work of Doris Lindner stands out, such as *Dancers* in 1934, and her series of horses. Freda Doughty specialised in creating models of children.

Following WWII Worcester continued to offer a wide range of products as well as introducing some contemporary patterns. In 1958 Royal Worcester bought the Palissy Pottery.

In 1961 a factory was established in Jamaica to

Vase painted with Highland Cattle by Harry Stinton, 1929. Reproduced by kind permission of The Worcester Porcelain Museum

make Island Worcester. At an exhibition in London in 1967, Worcester launched a number of limited edition figures alongside a shape range, *New Palladian*, which was based on the Italian Renaissance style and successfully mixed the traditional with the modern. Also launched were two new fish models called *Bluefin Tuna* and *Swordfish*, as well as two Victorian lady figures, *Elizabeth* and *Madeleine*.

In 1974 Royal Worcester and Spode Ltd. merged and soon after, the new company name Royal Worcester Spode Ltd. was formalised, although both companies run separately from each other.

• The majority of Royal Worcester ceramics appeal to the higher end of the market. In particular look out figures by Doris Lindner.

Further Reference

Sandon, H., *Royal Worcester Porcelain: From 1862 to the Present Day.* Barrie & Jenkins, 1979

www.royal-worcester.co.uk

Above:
HRH Princess Elizabeth on Tommy, *designed by Doris Lindner in 1948*

Group of Rye Pottery including a large mug decorated with the Mosaic *pattern and a smaller mug decorated with the* Cottage Stripe *pattern, all c.1956*

RYE POTTERY

Records exist of pottery works in Rye for many years. In 1840, the Cadborough Pottery in Rye was purchased by William Mitchell. In 1869 William's nephew Frederick Thomas Mitchell ran the business, under the name Bellvue Pottery, with help from two potters Fred Masters and Edwin (Bert) Twort. After F.T. Mitchell's death in 1920, Twort stayed on and worked closely with Frederick's widow Edith. In 1930 the business was bought by Ella Mills; again Twort stayed on, playing a central role in the pottery, which continued to produce mainly simple pieces of Sussex Rustic Ware and Sussex Art.

Defence Regulations shut the Works down in 1939, and it was not until 1947 that the pottery was resurrected when it was purchased by brothers John (Jack) and Walter (Wally) Cole, who renamed it the Rye Pottery. Both were experienced craft potters who had worked in sculpture and studio potting in London, mainly in stoneware. John was Headmaster at Beckenham Art School and Wally had taught part time at the Central School as well as working on the

1946 Britain Can Make It Exhibition at the V.&A. Although the Coles introduced a completely different style to Rye, several of the traditional Rye shapes were still made, such as the Sussex Pig, small jugs and mugs. They also encouraged Bert Twort to return to Rye and teach the young apprentices how to make the old shapes. The pre-war lead glazes were now illegal, instead the pottery was decorated in the 17th century Lambeth Delft style – a white glaze decorated with freehand brushwork. Apprentices, including Raymond Everett, Dennis Townsend and David Sharp, were taken on, all later setting up their own potteries within the town. In 1949 Rye made prototypes of jugs, ashtrays and condiments, all with an applied company motif, for the brewers Whitbread & Co. Ltd.

During the '50s new patterns and shapes were produced and more staff employed. The progress of Rye Pottery at this time must have been quite significant as fifteen pieces were shown at the 1951 Festival of Britain in London. For the first few years of the '50s John and Walter Cole then developed a new range of pottery that was both hand thrown and

Rye pottery lamp base, height 8in (20.3cm), c.1956

Group, where he encouraged everyone taking part to have an input in the designs. The Cole brothers worked in tandem, with Jack producing the theory and pattern suggestions, while Wally supervised the factory output and the standard controls in both shape and decoration. At the same time a new line of vases, bowls, lamps, jardinières and dishes were being painted in the sgraffito textures for which Rye became particularly known. (Sgraffito is a method of applying colour all over the glazed area, this is then scratched through to reveal the glaze beneath.) Some inspiration came from the sea with items including a fish dish decorated in red and green and a blue slipware plate featuring a fish border and seaweed. Over the years, Rye produced a loving cup with various patterns, often complemented by words and sayings. In 1956 David Sharp left the company to set up the Cinque Ports Pottery with George Gray. From the late '50s to the early '60s the company concentrated on complete ranges of tableware, starting with the *Cottage Stripe*, *Candy Stripe* and floral designs.

By the '60s Rye was exporting all over the world especially to the U.S.A. Over the years Rye also produced a considerable number of commemorative items winning the Council of Industrial Design Award for their engraved dishes and hand-lettered plates for the Prince of Wales's Investiture in 1969. Rye also produced commemoratives for Queen Elizabeth II's Silver Jubilee in 1977 and her Golden Jubilee in 2002.

During the '70s, when the impact of the miners' strike forced the Government to impose a three-day working week, the pottery was forced yet again to change direction, leaving tableware behind and concentrating on a range of collectable figures and animals. In 1978 Walter Cole retired leaving the business in the capable hands of his son Tarquin.

In the '70s Gordon Davies, at the suggestion of Canterbury Cathedral, had produced the *Wife of Bath* figure, but when he was unable to continue the range in the early 1980s, Tony Bennett, who had trained at the Royal College of Art, was asked to take over. He subsequently designed over 30 characters from Chaucer's *Canterbury Tales*, such as *The Cook*, *The Doctor* and *The Miller*. The figures were all inspired by contemp-

slip cast alongside new patterns. With a clear reference to the pioneering work of the studio concept of several Scandinavian potteries, Rye Pottery created a range of shapes that skilfully united both the simple patterns and undemanding practical shapes that appealed to the customer.

One of the most popular lines was *Cottage Stripe*, a deceptively simple vertically-striped design in various colours, which has been in continuous production for over 50 years. Two other popular designs of this period were the complex traditional *Lambeth*, a hand-painted chequer board with stars inside a latticework and the modern *Mosaic*, which was the result of Jack Cole's Saturday morning sessions with the Rye Design

Hand painted earthenware figure of The Wife of Bath, *from* The Canterbury Tales *series, 7½in (19cm). Designed by Gordon Davies, 1970s*

orary medieval sources, and were hand-painted in a tightly managed colour range. Tony Bennett is also responsible for most of Rye's animal figures.

Neal French, who had previously designed for Royal Worcester, created a range of figures for Rye, starting with *The Rye Lovers* and his *American History* series, which included *George Washington* and *Thomas Jefferson*, both mounted on horses, in 1988. French also designed a range of *Lovers* and *Edwardian Country House* figures, all painted in Rye's soft, lustrous colours.

Rye Pottery is still active, introducing new collectables each year, maintaining the high quality and originality on which its reputation has been built for the past 200 years.

• The Rye Pottery is well known today for its wide range of simply decorated pottery and latterly for its figures, all of which have a unique style that has made them very popular with collectors for a number of years.

• *Cottage Stripe*, which has been in continuous production for over 50 years is highly sought after by collectors. Items from the '50s proving the most popular.

• The products of the '50s are probably the most sought after by collectors today, in particular the *Rye Festival Jug* is very collectable.

• *The Cock Vase*, first issued in 1954 but in regular production for more than 20 years is a much-collected item today.

• Look out for figures from the range of *Canterbury Tales* by Tony Bennett. The collection at present numbers over 30 pilgrims and is widely collected.

Further Reference
www.ryepottery.co.uk

Rye backstamp, 1950s

137

Bone china Vogue *shape part tea set for two, decorated with the* Sunray *pattern, designed by Eric Slater, height of teapot 4⅓in (11cm), c.1930*

SHELLEY POTTERY

The Shelley Pottery is very well known today for its diversity of products and styles, from the Deco styles created by Eric Slater to the nursery wares by Mabel Lucie Attwell.

Originally known as Wileman and Co., the company was founded in 1853 by Henry Wileman. In partnership with John King Knight, it traded as Wileman and Knight for three years until Knight retired from the business. In 1860 Henry Wileman established the Foley Potteries, which was run by his two sons James and Charles on his death. Charles resigned in 1870. In 1872 Joseph Shelley, who had

worked successfully as a sales rep for the firm for ten years, was offered a partnership with James Wileman.

Joseph's son Percy Shelley joined the firm in 1881, eventually taking over the company in 1896, and was instrumental in improving the quality of tableware and introducing exciting ranges of Art Pottery that were sold through Liberty's. In 1905 Walter Slater, who had previously worked at both Mintons Ltd. and Doulton & Co., joined the company as Art Director.

Slater introduced a second series of the popular *Intarsio* range, the first series having been introduced by his predecessor Frederick Rhead, alongside patterns such as *Hunting Scenes* and the

Festival of Empire series, c.1911. He also experimented with lustres for a series of ornamental pieces launched at the British Industries Fair c.1920. At about this time his son, Eric Slater, joined the company in order to learn the various skills and processes of pottery manufacture.

In 1925 the firm changed its name to Shelley, becoming a limited company four years later, with Percy Shelley's three sons becoming equal shareholders. The late '20s saw the introduction of charming nursery wares designed by both Mabel Lucie Attwell and Hilda Cowham. These ranges, with various themes, proved to be enormously successful and were in production for several years, certainly up until the outbreak of WWII; a number of items were continued during the post-war period. Since the early 1900s, the company had also been producing jelly moulds and advertising ware.

In 1926 art director's son, Eric Slater, modified an old shape called *Antique* to develop the *Queen Anne* shape, which was decorated with patterns such as

Archway of Roses. One of his most successful patterns was *Sunset and Tall Trees* introduced in 1929.

In 1928 Eric Slater was promoted to the position of Art Director and soon developed a new modern range of pottery with a clear understanding of what the public wanted, carefully balancing the demand for the traditional whilst introducing new ideas. In 1930 Shelley launched the *Vogue* shape. A strikingly modern form unlike anything the company had produced before, *Vogue* was decorated with suitably fashionable patterns, such as *Blocks* and *Sunray*. This was soon followed by a slightly modified version, *Mode*, which retailed at a slightly cheaper price. Neither shape proved practical: the handles of the cups were rather difficult to hold and the *Vogue* teacup allowed hot drinks to cool too quickly. A new interpretation, *Eve*, was introduced in 1932 in order to address these problems.

Also launched in 1932, *Regent* was possibly the most important shape Shelley ever produced and was still in production in the '50s. This softer form

Bone china Vogue *shape part tea set, decorated with an abstract pattern, 1930*

was decorated with over 100 patterns, including *Phlox* and *Syringa*. In contrast to these delicate florals, *Harmony* art ware was launched in several appealing colour variations that evolved from the drip ware technique. The success of the *Harmony* range prompted the introduction of other vases and lamp bases decorated with various patterns such as *Moresque* and *Flora*.

During WWII Shelley Pottery produced wares for the export market whilst planning the modernisation of the works. A number of new patterns that incorporated aerographed and sgraffito decoration of stylized leaves and feathers were developed by Eric Slater with some shown at both the Britain Can Make It exhibition in 1946 and the Festival Of Britain in 1951.

Slater recognised that tastes had changed and new patterns were targeted at the important foreign markets, which demanded traditional floral styles allied with the highest quality of new shapes such as the *Henley* and *Perth* shapes.

One of the most distinctive patterns was the simple *Pole Star*, produced in a number of colourways in 1955. This was followed a year later by the *Stirling* shape, which was decorated with stylish patterns such as *Pastoral* and *Snow Crystals*. In 1964 the new *Avon* shape was launched decorated with several patterns including *Hathaway*, a large sunflower motif, and *Naples*.

In May 1965 the Shelley Potteries Ltd. changed its name to Shelley China Ltd. Within in a year the company was taken over by Allied English Potteries (A.E.P.), owned by the parent company S. Pearson & Sons Ltd. At this point the Shelley family connection with the company ended and the Shelley site was used for the production of Royal Albert bone china. In 1971 A.E.P. merged with the Doulton Group.

- Art pottery ranges can be expensive to collect, but examples of Shelley Pottery from 1910-1920 are still affordable.
- Of Shelley Pottery's diverse range of wares, the Art Deco tea sets are probably of most interest to collectors today. Patterns such as *Blocks* and *Sunray*, a typical Art Deco motif, on the *Vogue* shape are in demand.
- Post-war patterns and shapes are less sought after than the products of the '20s and '30s.
- The range of nursery wares by the famous Mabel Lucie Attwell are well worth looking out for, though collectors should watch out for copies and fakes.

Further Reference

Hill, S., *The Shelley Style*. Jazz Publications, 1990

Knight, R. and Hill, S., *Wileman: A Collectors' Guide*. Jazz Publications, 1995

Watkins, C., Harvey, W. and Senft, R., *Shelley Potteries: The History and Production of a Staffordshire Family of Potters*. Barrie & Jenkins, 1980

www.shelley.co.uk

Shelley nursery ware tea set designed by Mabel Lucie Attwell, height of Boo Boo *character milk jug, 5⅛in (13cm), c.1926*

Bone china Queen Anne *shape trio decorated with the* Sunset and Tall Trees *pattern, designed by Eric Slater, c.1929*

Two earthenware ginger jars, decorated with the Harmony *range, height of the larger jar 9½ in (24cm), c.1932*

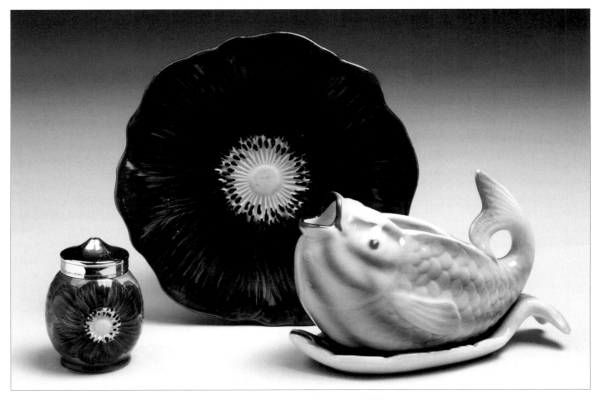

Collection of earthenwares including gravy boat in the form of a fish, c.1930s

SHORTER AND SON

Shorter and Son is very well known for its wide range of novelty wares. The company was founded by Arthur Shorter in the 1870s and based in Hanley. In 1878 he joined forces with James Boulton, who had previously worked at Josiah Wedgwood and Sons Ltd., and they traded under the name Shorter and Boulton. This new business moved to the Batavia Works in Stoke-upon-Trent with the earliest productions including majolica wares and various domestic wares, which were mainly exported to other countries within the Empire.

In 1885 Arthur Shorter took over the running of the A.J. Wilkinson Ltd. factory following the death of the owner, leaving James Boulton to take charge of the Shorter factory. Boulton retired in 1897, and was eventually succeeded by Arthur Shorter's son Guy in 1900; Arthur's other son, Colley, took responsibility for A.J. Wilkinson Ltd. in 1906.

The company's association with A.J. Wilkinson Ltd. was a boost, especially because of its well-known designer Clarice Cliff, who from time to time created a number of shapes for Shorter's such as the famous *Fish* tableware set, c.1927, which included plates, cover dish, and sauceboat and stand. Shorter also used a number of Clarice Cliff's shapes, such as her *Viking boat* from the late '20s, finished with matt glazes.

In the 1932 Harry Steele was appointed as Manager, with the challenge of bringing the company's range of goods up to date with the fashions of the decade. Steele's innovative ideas allied with an understanding of market needs was a recipe for success. Under Steele's direction Shorter's produced a range of Art Deco styled vases such as *Pyramus*, *Rhomboid* and *Olwen*; quite different from anything that they had created before.

In 1933 a young designer, Mabel Leigh, joined

Shorter's. Her patterns and shapes reflected an innovative use of design, rejecting, as she did, the brash colourings of the Art Deco movement. Her striking range of decorative wares, launched in 1933 as *Period Pottery*, was inspired by the Middle East, Central America and Africa. Encompassing patterns such as *Medina*, *Anglo Afrik*, *Aztec* and *Moresque*, the range stood out among other wares available at the time and proved very popular.

In contrast to these artistic wares the factory also produced a wide range of moulded wares, similar to those produced by other manufacturers, including several tableware ranges such as *Wild Rose*, *Anemone*, *Waterlily* and *Dahlia*. Mabel Leigh also produced two sets of moulded wares: *Pagoda* and *Shantee*.

In 1949 Shorter's launched an extensive range of *Gilbert and Sullivan* figures, which had originally been modelled by Clarice Cliff in 1940. The range, reproduced by permission of the D'Oyly Carte Opera Co., included figures from several operettas such as the *Pirates of Penzance* and *The Mikado*.

Many popular patterns were continued after WWII, though the early '50s also saw the introduction of a series of organically-styled, matt-glazed wares with some moulded decoration. Further examples were added during the '60s, alongside more moulded wares, often advertised in the trade press alongside the current range from A.J. Wilkinson Ltd. New product lines were still being introduced, including the new oven-to-tableware called *Jackpot*. In 1964 Shorter and Son was taken over by Crown Devon. The factory closed in 1974.

• Mabel Leigh's striking range of decorative wares, launched in 1933 as *Period Pottery*, included patterns such as *Medina*, *Anglo Afrik*, *Aztec* and *Moresque*. The range stood out among other wares available at the time and proved very popular. Leigh left Shorter's after just a few years, though her patterns were continued with new interpretations being added to the product range. Collectors should be careful to identify her original patterns.
• Look out for examples of ranges such as *Stag Ware* and *Shell* tableware, from 1938, as well as a

Large earthenware rabbit decorated with a matt yellow glaze, height 12¼in (31cm), possibly 1930s

whole range of novelties including wall plaques, nursery wares, flower troughs and book ends, all of which are clearly marked.
• Another popular range for collectors is the extensive range of *Gilbert and Sullivan* figures, which were modelled by Clarice Cliff in 1940 but not launched until 1949. Figures include those from several operettas such as the *Pirates of Penzance* and *The Mikado*. Collectors should note that these were also later reissued in 1961.
• A series of organically-styled, matt-glazed wares with some moulded decoration were produced in the early '50s, these are now sought after by collectors.

Further Reference
Hopwood, I. and Hopwood, G., *The Shorter Connection*. Richard Dennis, 1992

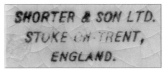

Standard Shorter & Son backstamp, there were many variations

Left:
Recent example of the long running Blue Italian *pattern*

Opposite:
Velamow *cat, c.1930, designed and modelled by E.B. Olsen*

SPODE
Copeland

The world-renowned reputation of Copeland, better known today as Spode, was gained through the production of high-quality design over many years of trading. Josiah Spode established the company during the late 18th century, selling a three-quarter share of the business to William Copeland in 1811. Following Copeland's death, his son William Taylor Copeland ran the company together with Josiah Spode II. In 1833 the Spode family sold its share of the company to William Taylor Copeland, who then entered a partnership with Thomas Garret, the business thereafter being known as Copeland & Garrett. From 1847 the company traded as W.T. Copeland Ltd. and, between 1868 and 1913, '& Sons' was added. (Ironically, the company name reverted to Spode Ltd. in 1970.)

The company produced a selection of top-of-the-range wares including figures, decorative tiles, domestic wares and vases, decorated with hand-painted botanic studies and landscapes; the *Blue*

Italian pattern, first introduced in 1816, is still in production today.

At the start of the new century demand for Copeland's highly specialised and expensive hand-painted wares was declining, although the blue printed wares remained popular. The *Geranium* pattern, also printed in blue, sold very well in Europe and North America. In 1912, following the death of Robert Frederick Abraham, Thomas Hassall was appointed as Artistic Director. Hassall supervised the introduction of several modern ranges. Whilst continuing to produce the more traditional lines, he often adapted or simplified them to make them less expensive.

The '30s saw the introduction of new patterns, such as *Chinese Rose*, a reworking of the *India* pattern, dated 1931, and *Lauriston* in 1939. This best-selling pattern proved so popular that it was introduced on bone china a few years later. Another popular pattern was *Herring Hunt* reproduced from original paintings by J.F. Herring).

The new shape *Empire*, launched in 1933, was specifically designed to suit the modern patterns of the time. Several patterns issued by the company in the '30s were simple banded or dotted patterns similar to those of their competitors. In 1935 Thomas Hassall introduced the *Anemone* pattern, a central motif in shades of blue, alongside *Reindeer* by Harold Holdway. Further patterns were commissioned from the London design consultant Agnes Pinder Davies who created, amongst others, *Country Souvenir*, in 1937, and *Shepard's Hey*, in 1938. Copeland also commissioned the modeller and designer Eric Olsen, who had previously worked at Josiah Wedgwood and Sons Ltd., to create a series of bowls, vases and jugs finished with matt glazes, as well as a group of animal sculptures.

In 1940 Harold Holdway became chief designer, following the death of Thomas Hassall. Holdway created the subtle yet modern *Queens Bird* pattern on the *Lowestoft* shape, which found favour with the Royal family. His other successful pattern was *Christmas Tree*, which was originally conceived for the American market. Launched in 1938, several new shapes were added to the range over the years, including a punch set in 1954, which is still a best seller for the company over 50 years later.

During the immediate post-war period the company enjoyed excellent sales, particularly to the export market, which wanted the traditionally styled patterns and shapes from the 18th century.

Notable new patterns by Harold Holdway from the late '50s included the printed *Oklahoma* pattern decorated on *Strathmere*, a modern coupe shape, and *Fortuna*, a series of fluted vases and bowls.

In 1958 the company agreed to produce a shape range created by students at the Royal College of Art. The two students selected were Neal French and David White, who together developed the set originally dubbed the *Royal College Shape*; it was renamed *Apollo* on receiving the Design Council Award. The shape was decorated with several patterns such as *Gothic*, designed by Michael Kitt, *Green Velvet*, by Harold Holdway, and *Persia*, by David Jackson.

During the '60s Christopher Bolton created a number of new lines including *Wayside Flowers* and *Cutie Kitten*, a nursery ware pattern that was printed

on the contemporary *Tricorn* shape designed by Harold Holdway; this shape had also been used for the *Barbeque* pattern in 1957. At this time the best-selling bone china patterns included *Maritime Rose*. A new pattern, *Trade Winds*, was launched c.1965.

In 1966 Spode became part of the Carborundum Group of Companies. Four years later it celebrated its bicentenary. In 1978 the company merged with Royal Worcester.

* Some of the most popular patterns, such as *Blue Italian*, first introduced in 1816 and *Christmas Tree*, 1938, are still in production today. Collectors are particularly keen on the earlier examples.
* Look out for the matt-glazed items and animal figures by Eric Olsen, which are highly collectable today.

Further Reference

Spours, J., *Art Deco Tableware*. Ward Lock, 1988

Wilkinson, V., *Copeland*. Shire Publications, 1994

Wilkinson, V., *Copeland-Spode-Copeland: The Works and Its People, 1770-1970*. Antique Collectors' Club, 1999

www.spode.co.uk

Earthenware bowl, decorated with a printed floral design, diameter 10in (25.4cm), c.1947

SWINNERTONS

Over the many years of production Swinnertons created many outstanding patterns and shapes with both modern and traditional designs to appeal to a wide market; the emphasis was on moderately priced pottery.

Based at Burton Place in Hanley, Stoke-on-Trent, Swinnertons was founded in 1906 by B.J. Swinnerton. As it became increasingly difficult to obtain sufficient amounts of blanks, Swinnerton entered into partnership with W. Lindley, a practical potter, to purchase the Old Chelsea Works manufacturing plant, in 1911. The factory only produced hollowware, so an extension housing a biscuit oven was added for the manufacture of flatware. Following B.J. Swinnerton's death, Mr. Alcock joined the company as Chairman, working closely with W. Lindley.

During the early part of the 20th century the company produced a selection of tablewares, vases, and toilet wares and matching trinket sets. Shapes, including *Don* and *York*, were decorated with printed florals. As business increased, the company purchased several small pottery works, including the

Washington Pottery during WWI, the Victoria Works, and the Scotia Pottery in Burslem in 1925; a new factory was also built for the manufacture of Rockingham and Samian teapots. Following WWII, the company boasted the latest machinery for pottery production and went on to purchase the Davison & Son Ltd., in 1952.

One of the company's earliest and most popular patterns was *England Gardens*, which was bought by both Queen Mary, wife of George V, and her daughter, the Princess Royal. *England Gardens* was revised during the post-war period and relaunched alongside a new range of traditionally-styled floral patterns such as *Autumn Spray*, on the *Luxor* shape, and conventional border designs on the plain *Imperial* shape. Further designs included the *Bungalow* shape covered dish as well as the *Ascot* pattern, a hand-painted floral design in bright colours. In 1958 the company launched a nursery ware range called *Funny Bunny*.

By contrast, in the same year, Swinnertons also launched a range of typically styled '50s hand-painted patterns with abstract leaves on a plaid background on modern rimless shapes.

Swinnertons was taken over by the Lawley Group in 1959, though production continued as normal. In 1963 the new *Moonglo* range was launched, comprising a series of cups and saucers decorated in single bright colours; the intention was that they could be mixed and matched. In 1966 new patterns included *Aztec, Harvest, Fruit, Monaco* and *Biarritz*. The company was eventually taken over by Royal Doulton.

Further Reference
'Earthenware with a Reputation, 40 years of growth', *Pottery and Glass,* December 1953, pp 354-356.

Swinnertons backstamp from the '40s

Group of preserve pots, tallest 5½ in (14cm), 1950s

SYLVAC
Shaw & Copestake

Though the name SylvaC is well known amongst collectors today chiefly for the very popular 'bunnies' with big ears, which the company introduced during the '30s, SylvaC has also produced many other important and popular ranges that are ideal for collectors.

The history of SylvaC began with William Shaw setting up the Sheaf Pottery in 1894. Around 1902, having moved to Commerce Street in Longton, Shaw went into partnership with William Copestake to form the company Shaw & Copestake; Copestake left a mere six months or so later. His place was taken by Richard Hull (Snr.) in 1903, though there was no change to the company name. After two years the factory moved to a new site on Commerce Street, Longton.

From the commencement of production until the '20s the factory produced all sorts of vases, jugs, plant pots, clock sets, and toilet sets. These ranged from the very plain to the very ornate, such as *Unique*, *Holborn* and *York*, which were decorated with floral patterns from as early as 1904. Other typical pattern themes included rural scenes, ploughing, Dutch scenes and shrimping, some featuring high glazes and heavy gilding to reflect the taste at the time.

In the late 1920s some of the wares were being produced using a cellulose, or painted, finish. At about the same time animals, figures and novelty pieces were gradually being introduced. These were followed by Deco shapes in a wide range of items, such as candlesticks, flower troughs, vases and jugs moulded as budgerigars, stags and rabbits, which were decorated in single-colour matt glazes developed by Richard Hull (junior). By the early '30s the glaze was available in green, fawn, blue, brown and pink, and was used on various products. The single-colour matt glazes, particularly the green and fawn, were a commercial breakthrough and soon became a company trademark, instantly recognisable decades later.

Richard Hull (junior) brought back a ceramic rabbit figure from France on one of his many trips abroad to buy examples of pottery. This gave him the idea to produce a similar range of fancies, which proved to be an outstanding success resulting in hundreds of mass-produced wares, including bowls, vases, plates, cups, jugs, troughs, wall plaques and domestic wares, bearing rabbits, both comical and natural. Around 1935 the 'SylvaC' name was adopted and used to market these new lines. The new name was not impressed into many of the products until after WWII; prior to this the company used a stick-on paper label.

In the '30s SylvaC introduced 'bunnies' in green, blue, fawn and pink. Their success led to SylvaC also producing many other comical animals, including over 200 dog figures. Of these the most notable are the *Sammy Spaniels*, the *Mac* dogs, the *howling dog*, the comic *hunchbacks* and the *Toothache Dogs*, the latter modelled by Stephan Czarnota. Other popular ranges were the *Wild Duck* series from 1931, which included 20 different items, and the *Harvest*, *Cornflower* and *Poppy* ranges. Some examples were discontinued in 1940.

In about 1938 SylvaC merged with the pottery company Thomas Lawrence (Longton) Ltd., which traded under the name Falcon Ware. Lawrence's designer Reginald Thompson, who had joined the company in 1917 and been appointed to the position of decorating manager in 1922, was responsible for a lot of SylvaC designs following the merger. In 1935 Richard Hull Snr. died and his son became the new partner.

During WWII the Government requisitioned the SylvaC factory, so production was moved to the

other site allowing them to maintain their strong export market. Throughout the '50s novelty items and many new lines, including a number of tableware lines reminiscent of Poole Pottery, were added to the company's wares. In the '60s SylvaC launched a series of bowls, jardinières and the embossed range *Begonia*. The new *Fiesta* and *Coral* patterns were added to the already popular *Apple Blossom*, *Hyacinth*, *Shell* and *Pebbles*; 1969 saw the launch of the *Manhattan* range.

In 1982 SylvaC went into voluntary liquidation. The company was bought by the North Midland Co-operative Society and then leased to Longton Ceramics. The factory was later taken over by the Co-operative Society and became Crown Winsor, which eventually closed in 1989.

- Most popular today are the various rabbits or 'bunnies', which were introduced in the early '30s in green, fawn and blue; other colours, including pink, are less well known. The rabbits were produced in different sizes with a popular example being Harry the Hare. Collectors should note that some examples were discontinued in 1940 although most collectors don't make any distinction between the early or later rabbits. New models were still being introduced as late as the '70s and in 1981 George Mathews created a rabbit moneybox.
- Freelance designer Otakar Steinburg, from Czechoslovakia, created several popular models. His Scottie dog called *Mac*, initially produced in five different sizes, is popular amongst collectors today.

Further Reference
Collins, M. and Collins, D., *SylvaC Animals*. SCC Publications, 2004

Van der Woerd, A., *Shaw and Copestake: The Collector's Guide to Early Sylvac 1894-1939*. Georgian Publications, 1992

Verbeek, S.J., *The Sylvac Story*. Pottery Publications, 2002

www.sylvacclub.com

Examples of the popular SylvaC bunny series first issued in the '30s

Art Deco earthenware vase, decorated with a hand-painted pattern, height 7¼in (18.4 cm), c.1937

WADE

The history of the Wade companies through the 19th century is rather complex. Albert J. Wade, George Wade & Son and Wade & Co. were all operating as separate companies in the Burslem area in the late 1800s. By the early part of the 20th century, there were two separate companies Wade, Heath & Co. and A.J. Wade Ltd., both run by the same family. The companies merged in 1935 to become Wade Potteries Ltd.; in 1958 the company was renamed Wade Potteries.

Whilst still operating as separate businesses, both companies expanded their range of wares throughout the '30s. In particular Wade Heath & Co. produced a wide range of overtly Art Deco shapes, including vases, jugs and wall chargers, that were decorated with brightly coloured patterns in the same vein as Myott Pottery. They also issued several moulded jugs that featured low-relief motifs of stylised animals and landscapes.

In contrast to the Art Deco novelties, Wade Heath

Small figure of a tree with bird, height 4in (10.2cm), probably 1950s

Earthenware starfish novelty dish, which was in production from 1959-1961 (Wade Heath) with a re-issue in 1973 (Wade Ireland), 4½ in (11.4cm) across

introduced a selection of elegant and stylish figures with many designed by Jessie Van Hallen. Examples ranged from classically styled figures dressed in the latest fashions, typified by *Summertime,* to the simple and traditional crinoline lady. Some of these figures were decorated with the new 'Scintillite' coating that made it possible to avoid glaze firing, thus making them cheaper than similar examples being produced by rivals such as Royal Doulton.

During the mid '30s Wade, Heath & Co. secured the rights from Walt Disney to reproduce the image of Mickey Mouse for a range of toy tea sets and figures that proved very popular. In 1939 the company produced a number of wares based on Disney's soon to be released film, *Snow White and the Seven Dwarfs*. The wares included a full set of characters, designed by Jessie Van Hallen, with *Snow White* at nearly 7 inches (17.8cm) high, a toy tea set and a less well-known moulded range of tea wares including a butter dish in the form of a cottage, as well as a lamp base and other associated items. Later examples from the early '60s included characters from the Walt Disney films *Lady and the Tramp, Bambi* and *Sword in the Stone*.

1953 saw the introduction of the new range of Wade *Whimsies*, which proved such an outstanding

success that the range was extended for several years with new additions created by Bill Kemp. There were ten different sets: the first comprising a horse, poodle, spaniel, stag and squirrel. Further examples included a range of dogs, a monkey, camel, lion cub and llama.

Other lines produced in the '50s included the *Flying Birds* set and *Aqua Dishes*, the *Quack Quack Family*, designed by Robert Marlow in 1952, *Yacht wall plaques*, in 1955, and *Minikins*, in 1956.

Wade also embraced the contemporary style of the '50s with brightly coloured patterns decorated on organic shapes, which were in total contrast to the *Whimsies*. These new shapes were thoughtfully planned rather that just sticking modern motifs on traditional shapes as was often the case with other manufacturers. The most popular range was the *Harmony* shape available decorated in one of four patterns: *Carnival, Fern, Parasol* and *Shooting Star,* or with two-tone coloured glazes. The same shapes were used for the popular *Zamba* line, depicting tribal dancers, printed on a selection of white wares with black interiors, from 1957.

Rowland Emett produced a variety of comical patterns for a series of dishes similar to those of Crown Devon with later shapes including *Mode* and *Flair*, the latter from 1956. Robert Morley, who

Novelty pebble vase, 1950s

Group of earthenware National Westminster piggy banks, from 1984.

joined the company in the mid '30s, became Chief Designer in the '60s and worked closely with Georgina Lawton to develop new patterns such as *Sunflower*, *Red Polka* and *Galaxy*. However, the demand for this sort of ware diminished during the late '60s and early '70s. In 1969 the company formed its own design and marketing company, Wade PDM.

In the '80s Wade was commissioned by the National Westminster Bank to produce piggy banks to encourage young people to save. Issued between 1984 and 1989, these proved extremely popular.

Renamed Wade Ceramics in 1989, the company is still in operation.

- Wade has produced a staggering range of collectables over the years. As well as the famous whimsies and Westminster piggy banks, look out for the figures produced in the '50s, such as the *Quack Quack* family.
- Wade is probably most famous for its *Whimsies*. These are eagerly sought after by a growing number of collectors, especially in the originally boxes. Unfortunately such popularity has resulted in fakes appearing on the market, so collectors should be cautious.
- Look out for the moulded *Big Bad Wolf* musical jug featuring the wolf as the handle, c.1935. Note that this is very similar to the examples by Burgess and Leigh Ltd.
- Whilst being highly collectable today, many of the National Westminster Piggy Banks, 1984-1989, are still relatively low priced. Only a few of the rarer examples command higher prices at the moment.

Further Reference

Jenkins, S., *Ceramics of the 50s and 60s. A Collectors Guide*. Millers 2001

Prescott-Walker, R., Salmon, F., and Folkhard, J., *The Wade Collectors Handbook*. Francis Joseph, 1997

www.wade.co.uk

Bone china ginger jar and cover decorated with a Fairyland Lustre *pattern by Daisy Makeig-Jones, c.1920*

JOSIAH WEDGWOOD AND SONS LTD.

Through continued investment in design, Josiah Wedgwood and Sons Ltd. have remained at the cutting edge of the British pottery industry for over 100 years and, as a result, they have created some of the most sought after ceramics of the 20th century.

The company was established by Josiah Wedgwood in 1758, based at Etruria in Stoke-on-Trent. By 1891 a new partnership had been formed between Laurence, Cecil and Francis Hamilton Wedgwood. With the realisation that the firm's

designs were still deeply rooted in the 19th century, Wedgwood appointed John Goodwin as Art Director c.1904, who ensured that a good balance between the traditional and modern was maintained.

The start of the 20th century was marked by the introduction of a number of hand-painted patterns suggested by the well-known artists and designers Alfred and Louise Powell, who were based in London. In 1907 Wedgwood set up a studio in London, supplying blanks, so that the Powells could develop new patterns. These proved so popular that Wedgwood decided they should be produced on a commercial basis. A studio was set up with several decorators working on patterns designed by the Powells, such as *Rhodian*. Eventually a Hand Craft studio was established in 1926.

From the early '20s Daisy Makeig-Jones designed some of the most outstanding lustre wares for Wedgwood. Success with her first series of *Ordinary Lustres* prompted her to dream up dazzling and unusual landscapes combined with characters from children's books, mixed with myths and fables that were popular at the time. *Fairyland Lustre* included patterns such as *Ghostly Wood*, *Firbolgs*, *Candlemas* and *Bubbles*. This range, decorated on various bone china vases, ginger jars and bowls, had a great appeal amongst the fashionable upper classes who were able to afford such expensive items. As popularity for these patterns increased, several other firms, such as Crown Devon and Carlton Ware, imitated them.

The Wall Street Crash in New York in 1929 and a massive trade slump prompted a rationalisation of the firm's products by the new management team, which resulted in many of the more expensive lines being withdrawn. On his death, Major Frank Wedgwood was succeeded as Managing Director by Josiah Wedgwood V, who was determined to introduce new designs in line with contemporary taste and, hopefully, thereby restore the profit margin.

Several freelance designers created outstanding shapes. John Sheaping produced a number of art deco styled animal figures for Wedgwood in the late '20s. In 1934 Victor Skellern was appointed to the position of Art Director and he skillfully combined Wedgwood tradition with the Art Deco style to

Group of bone china coffee pots decorated with various patterns, including a floral lustre design by Louise Powell (front), c.1930

Four examples of the shape (3081) designed by Keith Murray, decorated with matt glazes, height 5⅞in (15cm), 1933

Earthenware jug and mug, decorated with the printed Alphabet *pattern, designed by Eric Ravilious, c.1937*

create outstanding patterns such as *Snow Crystals* on the *Globe* shape, *Wood Magic*, *Forest Folk* and *Seasons*. He worked alongside Millicent Taplin, who had previously been in charge of the Handcraft studio but by the early '30s was creating her own patterns such as *Sunlit* and *Papyrus*. Her best-known patterns were *Falling Leaves*, *Moonlit* and *Green Lattice* decorated on a wide range of tea sets, coffee ware and breakfast sets. Her later patterns included *Briar* and *Dahlia*. Unfortunately, the company policy did not allow the names of in-house designers to be included in the backstamp, so attribution proves rather difficult; however, freelance designers were named on the backstamp.

During the early '30s Wedgwood commissioned architect Keith Murray to develop a tureen for the *Annular* shape, designed by Tom Wedgwood and John Goodwin. (Collectors should be aware that this range, decorated with various matt glazes, is not by

Backstamp used by Wedgwood during late 1930s and 1940s

Murray.) Shortly afterwards he started developing new modern vases and bowls featuring incised bands and decorated with matt glaze colours, such as matt straw, blue and green, which were pioneered by Norman Wilson, Works Manager. This range, first shown in 1933, was marked, 'Keith Murray, WEDGWOOD, MADE IN ENGLAND.' Collectors should note that other marks were also used for his ware including his initials 'KM'.

In response to the market demands, Murray created a number of cheaper slip-cast items such as inkstands, ashtrays, cigarette boxes, powder bowls and even a denture box. At the same time beer mugs decorated with either an ivory or champagne glaze, retailed at half the price of the earlier hand-thrown versions. He later used the same method for several classically-styled vases that were dipped in celadon slip, then turned on the lathe to reveal the cream clay underneath, part of a process called the two-coloured clay method. Norman Wilson produced a wide range of vases, ornamental bowls and snack trays decorated with unusual glazes, known as *Unique Ware*, from 1932-39 and again from 1954-63.

An important contribution was made by Eric Ravilious who, in the brief time he worked for Wedgwood, created several designs that did much to

A set of three resist lustre patterns, designed by Millicent Taplin on a shape designed by Keith Murray c.1951-52.

raise the profile of the company. His first design, in 1936, was for the commemorative mug for the forthcoming coronation of Edward VIII. The *Coronation Mug* was, of course, immediately withdrawn on the announcement of The King's abdication. The pattern was later adapted for the coronations of George VI in 1937 and of Queen Elizabeth II, in 1953.

One of Ravilious' most enduring designs was the *Alphabet* range from 1937. Consisting of two bands of motifs placed under the individual letters, it was available on items such as a plates, porringers and mugs. His name was included on the backstamp. Ravilious' most outstanding design was the *Boat Race Day*, produced in 1938, which featured individual scenes from the famous Oxford and Cambridge boat race. Rare patterns, not seen often on the market include *Garden Implements*, launched in 1939, which was designed specifically for a lemonade set. His tableware patterns, such as *Persephone*, *Garden* and *Travel*, were produced in large quantities, mainly in the '50s. One of the last patterns by Ravilious was the *Barlaston Mug* designed to commemorate the relocation of the works from Etruria to Barlaston in 1940. More recently Wedgwood has produced official

reproductions for special exhibitions; these are clearly marked.

Other notable contributions to this period were the special range of figures by Arnold Machin, including *Zodiac the Bull*; a mug decorated with a pattern designed by Norman Mackinson (often wrongly attributed to Eric Ravilious), which was issued to celebrate the Festival of Britain in 1951; *Queen's ware* mug designed by Richard Guyatt to commemorate the coronation of H.M. Queen Elizabeth II in 1953; a series of 6 designs called *Outlines of Grandeur* by Laurence Whistler, which featured architectural achievements in British history. A lesser-known design, the *Heartsease*

The Shakespeare *earthenware mug, printed and hand coloured in blue and yellow. Designed by Victor Skellern for Josiah Wedgwood and Sons Ltd., 1964. Height 4⅝in (11.8cm).*

Set of bone china plates entitled Variations on a Geometric Theme, *limited edition of 200, designed by Eduardo Paolozzi, diameter 12½in (31cm), c.1970*

pattern, was designed by Edward Bawden for the Orient shipping line in 1952.

As early as the late '30s discussion had taken place regarding the introduction of printing. This finally came to fruition during the '50s with the resultant patterns such as *Asia* by Skellern and a series of traditionally styled patterns being typical. Like many other companies Wedgwood introduced its own oven-to table ranges, including *Pennine*, in 1965, and *Blue Pacific*, in 1969.

To celebrate the 225 year history of the company Wedgwood released the striking *225* shape by Jeremy Gould in bone china and black basalt in 1983.

During the latter part of the 20th century, Wedgwood maintained its reputation for employing cutting-edge designers and artists, including Eduardo Paolozzi and Glenys Barton.

During the '90s Wedgwood produced a wide range of subtle patterns targeted at the wedding market. The company continued to develop special collectors' items and commissioned new freelance designers, such as Paul Costelloe and Nick Munro, in the 21st century.

- The work of architect Keith Murray, who started designing for Wedgwood in the early '30s, is popular among collectors today. His early wares are the most sought after, devoted collectors are particularly keen on his limited range of shapes such as bowls, tobacco jars and his coffee set in black basalt. Collectors should note that some of his shapes were used by other designers for other patterns and, in particular, a set of commemorative wares.
- Look out for the commemorative mug issued for Edward VIII's forthcoming coronation. On the announcement of his abdication in December

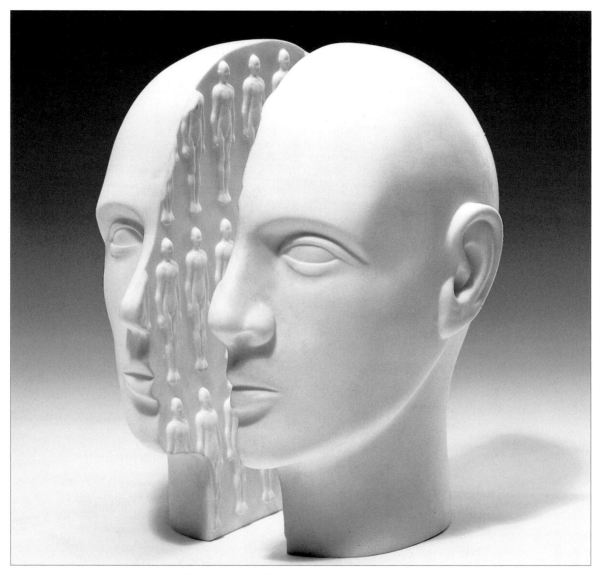

Innovative ceramic art created by Glenys Barton. The head is in two sections with relief figures, limited edition of 4, height 6⅓in (16cm), 1977

1936, the mug was immediately withdrawn, and is now highly sought after.

- The wide range of products introduced during the '50s and '60s have yet to catch the eye of the collector despite some of these being at the forefront of modernity. In particular, Robert Minkin created stylish black basalt coffee wares and a range of experimental items called *Design '63*.

Further Reference

Batkin, M., *Wedgwood Ceramics 1846-1959. A New Appraisal*. Richard Dennis, 1982

Reilly, R., *Wedgwood: The New Illustrated Dictionary*. Antique Collectors' Club, 1996

www.wedgwood.com

Earthenware tea set decorated with an Art Deco style hand-painted pattern, c.1930s

WEDGWOOD & CO.

This company is often confused with its competitor Josiah Wedgwood and Sons Ltd. The firm of Wedgwood and Co. was founded c.1855 and based

Modern Wedgwood backstamp

at the Unicorn and Pinnox pottery in Tunstall. Initially it manufactured toilet and domestic wares often decorated with transfer printed patterns. In about 1900 it became an incorporated company; from 1965 it became known as Enoch Wedgwood (Tunstall) Ltd.

By the early '20s Wedgwood & Co. was offering a wide range of wares: shapes such as *Richmond* decorated with printed border patterns including *Dorothy* and *Dresden*. Simple border patterns were also used on the *Turin* shape; later a new Art Deco shape called *Farnol* was launched. One of the most popular lines was *Asiatic Pheasant* a traditional printed pattern that remained in production for many years.

Small earthenware plate, printed with the Asiatic Pheasant *pattern, diameter 7in (17.8cm)*

Following WWII, the company employed several artists including Hans Strasser, John Clarkson, the Principle of the Newcastle School of Art, Professor Karl Vogl and Nancy Catford. Roy Smith created serviette rings moulded as farm animals alongside figures such as *The Flower Girl* and *The Rake Figures*. In 1954 the company launched the new *Patio* range, available in a wide variety of items such as tea, coffee and dinnerwares with patterns such as *Tanglewood*, *Cadenza* and *Gingham* being typical. A series of special items was also manufactured for the cosmetics company Avon, including Christmas plates.

In 1974 the company bought out A.G. Richardson (Crown Ducal). In turn, in 1980, Enoch Wedgwood was itself taken over by Josiah Wedgwood and Sons Ltd., from which time the works became known as the Unicorn Pottery. Subsequently David Queensbury, of the Queensbury Hunt Partnership, developed a new shape range called *Marquess*. This shape was also used by the Johnson Brothers (who had been taken over by Wedgwood in 1968) for the *Jessica* pattern designed by Jessie Tait.

♦ Despite producing a wide range of patterns and shapes, this company is relatively unknown. There is, however, a growing market for its range of Avon plates.

Earthenware Stamford *shape tea set, decorated with the hand-painted* Trees and House *pattern, designed by Clarice Cliff, height 4¾in (12cm), 1929*

A.J. WILKINSON LTD.

Though probably best known today for Clarice Cliff's *Bizarre* ware, which captured so well the mood of the '20s, A.J. Wilkinson Ltd. actually produced a wide variety of high-class pottery for an international clientele alongside its range of artistic wares.

The company was established by Arthur Wilkinson in 1885, and based in Burslem trading as Royal Staffordshire. Wilkinson died in 1891 and the firm was eventually taken over by Arthur Shorter, a member of the Wilkinson family, in collaboration with Edmund Leigh in 1894.

A.J. Wilkinson Ltd. became increasingly profitable before WWI, prompting expansion of the business. The company produced a wide range of products, including vases, dinnerware and toilet wares, shapes included *Sophie* and *Rye*. There was also a selection of floating bowls complemented by a series of naturally coloured birds on rockery stumps, which served as holders for floral arrangements.

The Art Director John Butler, who had joined the company in 1904, created some of the most decorative items, including *Tibetan* and *Rubaiyat* wares. The *Oriflamme* range, designed c.1910 encompassed several patterns, including *Golden*

Mean, *Medice*, *Ruby* and *Opal*, some of which were shown at the various domestic and international trade fairs. Collectors should note that Butler's wares were not typical of the main Wilkinson products.

Fred Ridgway created a number of patterns for plaques that included *Old London Cries* and *The Conference* series. His *Eastern Soudan* pattern, depicting figures of Arabs in their robes, buildings and the desert sands, in realistic colours, was illustrated in the trade press in 1927.

Clarice Cliff joined A.J. Wilkinson's c.1917. When her skills as a talented painter were recognised she was moved from the general decorating shop to work alongside John Butler and Fred Ridgway. Cliff was very interested in French design and was greatly influenced by the bright colours and interesting shapes that were so different from the many drab British pots that she had seen. Inspired to create a new look, she was allowed to experiment on the unsaleable ware that came with the purchase of the Newport Pottery in 1920. The paint was applied thickly to cover up the defects in the pottery and to emphasise that the wares were hand-painted. Sold as the *Bizarre* range, it caused a sensation. Despite

Earthenware Tankard *shape coffee pot decorated with the* Mondrian *pattern, designed by Clarice Cliff, height 7½in (19cm), 1929*

Earthenware biscuit barrel decorated with the Orange House *pattern, designed by Clarice Cliff, 1930*

initial doubts from the salesmen it proved to be an outstanding success.

The *Bizarre* name encompassed pattern ranges such as *Archaic*, *Latona* and *Inspiration*. To achieve a distinctive look Cliff realised that she would need new, modern shapes; the result was the dramatic *Conical* shape, introduced in 1932. Many of her Art Deco patterns, such as *Blue Autumn*, *Red Roofs*, *Summerhouse* and the popular *Trees and House*, featured landscapes scenes with the cosy cottage. Several abstract patterns such as *Melon*, *Sliced Circle* and *Tennis* were also very popular. The *Fantasque* range was introduced in 1929 with the first patterns including *Broth* and *Lily*, *Orange House* and *Carpet* followed. The popular *Crocus* pattern was also introduced in 1929, remaining a best seller for over thirty years. Responding to the demand for novelty and variety, Cliff created a range of fancies including the *Age of Jazz* figures, introduced in 1930.

When tastes changed in the mid '30s Cliff followed a new direction typified by the *My Garden*

Earthenware charger decorated with the Aquatic *pattern, from the* Tahiti *range designed by John Butler, 1928-1929*

Earthenware plate decorated with the rare Carpet *pattern, designed by Clarice Cliff, 1930*

range. Encompassing various items, including vases, bowls, trays, candlesticks and fancies, the range featured moulded flowers and fruits on the handles and on the base of each piece. Other moulded wares included *Celtic Harvest* and *Waterlily*, whilst hand-painted patterns such as *Rhodanthe* and *Coral Firs* were popular.

Business was still slack in the late '30s and, with the advent of war, it became apparent that further production of new ranges would not be possible.

After WWII there was some modernisation of the factory and the company began the production of dinnerware using the 'Royal Staffordshire' mark, chiefly for the export market. By far the most popular pattern on the North American market was *Tonquin*, a traditional landscape print. This was soon

Single-handed Lotus *jug, decorated with a hand-painted* Bizarre *pattern designed by Clarice Cliff, height 11⅝in (30cm), 1928-29*

162

Conical *shaped bowl decorated with the* Crocus *pattern, designed by Clarice Cliff, from 1928*

followed by the *Chelsea Basket*, *Rural Scenes* and *Harvest* patterns.

In 1951 Eric Elliot was recruited to develop new designs such as his *Sunkissed* pattern depicting large hand-painted fruit motifs, *Magnolia*, *Paris* and *Clematis*. Television sets, comprising a cup on a large, assymetrical saucer/plate, were decorated with patterns such as *The Memories of the Past* series, featuring various vehicles such as a hansom cab and a mail coach. New shapes were launched, including the *Devon* range in 1956, and the *Clayton* range in 1957.

Following the death of Colley Shorter, the works were eventually sold in 1964 to W.R. Midwinter Ltd.

- Wilkinson's is best known for the brightly coloured *Bizarre* wares by Clarice Cliff, which are mainly sold at specialist sales.
- An alternative choice for the more modest wallet is Cliff's popular *Crocus* pattern, introduced in 1929. Collectors should note that different versions were produced over the years, the earliest examples being the most sought after.
- Collectors should also look out for the less well-known designs by John Butler.
- American collectors today are eager to purchase *Tonquin*, a traditional landscape printed dinnerware with the 'Royal Staffordshire' mark.

Further Reference

Griffin, L. and Meisel, L., *The Bizarre Affair*. Thames and Hudson, 1988

Griffin, L., *Clarice Cliff – The Art of Bizarre*. Pavilion, 1999

Slater, G. and Brough, J., *Comprehensively Clarice Cliff*. Thames and Hudson, 2005

www.claricecliff.co.uk

ARTHUR WOOD & SONS (LONGPORT)

The formation of the Arthur Wood came about through a partnership with Capper and Wood in 1884; by 1900 Arthur Wood was the sole owner. The factory was based at the Bradwell Works in Longport and traded under the Royal Bradwell name.

During the early part of the 20th century the company built a good reputation for producing teapots, praised for their plainness and practicality. These came in all varieties and sizes including the famous brown teapot, often decorated with simple bands, that was popular with hotel and café owners.

In 1928 the business was registered as a limited company and renamed Arthur Wood (Longport Ltd) 1928, with Arthur Wood as Chairman with his son Gerald as Managing Director. On Arthur's death two years later, Gerald succeeded him as Chairman. Under the new management there was a definite move to expand the product line with several new fancies introduced, as well as a wider range of earthenware teapots, jam pots and cheese dishes. The variety of goods included an *Octagon* shaped set decorated with the *Futurist* pattern introduced in 1931. The new lines, made in earthenware rather than bone china, necessitated the introduction of new manufacturing machinery.

During the immediate post-war period the trade press highlighted that the company had installed new equipment, updated its offices and showroom and that the number had staff had increased from 50 in 1930 to over 200 in 1953. A wide range of products was on offer, including biscuit barrels, cigarette boxes and tankards decorated with *Dickens Days* and *Hunting Scenes*. In 1948 new teapot shapes including *Stanley* and *Wedgwood* were introduced alongside a new line of embossed wares, such as *Blossom Time*. The *Queen Anne* teapot shape, first introduced c.1953, was decorated with various forms of decoration including silver lustre with handles and knobs painted black, and various stylised floral patterns with gold decoration. Other teapot shapes included *Melon* and *Aladdin*, the latter

Typical example of a '30s moulded and hand-painted jug by Arthur Wood Ltd.

Image courtesy of Dorling Kindersley Limited and Judith Miller, and by kind permission of Beth Adams

decorated in a deep-blue glaze with stylised flowers in gold. Also produced were musical tankards decorated with sports themes and other subjects, which played a tune when lifted off the table. In contrast to the popular novelty lines the company also produced a series of plain and stylish matt glazed ornamental wares including the *Crown* bowl and *Oakland* jug.

In 1967 Arthur Wood & Son purchased the popular Carlton Ware Ltd., but sold it again in 1987. In 1974 the company produced *Samarkand*, a range of wares decorated in deep colours with patterns such as *Caspian*, *Sienna* and *Forest Green* being typical. It also introduced a number of novelty items including a string dispenser in the form of a dove.

♦ Though Arthur Wood & Sons is still not very well known, some of the wares from the '50s are now attracting interest from collectors.

WOOD & SONS LTD.

Wood & Sons were a famous pottery family, running several pottery businesses from the early 19th century. In 1865 it established a company based at the Trent and New Wharf Potteries in Burslem, which traded as Wood & Sons from 1910. Wood's produced a wide range of domestic, toilet and hotel wares.

The driving force behind the success of Wood and Sons, during the early part of the 20th century, was Harry J. Wood. He employed artists and designers such as Frederick Rhead, who was appointed Art Director in 1912. This prominent designer, who came from a family of potters, had previously worked at a number of pottery factories and brought with him the skill of tube lining, a form a slip trail decoration, which he used on a number of wares including *Trellis* and *Elers*. One of the company's most famous patterns, and still in production today, was *Yuan*, designed by Frederick Rhead in 1916, and printed in blue on the earthenware *Paris* shape.

When his designs proved popular, Frederick Rhead persuaded Harry J. Wood to purchase the redundant Crown Pottery that was adjacent to the Wood's site, with the intention of setting up an art studio to develop new wares. Once purchased, a new company called Bursley was established. The Bursley Works produced a range of decorative wares during the thirties in the Art Deco style. Not only did this provide an ideal opportunity to create new innovatory designs, but also an opportunity for his daughter, Charlotte Rhead, to work as a designer. Initially training the decorators on how to tube line, she soon developed popular and successful patterns such as *Persian* and *Seed Poppy* alongside creating several patterns decorated with tube line patterns for the Elgreave Pottery, purchased by Wood's in 1921. Interestingly, from c.1923, the back stamp for the Elgreave products reads, 'Lottie Rhead Ware'. These wares are much sought after by collectors today.

Group of earthenware pottery decorated with the Yuan *pattern, designed by Frederick Rhead, c.1916*

By the '20s Wood and Sons was promoting the latest dinnerware lines on the *Dorchester* and *Duke* shapes, which included patterns such as *Woodland* and *Alva*. In 1926 Charlotte Rhead left Wood's to work for Burgess and Leigh Ltd., three years later her father, Frederick Rhead also left the company.

In 1930 John Butler, who had spent the last 20 or so years as designer at A.J. Wilkinson Ltd., took up the position of Art Director at Wood and Sons. Little is known about his work during this period; he died in 1935. During the '30s Eddie Sambrook, whose father was the Chief Modeller for Wood's, took charge of the artistic side of production.

During the early '30s Harry J. Wood offered Susie Cooper space at the Crown Pottery. A few years later Susie Cooper designed a few patterns for them, including *Academy*, *Cavendish*, *Cromer* and *Charnwood*, which were generally marked with the Wood's back stamp and the words 'DESIGNED BY Susie Cooper'. These patterns were decorated on the *Wren* shape, which Susie Cooper had designed for Wood's, as well as a modified version called *Jay*.

Probably the best-known of Wood's products was *Beryl Green Ware*. Launched c.1939, this was a practical range of domestic wares finished with an over-all green glaze on the *Burlington* shape. The range proved popular in cafés and with average householders; it is still in production. Later alternative colour versions included *Jasmine*, with a yellow glaze on the *Jay* shape *with* Portland cups and saucers, and *Iris*. A range of transfer-printed floral patterns such as *Doris*, *Chatham* and *Bideford*, as illustrated in a company sales catalogue, were typical of the period.

In 1942 Charlotte Rhead was offered a position by Harry J. Wood at H.J. Wood Ltd. This company had originally been run by Percy Wood producing teapots. When demand for stock declined, the company faced financial difficulties and was bought by Wood and Sons. Rhead developed a series of tube-lined designs that were marketed under the newly created *Bursley Ware* trade name. Typical patterns included *Daisy*, *Trellis* and *Arabesque*, many of which were still for sale in the early '50s.

Opposite:
Cube *shaped part tea set decorated with an Art Deco style pattern, 1930s*

Right:
Bowl decorated with the Hedgerow *pattern, diameter 8in (20.3cm), c.1953*

At the same time Edward Radford was working in the same building developing his range of wares; he retired in c.1948.

During the immediate post-war period Wood's started to develop a new shape range called *Ringwood* decorated with a wide range of contemporary patterns such *Polka Dot*, *Carnival* and *Hedgerow*. The *Piazza ware* range of vases and ashtrays, decorated with hand-painted stylised patterns, echoed the shapes emanating from America. At the same time the company still promoted its traditional range of goods, including the *Seaforth* pattern on the *Grenville* shape and *Blue English Scenes*. From 1954 the company was known as Wood and Sons (Holdings). Eddie Sambrook left Wood's c.1959/60 to take up a new position as Art Director at Ridgways.

Wood's launched *Atlanta* in 1966. This new shape, designed by Tom Arnold, was decorated with a range of patterns including *Pierrot*, *Mexicana*, *Richmond*, *Albany* and *Satellite* – the latter designed by Michael Brennan. Other Wood's designers included Alan Swale and Alan Scott. In 1969 another shape range was launched called *Argos* along with new patterns including *Morocco*, *Blue Grotto* and *Moonlight Rose*. The business continues today.

- Collectors are particularly keen on the earlier tube-lined designs by Frederick Rhead and his daughter Charlotte Rhead from the early part of the 20th century.
- Collectors should note that examples of Charlotte Rhead's work marked 'BURSLEY' date from the post-war period, and not from the '20s.
- Collectors should be cautious as several patterns similar to Susie Cooper's work, but not by her, were produced by Wood's through to the '50s. Patterns by Susie Cooper are clearly marked.

Wood and Sons backstamp

Earthenware plate shape 'S' designed by Ulla Procope in 1960, decorated with the Pomegranate *pattern designed by Gunvor Olin-Grönqvist, diameter 7⅞in (20cm), early 1960s*

CHAPTER 2

EUROPEAN MANUFACTURERS

ARABIA

The Arabia factory came to the forefront during the late '40s and '50s with its design-conscious pottery born from the principles of modernism in the inter-war period. The company was characterised by the plain whiteness of its wares.

Arabia, based in Helsinki, Finland, was founded, as a subsidiary to the famous Swedish company Rörstrand, in 1874, in the hopes of breaking into the nearby Russian market. The earliest examples of Arabia pottery were very similar in style and shape to the parent company's wares, which also supplied the transfer prints. Arabia developed a wide range of practical and functional wares and was awarded a gold medal in Paris in 1900. In 1914 Arabia became an independent company giving it the opportunity to assert its own distinctive look.

The first moves towards modernism began during the early '20s with the increased number of outside artists and designers, such as Friedl Holzer-Kjellberg, who joined c.1924. In 1932 Arabia appointed Kurt Ekholm as artistic director. Ekholm set up an art department and invited artists to develop new ideas without consideration for the commercial side of the business. Greta-Lisa Jäderholm-Snellman, who joined Arabia during the late '20s, made a lasting con-tribution to the company and designed several important ranges. Arabia ran a world-class art studio from 1932 to the 1980s that employed a number of important artists including Toini Muona, Annikki Hovisaari, Kyllikki Salmenhaara and Rut Bryk. In particular the studio wares from the '50s and '60s were very influential. Birger Kaipiainen's studio wares were displayed at the Paris Exposition in 1937.

As Finland remained neutral during WWII, pottery manufacturers were able to continue production. In 1940 Arabia merged with the Wärtsilä Oy Group, which produced domestic and sanitary ware. In 1945 Kaj Franck, who was now in charge of design,

commissioned many new designers, including Kaarina Aho and Goran Bäck.

One of the most important ranges by Arabia in the post-war period was *Kilta*, designed by Kaj Franck in 1948, though not put into production until 1952. The range consisted of various simple and functional shapes decorated in a range of colours. *Kilta* remained in production until 1974. In contrast, Birger Kaipiainen created the decorative *Tapetti* (*Tapestry*) pattern printed on stoneware in 1953. *Ruska* stoneware, which was decorated with mottled brown glaze, was one of the company's most successful lines in the '60s and is still in production today. During the '60s the company started to export the wares to the UK, with great success. Notable examples from the early '70s include *Sinlkukka* (*Blue Flower*) tableware range and the *Black Ribbon* pattern, both designed by Peter Winquist. Interestingly the company also produced a number of sculptural forms including *Slpullt* (Onions), a stoneware form, made by Gunvor Olin-Grönqvist in 1982 and *Signs of Storm* made by Kati Tuominen in 1984. Arabia eventually remerged with its parent company Rörstrand.

Further Reference

Cameron, E., *Encyclopedia of Pottery and Porcelain, The 19th and 20th centuries*. Faber and Faber, 1986

Hellman, Å. (ed.), *Ceramic Art in Finland*. Thames and Hudson, 2005.

Opie, J., *Scandinavia: Ceramics and Glass in the Twentieth Century*. V&A Publications, 1989

www.freeformusa.com

Arabia backstamp

Form 2025 *teapot, designed by Heinrich Löffelhardt, 1957*

ARZBERG

The Arzberg Pottery has been associated with good design from the beginning of production in Germany in the 1880s. The company manufactured high-quality porcelain that was comparable to similar wares by the famous Limoges factory. From the '30s through to the latter part of the century the company continued to be associated with great artistic achievement.

Established by Theodor Lehman in 1886, the business grew steadily and by 1905 the company was employing over 560 people. Production was focused on tea and coffee wares until 1930. The new designs showed a clear understanding of the Bauhaus principles of modern design, which rejected decoration. As a result, the shapes were simple and architecturally styled.

Hermann Gretsch, who began his career as an architect in Stuggart, was appointed as artistic consultant for Arzberg in 1931, soon becoming one of the company's designers. In 1932 he created a new shape range called *Form 1382*, which proved an outstanding success, winning such coveted awards as the Gold Medals at the 6th Triennial in Milan and the 1937 Paris Exposition. In fact his shapes were so successful that by 1939 production was concentrated entirely on individual shapes designed by Gretsch. In 1945 he left the company to continue his career in architecture.

Heinrich Löffelhardt was appointed Head of

Form 3000 *teapot, decorated with the* Sicilia *pattern, shape designed by Hans Theo Baumann, height 5in (12.5cm)*

Design in 1952. Two years later Löffelhardt's shape range *Form 2000* was launched and was awarded a Gold medal at the Triennial in Milan; his *Form 2025* winning a gold medal at the Milan Triennial in 1957. *Form 2000* was later selected as the West German Federal Chancellery's conference service in the late '60s.

During the early '60s, with a workforce of over 1,500 people, the factory was completely modernised with the installation of gas tunnel kilns. Arzberg also supplied domestic wares suited for hotel and catering. In 1966 a new shape range called *Schönwald* was launched decorated with patterns such as *Nizza* and *Braun Seidenmatt*.

Recent shape ranges, including *Tric* (designed by Dieter Sieger in 1993) and *Cult* (designed by Dieter's son, Michael Sieger in 1994), continue the modern approach to design that has proved both popular and commercially successful for Arzberg. The factory currently operates under the umbrella of the company Hutschenreuther AG.

◆ Look out for the well-known shapes such as *Form 2025* and *Form 2000*.

Further Reference
www.skv-arzberg.com

Arzberg backstamp, 1950s

Group of earthenware cups and saucers

Boch Frères backstamp

BOCH FRERES

The pottery manufacturer Boch Frères has an illustrious history going back to the mid-18th century. It is best known today for its range of colourful and innovative wares from the '20s and '30s such as vases and ornamental plaques, which are much sought after by the higher end of the collectors' market. These artistic achievements presented the best in Belgian Art Deco design.

Boch Frères was initially part of a larger group of pottery companies founded in 1767 at Sept Fontaines in the Saarland region of Germany under the direction of Pierre-Joseph Boch. In the early part of the 19th century Eugène Boch merged the company with another to create Villeroy and Boch. Following border changes in 1839 there was a split and the Boch side of the business broke away to set up an independent manufactory at La Louvière.

The new business, using the trade name Keramis, was established in 1841. (Unfortunately, little is known about the history of the company due in part to the fact that many important company records were destroyed during WWII.) In 1906 Charles

Catteau joined the company and, within a year, was promoted to Artistic Decorator. Over the following years he introduced a range of popular lines, new decorative finishes and re-introduced hand throwing in order to replace the old moulds.

Earthenware saucer decorated with a blue spot design, 1920s

Right:
*Earthenware vase,
designed by Charles
Catteau, c.1925*

Far right:
*Earthenware vase,
designed by Charles
Catteau, height 11⅜in
(29cm), c.1925*

After WWI Boch Frères found a new impetus, its shapes decorations and glazes were renewed, leading the company to exhibit at the 1925 Exposition Internationale des Arts Décoratifs et Industriels Modernes in Paris, at which it was awarded a Grand Prix. The Art Deco wares of the '20s were stylish and distinctive, achieved by a decorative process that was unusual for the period. First the pattern was incised into the ware and then covered in a thick crackle glaze, known as *craquelure*, before the piece was hand-painted by a decorator. Many of the patterns featured abstract and stylised floral motifs. Marcel Goupy created some of the company's Art Deco designs.

In contrast to these high-class Art Deco wares they also manufactured tea wares and other domestic lines but these are less well known as examples are often difficult to spot. Probably during the late '40s

and early '50s the company produced a range of self-coloured wares in soft shapes.

Little is known about the general history of the company after WWII.

◆ The brilliant and colourful Art Deco wares, especially those by Charles Catteau are the most sought after and, as a result, most expensive examples of Boch Frères ceramics.

Further Reference

Cameron, E., *Encyclopaedia of Poetry and Porcelain, The 19th and 20th centuries*. Faber and Faber, 1986

De Pauw, C. and Stal, M., *Catteau*. King Baudouin Foundation, 2001

www.royalboch.be

*Art Deco figure of a seated woman by Stefan Dakon,
height 10⅝in (27cm), 1920s*

GOLDSCHEIDER/
GOLDSCHEIDER POTTERIES (STAFFS)

During the '20s and '30s several European factories
such as Goebels, Katzhütte and Royal Dux manufactured a range of Art Deco figurines, but the
productions of the Austrian pottery firm Goldscheider
are the most well known and sought after today for
their superior quality, elegance and style. Goldscheider
figures and masks so elegantly evoke that magical
era of the interwar period and the Art Deco style that
has become so popular today.

With factories already in Pilsen and Carlsbad in

Bohemia, Friedrich Goldscheider set up in Vienna in
1885. Initially focusing on the production of earthenware and porcelain, the company expanded its range
to include dessert wares, tea and coffee sets and toilet
wares. Besides making reproductions of classical
sculpture based on examples in museums, Goldscheider
also made a series of terracotta figures and plaques
that would be the precursors to the products of the
early 20th century. In 1891 the company patented a
bronze plating process and, within a year, had
established a bronze factory in Paris.

By the start of the 20th century Goldscheider's
many factories were producing a wide range of
products with trade outlets in Berlin. Following the
death of the founder c.1897 the business was run by
his widow, Regina, with help from her brother,
Alois, and her son, Walter.

From 1920 Walter was assisted by his brother,
Marcel Goldscheider, and they employed several
accomplished freelance artists and modellers
including Susi Singer and Hertha Bucher who had
also produced work, on a freelance basis, for the
Wiener Werkstätte. Other designers included Ida
Schwetz-Lehmann and Ida Erdös-Meisinger.

Goldscheider is best known for its range of

Face mask, height 12⅖in (32cm), 1920s-1930s

decorative polychrome pottery figures, which were produced during the Art Deco period. Typical examples included figures of stylish women wearing the latest fashions and female dancers. Goldscheider also produced an extensive range of terracotta face masks that were more stylised and showed the influence of African art, which had been popular in Paris since the early part of the century. These masks were often painted in a natural style and finished with a glossy glaze. Many of these figures were designed by Josef Lorenzl with some acknowledged to Stefan Dakon, an Austrian sculptor.

In 1938 the family, including Walter, moved to America to set up a factory in Trenton. The business floundered and went into liquidation within a few years due to various factors including the fact that his wares were dated and unsuccessful on the American market. He returned to Vienna in 1950.

Marcel Goldscheider left Austria in 1939 to live in England as a refugee. He went to Stoke-on-Trent and formed an association with the Myott Pottery. At this factory he produced many ceramic figures and face-masks, which were clearly inscribed on the base. In 1950 Marcel Goldscheider formed his own company, Goldscheider Potteries (Staffs), in Hanley, Stoke-on-Trent. He concentrated on the production of figures and decorative wares in bone china, which were reminiscent of his work from the '30s. A company catalogue from 1951 boasted over 800 models, including Toby jugs, jugs, birds and some novelty wares such as a cartoon-style elephant. The factory closed in 1959.

* Goldscheider produced the very best range of Art Deco figures, which were often copied. Collectors should be aware that high-quality fakes are on the market that are very hard to spot – always buy from reputable dealers and auction houses.
* Look out for the polychrome pottery figure of the *Butterfly Girl*, which was produced in three sizes.
* The terracotta face masks are very popular, but perfect examples are rare as they are fragile and easily damaged.
* The products of Goldscheider Potteries (Staffs) are very rare and do not have the same collecting interest as the Art Deco figures by Goldscheider.

Figure of girl on a drum, by Josef Lorenzl, height 14½in (37cm), 1920s-1930s

Further Reference

Miller, J., *Collectors' Guide to Art Deco*. Dorling Kindersley, 2005

www.goldscheider.de

Earthenware vase from the Argenta *range, designed by Wilhelm Kåge, height 6⅓in (16cm), 1930*

GUSTAVBERG AB

Gustavberg is recognised for its pioneering approach to modern design over the last century typified by its range of functional and practical wares, which set a new standard in Swedish design and influenced European industrial design. Many examples of Gustavberg pottery are considered to be classics and are sought after by those collectors interested in modern design.

The Gustavberg factory was established in Stockholm, Sweden in 1825, based at an old brickworks, which was operating as early as 1640. The factory produced earthenware and bone china in the English style with the raw materials being imported from England.

By 1867 Gustavberg was at the forefront of international design, exhibiting the latest lines at the Paris exhibition. Gunnar Wennerberg, a painter from the Stockholm Academy, joined the company in 1895, bringing with him a new approach to pottery production. He abandoned the period styles and instead looked to natural forms and nature for inspiration to develop decoration. As a result, simpler hand-painted patterns, using brighter colours, were introduced. This marked the start of the Scandinavian tradition.

In 1917 Wennerberg was joined by Wilhelm Kåge, originally an artist working as a poster designer in the large cities of Sweden. Within a few months of joining the company, despite having no previous experience, Kåge had designed a new functional set aimed at the working classes. However, as with many new ideas, this proved costly to produce and so the wares never actually reached the working classes. Gustavberg was well known for its range of practical and stacking sets introduced during the '30s. Kåge's first earthenware set suited to oven use was called *Pyro*. Decorated in brown on various tea wares and storage jars and first shown at the important Stockholmsutställningen exhibition of art and industry in 1930, it remained in production for 25 years. A blue version called *Marina* was introduced in 1933. The same year also saw the introduction of another practical kitchen range, *Praktika*, which was intended for volume production and available with various decorations including *Weekend*, with simple green bands, *Camping* and *Kitchenette*.

Besides the functional wares, Gustavberg also created a wide range of decorative wares such as *Argenta* and *Farsta*, designed by Wilhelm Kåge, which used similar motifs to those by Orrefors Glass Company. Introduced in 1930 this stoneware range was decorated with a green or red glaze with inlaid silver decorative motifs of female nudes, male warriors, floral borders or sea creatures. *Argenta* continued in production into the 1960s.

During the late '30s Wilhelm Kåge developed a range of soft earthenware forms, clearly showing the move towards organic shapes and influenced by the work of Alvar Aalto. This important range was decorated with suitably simple patterns such as plain banding. In contrast Kåge also created a number of vases such as his *Surrea* series from 1940. Furthermore, examples of his work were exhibited at the New York World's Fair in 1939. From 1942 an

Gustavberg backstamp for the Pyro *range, 1930s*

Group of hand-painted wares designed by Stig Lindberg, height of tallest item 15¾ in (40cm), early 1950s

experimental studio was set up for individual designers to create new forms, which could eventually move into main production.

Although Kåge remained working at the company until his death in 1960, he handed over the art directorship to Stig Lindberg in 1949. Lindberg developed a wide range of bone china tableware, studio, stoneware and earthenware ranges. He created a range of decorative faïence patterns, such as stylised floral and banded designs that were applied to a range of organically shaped dishes and vases. This innovative work received international recognition and was featured, from the early '50s, in the British pottery trade press, in particular in the *Decorative Art Studio Yearbook*. His practical and stylish tablewares such as *LA*, *LB* and *LG*, the latter from 1955, contrasted with his outstanding range of innovative white stoneware vases such as *Veckla* and *Vinda*. His faïence designs, painted in bright colours, depicted stylised people and simple banded decorations. He also created popular patterns for tablewares such as *Berså*, a printed repeated panel of stylised leaves in green and black, from 1960.

Other notable designers included Karin Björquist who joined the company in 1950 and created patterns such as *Svart Ruter* (*Black Diamond*) for a tableware range in 1955, *Röd Kant* (Red Edge), in 1968, and *Bell*, in 1979. She was appointed Art Director in 1980. In 1987 Gustavberg was bought by Arabia and by 1988 the company was known as Rörstrand-Gustavberg AB.

- The *Argenta* and *Farsta* ranges, in particular the *Spirea* vase designed by Wilhelm Kåge, from the Art Deco period is highly sought after as are the tablewares from the '50s and '60s.
- Stig Lindberg's faïence designs and studio works, painted in bright colours, depicting stylised people and simple banded decorations, are very popular with today's collectors

Further Reference

Opie, J., *Scandinavia Ceramics and Glass in the Twentieth Century*. V&A Publications, 1989

www.freeformusa.com

www.gustavsberg.com

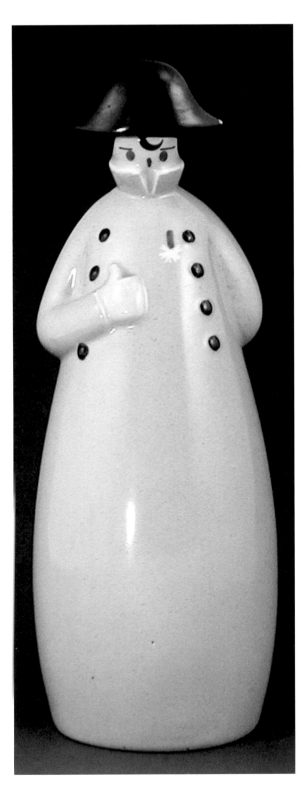

Decanter depicting Napoleon, *commissioned by Robj, height 10⅕ in (25.9cm), c.1929*

PARIS RETAILERS & MANUFACTURERS

During the early part of the century, and in particular the '20s and '30s, several pottery manufacturers produced decorative vases, plaques and tea wares often as exclusive lines, for a number of important department stores in Paris, which were similar to the London stores such as Heal's and Liberty. Only a few are well known today and that is partly due to examples being sold in the important decorative art sales across the world.

Paris has always held a reputation for fashion and style and, of course, is best remembered amongst today's collectors as being the venue of the all important 1925 Exposition Internationale des Arts Décoratifs et Industriels Modernes in Paris. It was here that designers from around the world saw the very best Art Deco designs in ceramics; it was a definite influence on the development of British ceramics and designers, such as Truda Carter. The design portfolios and pochoir prints created by French designers, such as Eduard Benedictus and E.A. Seguy, inspired these English designers.

The important French stores employed well-known or established designers to create fashionable new lines. They commissioned craftsmen to produce a wide range of wares for the home, including furniture, textiles and ceramics. Whilst these amazing designs are of great appeal to the collector today, at time of production they represented only a small segment of the higher end of the market. As there are so many retailers and manufacturers it is not possible to include them all here; three well-known examples are Primavera, Longwy and Robj.

Primavera was a very important manufacturer of Art Deco ceramics during the '20s. The studio was set up in 1912 by the important department store Les Grands Magasins du Printemps in order to offer high quality and exclusive items, which were manufactured at a factory at Sainte Radegonde, near Tours. The store commissioned various artists to create tablewares, figures and decorative wares such as vases and lamp bases, chiefly to complement the modern interior. Within the first year there were over 800 models in production, which had increased to 13,000 by 1928. Several designers including Jean Jacques Adnet, Marcel Renard, Léon Zack and René Buthaud created the ceramics. Buthaud was one of the most influential Art Deco designers of this period, running an art studio from 1923-25. His work was typified by his interest in stylised figures of African women and several examples of his work were displayed in the Primavera pavilion, in the form of a glass pyramid, at the 1925 Exposition Internationale des Arts Décoratifs et Industriels Modernes in Paris. Ten years later the trade press illustrated a set of stylised table decorations of horses and zebras made from metal and horn, created by Colette Gueden.

The **Longwy** factory, set up during the latter part of the 18th century, made decorative tiles and majolica-style wares. Although a much smaller concern than many others, the company's work was both innovative and attractive and from the '20s onwards Longwy supplied exclusive lines to the Paris stores, such as Le Bon Marché.

Importantly they produced a wide range of decorative ceramics, with the trademark crackled glaze, for Primavera with examples including large earthenware plaques depicting stylised naked figures and animals within a landscape alongside more practical wares such as tea and coffee sets.

The Paris retailer **Robj** commissioned a wide range of high-quality vases and smalls, such as ashtrays, lamps, and glass jars, often in the form of human figures. It enjoyed commercial success with a group of novelty musical bottles, which, when lifted, played the tune, "Show Me The Way To Go Home". The bottles were modelled as professional workers with each one given a specific beverage, such as gin, brandy and cognac.

There was also a lamp base modelled as a cowboy and a three-piece liqueur set modelled as golfing figures. Other examples were decorated with a

Longwy earthenware plaque, decorated with panels of stylised animals and trees on a craquelure glaze, diameter 14½in (37cm), 1920s

crackled glaze, which was popular during this period. A notable piece was a stylised figure of a *Spanish Dancer* by Marjerie from 1929. Robj also briefly sponsored an annual design competition from the late '20s to about 1931; the winning designs were put into limited production and manufactured by Sèvres. Many examples of the work produced by Robj were illustrated in the *Studio* yearbooks.

Further Reference

Benton, C., Benton, T. and Wood, G. (Editors), *Art Deco 1910-1930*. V&A Publications, 2003

Brunhammer, Y. and Tise, S., *The Decorative Arts in France: La Société des Artistes Decorators, 1900-1942*. Rizzoli, 1990

Cameron, E., *Encyclopaedia of Pottery and Porcelain, The 19th and 20th Centuries*. Faber and Faber, 1986

Gallagher, F., *Christie's Art Deco*. Pavilion Books Ltd., 2000

Blå Eld (Blue Fire) *serving set designed by Hertha Bengton, length of platter 15¾ in (40cm), 1951*

RÖRSTRAND

Rörstrand was established in 1726. In 1874 the company founded the Arabia factory (*see separate entry*) to try to break into the lucrative Russian market. Alf Wallander joined the company in 1895 and, within two years, became Art Director. His Art Nouveau-inspired tablewares and vases were outstanding and he was awarded a Grand Prix at the Paris Exposition in 1900.

Over the years Rörstrand employed several important designers who created striking patterns and shapes. Edward Hald, better known for his stylish designs for the Swedish glass company Orrefors, joined Rörstrand in 1917 and developed several patterns such as the *Halda* range, decorated with a transfer printed pattern, from 1919. Other designers included Louise Adelberg. In 1926

Rörstrand moved production to Gothenburg, relocating again to Lidköping within three years.

In 1931 Gunnar Nylund joined the company as Art Director. He created a variety of new lines from studio wares, such as his *Unic* range, a hand-painted relief wall plaque *The Nest*, and the *Cuprino* tea set from 1950. Four years later his new ovenware *Gratina* was introduced alongside his *Dala* and *Arena* patterns. He left the company in 1958.

Collectors of Swedish design, especially in Britain, are particularly keen on the more decorative wares that Rörstrand introduced during the '50s. One important designer of this period was Carl-Harry Stålhane, who designed a number of high-fired stoneware vases with a notable example being *Frozen Music*, decorated with contrasting matt glazes, from 1951. His domestic wares included *Blanca*, an undecorated set, and a coffee service decorated with the *Inca* pattern, both

Set of serving dishes and jug with red and green glaze, designed by Hertha Bengton, height of jug 9in (23cm), 1955

from about 1957. He used red clay for his *Siam* tea set, decorated with simple banded decoration, from about 1958, alongside a range of one-of-a-kind stoneware vases called *Magnific*. Other important designers included Marianne Westman and Hertha Bengton. Patterns by Marianne Westman include *Picknick*, which depicted stylised vegetables and herbs, and the *Pomona* range, both from 1956. Her *Mon Amie* pattern, a repeated design of blue flowers, from 1951, is still in production today and clearly inspired the *Roselle* pattern by W.R. Midwinter Ltd. Hertha Bengton created a number of new shapes from 1949 that included the *Blå Eld* (*Blue Fire*) ware, a moulded set decorated with a blue glaze, and the *Koka Blå* contemporary shape range. She also used red clay for her designs, typified by her *Cayenne* range with simple banded decoration, from 1958.

Rörstrand became part of the Uppsala-Ekeby Group in 1963 until it was bought by the Finnish company Wärtsilä Oy in 1984. In 1987 Wärtsilä Oy also bought Gustavsbergs porslinsfabrik; the Finnish Hackman Group acquired the company in 1990.

◆ Marianne Westman's post-war patterns, such as *Picknick* and *Pomona*, both 1956, are sought after. Collectors should note that *Pomona* was in production until 1971.

◆ Collectors should also look out for the strikingly contemporary designs by Hertha Bengton, such as *Blå Eld* (*Blue Fire*).

Further Reference

Opie, J., *Scandinavia Ceramics and Glass in the Twentieth Century*. V&A Publications, 1989.

www.freeformusa.com

Right:
Examples of the
Service 2000 *designed*
by Raymond Loewy
and Richard Latham,
introduced 1954

Below:
The TAC *shape*
designed by Walter
Gropius in association
with TAC (The
Architects
Collaborate), 1969

ROSENTHAL AG

Throughout the 20th century Rosenthal earned a worldwide reputation for its pottery, which is both avant-garde and sophisticated. With such a strong market the company has made an influential contribution to the world of ceramics. Philipp Rosenthal established the company in 1879, known then as Philipp Rosenthal & Co., in a small village in Selb, Germany. Initially the company bought in blank wares and decorated them, but moved to manufacturing within twelve years. One of the first successful lines was *Monbijou* (*My Jewel*) introduced in 1896 and still in production. This was soon followed by a number of Art Nouveau-inspired ranges, including *Donatello* from 1905.

By the start of the 20th century business was going well with over 1,000 people employed by 1904. In 1910 a new art department was set up. During the Art Deco period the company made a number of decorative figures, some designed by Dorothea Charol and Claire Weiss. In 1921 Rosenthal set up its own distribution company in America, Rosenthal China Corporation. During the late '20s business remained strong and it was reported in the American trade press that the company had offices and showrooms in New York. The article also noted the wide range of patterns, from a series called *Rhine Castles* to a number of floral border designs.

Due to Hitler's anti-semitic regime in Germany, Philipp Rosenthal was forced to resign from his own company in 1935.

In the early '50s Philip Rosenthal, son of the founder, joined Rosenthal. Initially in charge of marketing, he soon became involved in design. Breaking from the traditional styles, he moved the focus onto contemporary style using the latest designers and stylists from all over the world, including Raymond Peynet, Elsa Fischer-Treyden, Raymond Loewy, and the Danish designer Bjorn Wiinblad.

American industrial designer Loewy created tableware ranges *E* and *Undine*, both in 1952-53, followed in 1954 by the *Exquisit* range, decorated with several patterns including *Melodie*. The most important shape range was called *Service 2000*, developed with Richard Latham, and introduced in 1954. This collectable shape range was decorated with many different patterns created by various designers over the years.

British designer Lucienne Day, better known for her contemporary textile, carpet, wallpaper and dress materials for various companies including Heal's in London, was commissioned by Rosenthal after he saw one of her wallpaper designs for the German company Rasch. From the late '50s she developed a variety of patterns for the *2000* shape, including *Bond Street*, *Columbine* and *Regent Street*.

Rosenthal Studio-line vase, shape designed by Tapio Wirkkala in 1960 and pattern by Rosemonde Nairac in the 1980s, height 8¼ in (21cm)

These contemporary lines were marketed under the new *Rosenthal Studio-line* banner with the popular and traditional lines under the *Classic* collection alongside *Thomas* porcelain.

In 1960 the company set up the Rosenthal Studio House in Nurembourg. Rosenthal invested heavily in the development of new shapes and compositions of sets despite having no security that a new shape would be popular. Notable examples of Rosenthal's pioneering designs include *Variation* (1962), *Composition* (1963) both by Tapio Wirkkala, *TAC* by Walter Gropius (1969) and *Suomi* (1976) by Timo Sarpaneva.

During the '60s Philip Rosenthal invited a number of important and international artists to create limited edition patterns for the company: Victor Vasarely created a wall relief, Henry Moore devised

The Century *shape designed by Tapio Wirkkala, 1979*

The Cupola *shape, designed by Mario Bellini, 1984*

a stylised sculptural shape called *Moonhead*, Friedensreich Hundertwasser created a ceramic vase, and Eduardo Paolozzi produced a dog sculpture.

From the early '80s Rosenthal looked to Italian architects for new inspiration with the resultant designs including *Cupola* by Mario Bellini and *Il Faro* by Also Rossi. One of the best-known patterns from the '80s is *Flash*, a very decorative range of unusual shapes designed by Dorothy Hafner.

In the mid '90s Rosenthal started to work with well-known partners to develop innovative patterns to add to the standard range. Under the name, *The Rosenthal Lifestyle Collections* the company created several luxurious porcelain sets and high-quality accessories. The association with the Italian fashion house Versace resulted in an extravagant and stylish range of pottery designed by Gianni Versace himself; the range included *Le Voyage Marco Polo*, *Le Roi Soleil* and

Medusa. Further associations were formed with both the Italian jeweller Bulgari and with Fornasetti.

- Over the years, Rosenthal employed some of the best European designers. In particular, collectors should look out for shapes by Raymond Loewy.
- Lucienne Day's ceramic patterns are highly sought after, particularly as it is not a large body of work. Note that her name was not included on the backstamp.
- The artistic creations by Victor Vasarely, Henry Moore, Friedensreich Hundertwasser, and Eduardo Paolozzi were produced in limited editions and are highly collectable.

Further Reference

Jackson, L., *Robin and Lucienne Day, Pioneers of Contemporary Design*. Mitchell Beazly, 2001

Living with Art: A Homage to Philip Rosenthal. Rosenthal AG, 2003

www.rosenthalchina.com

www.int.rosenthal.de

An example of the company backstamp

Group of earthenware pots decorated with the Flash One *patten designed by Dorothy Hafner, early 1980s*

Girl with a Goose sculpted for Royal Copenhagen in 1903 by Christian Thomsen (1860-1921) (Modern production)

Aluminia. Arnold Krog joined the company as Art Director in 1885; his first job was to relaunch the well-known ancient *Blue Fluted* pattern, which is still associated with Royal Copenhagen today. Inspired by techniques from Japan, Krog concentrated on underglaze painting, developing a new style that combined Japanese imagery with European naturalism. Due to the high temperatures at firing, the colour range was limited to cobalt blue. As the technique was perfected, chrome green and a golden brown/red were added to the palette and the decoration tended to traditional Nordic motifs and landscape scenes that are still popular today. Examples of these wares were displayed at the important expositions such as Paris Exposition Universelle in 1889, where the company won the Grand Prix.

At the turn of the century Aluminia introduced faïence ware in the Art Nouveau style, particularly by designers such as Christian Joachim and Harald Slott-Møller. Around the same time the sculptor Gerhard Henning was producing elegant porcelain figurines with elaborate decoration, and Patrick Nordström was experimenting with stoneware glazes.

By the late '20s and early '30s, Royal Copenhagen was embracing Art Deco, but with a Danish interpretation – more subtle and simple than often found in the rest of Europe – that was a forerunner to the sparse functionality now associated with Danish design.

Following WWII the company offered a wide range of lines for the market. Of particular note was the work of Axel Salto, who made quite an impact with his original high-fired stoneware vases and bowls, including the *Solfatara* glaze. Other notable designers of the time included Thorkild Olsen, Gertrud Vasegaard, Nils Thorsson and Magnus Stephensen.

Grethe Meyer joined the company in 1960 and proved to be an important designer, creating several new lines including the *Blue Line* earthenware range of domestic and functional tablewares for Aluminia. Her porcelain service *White Pot*, a functional and

ROYAL COPENHAGEN

Royal Copenhagen was established as a private company in 1775 with support from the Danish Royal Family. The company gained a reputation for high-quality hard-paste porcelain exemplified by the *Flora Danica* service made in 1790-1802 intended for Catherine the Great. During the 19th century the company enjoyed some commercial success under the artistic direction of G.F. Hetsch. In 1882 Royal Copenhagen merged with the earthenware factory simple range introduced in 1971, quickly became a design classic.

In 1972 the company bought Georg Jensen Silversmiths. This was the first of a series of mergers: in 1985 with Holmegaard Glassworks; in 1987 with Bing & Grøndahl; and then with Swedish glassworks Orrefors and Kosta Boda to form the company Royal Scandinavia. These days Royal Scandinavia is made up of Georg Jensen Silver and Royal Copenhagen, which continues to produce a wide range of high-quality porcelain items.

* In 1908 Royal Copenhagen introduced the first of a long series of Christmas plates, featuring different images each year, finished in a soft blue glaze. Pattern names such as *Mother and Child* (1908, *Danish Landscape* (1915) and *Jingle Bells* (1984) are typical.
* Royal Copenhagen also produced a vast range of tableware, sculptural items and studio wares. In particular, collectors should look out for *White Pot* by Grethe Meyer.
* Particularly popular with Royal Copenhagen collectors are the high-quality figurines, those portraying children and animals being the most common.

Further Reference

Opie, J., *Scandinavia Ceramics and Glass in the Twentieth Century*. V&A Publications, 1989

www.royalcopenhagen.com

Hand-painted dish from the Tenera *series, c.1959*

An example of the company backstamp

The Desert *Christmas plate designed by Kai Large, 7in (17.8cm), 1972*

Range of kitchenwares showing the simple and practical approach to design in the early '30s

VILLEROY AND BOCH

In the early 19th century N. Villeroy and Jean François Boch amalgamated their companies to form Villeroy and Boch, which soon became the leading German manufacturer of pottery and, over the years, established an international reputation for outstanding quality and innovation in pottery design.

During the early 20th century the company produced a wide range of sanitary ware, and wall and floor tiles, not only for domestic bathrooms, but also for luxury liners and corporate and official buildings. The company also produced tableware as well as decorative items, including the well-known Mettlach Steins, and some of the most beautiful examples of Art Nouveau wares, known as *Jugendstil* in Europe. Important designers included Henry van de Veldes, Adelbert Niemeyer, Joseph Olbrich and Peter Behrens.

The shapes and designs of this time reflected an interest in the principles promoted by the Bauhaus

Example of the company backstamp used 1967-1979

Earthenware dish decorated with an Art Deco shape pattern, possibly 1920's

Plate decorated with Acapulco *pattern designed by Christine Reuter in 1967*

movement, as can be seen in a number of examples by Hermann Gretsch.

In 1928 the company set up an experimental studio research centre in Dresden.

The company also responded to the Art Deco style by producing a range of figural items of women and stylised animals.

During the '50s and '60s the innovative design team at Villeroy and Boch created new patterns and shapes that had more than a passing likeness to some Swedish manufacturers, a notable example is the tea service *Diamant*. During the '60s the company introduced a new fireproof porcelain tableware range that proved popular on the British market, with patterns such as the in-glaze *Cadiz*, designed by Christine Reuter. Another new shape, *Milano*, designed by Ludwig Scherer, was decorated with various patterns, in particular *Acapulco*, a printed design depicting stylised birds in trees by Christine Reuter.

One of the most original items from the early '70s was the *Kugel* (*Sphere*) range designed by Helen Von Boch in 1971. This ingenious range comprised an entire dinnerservice that could be stacked to form a ball.

◆ With such a long period of production, collectors have a wide selection of Villeroy and Boch wares from which to choose. In particular, some of the contemporary patterns from the late '60s and early '70s, such as *Acapulco*, are popular with younger, design-conscious collectors.

Further Reference

Desens, R., *Villeroy & Boch, 250 Years of European Industrial History, 1748-2005*. Villeroy & Boch Aktiengesellschaft, 2005

www.retroselect.com

www.villeroy-boch.com

CHAPTER 3

AMERICAN MANUFACTURERS

Examples of the Ring Ware *range, designed by Louis Ipsen, 1933*

BAUER POTTERY

Bauer Pottery pioneered the use of solid colour glazes on functional earthenware shapes, thereby influencing the entire North American ceramics industry.

Bauer was a family business, initially based in Kentucky, founded c.1885, producing stoneware and earthenware for domestic use. The factory closed following the death of John Bauer in 1898.

In 1905 the factory was reopened after considerable modernisation and became a limited company. Four years later the firm moved to California, close to major pottery manufacturers such as Gladding McBean and Vernon Kilns. In order to develop new designs and shapes the company employed the modeller Louis Ipsen, a Danish immigrant. Edwin Bauer, the son of the company's owner joined in 1914.

In 1929 the company employed Victor F. Houser, a glaze specialist, who went on to develop the all-

important brightly coloured glazes. The combination of practical shapes and coloured glazes developed into a range of mix-and-match dinnerwares, starting a new trend. The first range, launched in the late 1920s, *Plain Ware*, was intended for everyday use in the kitchen. Originally available in three colours, orange, green or yellow, it was later extended to include dinnerware and new colours were introduced.

Bauer enjoyed tremendous success with its next range, *Bauer California Pottery*, known today by collectors as *Ring Ware*. Designed by Louis Ipsen, the range featured simple banded indentations to the edge of the ware and was launched in a limited colour range, which included *Jade Green* and *Chinese Yellow*; other colours were added later.

Bauer Pottery closed in 1962. Today, the work of J.A. Bauer has been reintroduced by a ceramics studio in Los Angeles, just minutes away from the original plant. The new line, *Bauer 2000*, uses original pieces as models, with emphasis on items first produced in the '30s and '40s.

* The *Ring Ware* range by Bauer is one of the most sought after today, in particular the oil jars.

Further Reference

Leibe, F. (editor), Atterbury, P. (consultant), *20th Century Ceramics. Antiques Checklist*. Millers, 2003

Stern, B., *California Pottery: From Missions to Modernism*. Chronicle Books, 2001

Tuchman, M., *Bauer Classic American Pottery*. Chronicle Books, 1995

www.bauerpottery.com

BUFFALO POTTERY

Buffalo Pottery was set up by John D. Larkin in order to produce ceramic gift wares, known as 'premiums', for its parent company soap manufacturer Larkin Co. Group, established in 1875.

Set up in Buffalo, near New York, in 1901 under the direction of Louis Brown, production began in 1903 with the first premiums being sold with purchases of soap, as well as in shops and through mail-order catalogues. The first products were bone china dinnerware styled to imitate the traditional French designs being imported into the country. In 1905 the company introduced one of the most popular patterns, *Blue Willow*, an under-glaze transfer-printed design, used on a range of earthenware tablewares. Two other patterns of note were *Bangor*, c.1905, and *Vienna*, which was illustrated in the company catalogue in 1915. In 1907 the new backstamp featured the words "SEMI-VITREOUS BUFFALO POTTERY" and a drawing of a Buffalo.

A range of art wares, *Deldare Ware*, was launched in 1908. Encompassing tablewares, candlesticks, vases and toilet sets, it was decorated with a range of patterns designed by Ralph Stuart, who was inspired by colonial revival themes, such as *The Fallowfield Hunt* series. The patterns were printed onto the ware then hand painted with a high-gloss glaze. Another line, *Emerald Deldare*, followed in 1911. It featured a wide range of subjects such as horses, landscapes and figures with a distinctive geometric border design.

During WWI Buffalo manufactured bone china wares for the Government for use by the armed forces. In 1917 the factory was enlarged and the ranges were extended to encompass the production of military wares. In the early '20s the factory ceased to manufacture soap premiums. As time went on production focused on catering and hotel wares, although the company did produce a series of wares decorated with coloured glazes sold under the *Multi Fleure* label during the late '20s.

In 1940 the company became known as Buffalo Pottery Inc. and later, in 1956, Buffalo China Inc. In 1983 it was purchased by the Oneida company.

- Without a doubt, the earliest ranges, such as *Deldare* (1908), are the most sought after of Buffalo Pottery's wares. The *Deldare* range, easily identifiable through its predominant green colouring, is particularly sought after as it was only in production for a year. The *Abino* line, depicting several themes such as sailing ships and landscapes, is similarly popular as it was only in production for two years from 1911-1913.
- In 1910 Buffalo produced a calendar plate on the *Deldare* body. This is extremely rare and most eagerly sought after.
- In 1950 the company introduced its Christmas plates, though these were given to customers and employees rather than being sold commercially. These popular plates, now sought after by collectors, were issued every year until 1962, except 1961.

Further Reference

Altman, V. and Altman, S., *The Book of Buffalo Pottery*. Schiffer Publishing, 1997

Atterbury, P., Denker E.P. and Batkin, M., *Twentieth Century Ceramics: A Collectors Guide to British and North American Factory Produced Ceramics*. Millers, Octopus Publishing Ltd., 1999

Two eathenware plates. Left: decorated with the Bangor *pattern, printed with painted decoration, diameter 10⅛in (25.7cm), c.1905; right: the printed pattern* Vienna, *c.1915*

FULPER POTTERY/STANGL POTTERY

The Fulper Pottery, an internationally renowned company, was established during the early part of the 19th century. The extensive range of decorative vases and the many innovative glazes applied to these stylish forms have attracted many collectors to Fulper pottery not least because the classic shapes sit well in today's modern interior.

The pottery works, based in Flemington, New Jersey, were founded by Samuel Hill to produce drain pipes, storage vessels and paving tiles from local terra cotta earthenware clay. On Hill's death in 1858, the factory was purchased by head potter Abraham Fulper. At that time production included salt-glaze stoneware crocks, jugs and industrial containers. Fulper became a limited company in 1899, controlled by Abraham's sons George and Edward, and grandson William Hill Fulper II.

Fulper's primary production during the first years of the 20th century was in patented stoneware water filters, cooking ware and decorated whisky jugs. The success of these lines enabled the company to invest in developing an artware line. It produced a range of decorative wares such as vases, often two handled, and flower holders that began production in 1909, after much experimentation, with a range called *Vasekraft*. The notable achievements in the production of art glazes gave the company a leading edge over other manufacturers. The matt and high-gloss glazes,

such as *Café Au Lait*, used on a range of wares, proved popular with the American buyer. There was also a more expensive range using glazes attempting to recreate period styles such as the Chinese glazes.

The success of the glazes was at least in part due to the pioneering work of Johann Martin Stangl, a German glaze chemist, who joined the company in 1910. Stangl left the company in 1914 to work for Haeger Potteries but returned to Fulper in 1919.

With German imports stopped during WWI, Fulper developed production of porcelain doll heads. However, after the war Fulper could not compete with the doll heads once again being imported from Germany. Instead, Fulper concentrated on novelty porcelain lamps, dresser boxes, ashtrays and boudoir items, all marketed under the name *Fulper Porcelaines*. This was a wise move as the fashion for heavy stonewares, which had built up the business, waned considerably during the late 1910s and early '20s.

In 1926 Stangl became President of the company, and continued at the helm until his death in 1972. Stangl

Selection of Fulper Pottery brand vases decorated in Verte Antique, Jade, Venetian Blue, and Cinnamon Tan Flambé *glazes, height of tallest item 8¼in (21cm)*

Stoneware handled vase decorated in Rose and Green Flambé *glaze. Height 6¼in (15.9cm)*

Fulper stoneware two-handled vase decorated with Cat's Eye Flambé *glaze. Height of vase 8in (20.3cm)*

was responsible for the introduction of America's first open stock solid colour dinnerware, which was initially marketed as *Fulper Fayence*, but became known as *Stangl Pottery*. Production of this new, lighter-weight artware increased throughout the '20s and in 1928 another factory was acquired in Trenton. The production of all heavy Fulper Pottery art wares ceased in 1935 with the closure of the Flemington Works. From this point on the company only produced the *Stangl Pottery* lines, although the company continued to be called Fulper Pottery until 1955.

During the late '40s and early '50s the company introduced a number of contemporary patterns with several by Kay Hackett, Stangl's main designer. At the same time the company was producing moulded bird figures such as *Humming Birds*, *Shoveler Duck* and *Rooster*, several of which were designed by August Jacob; these figures were extended due to their popularity. Patterns such as *Golden Harvest*, 1953, and *Amber-Glo*, 1954, were typical as was the new coupe shape plate, which reflected modern tastes.

Johann Martin Stangl died in 1972; the pottery eventually closed in 1978.

• The range of vases and bowls from the '30s and '40s are highly sought after by collectors.
• In 1933 Tony Sarg designed his Stoby mugs.

These hand-painted character mugs, command high prices today.
• Stangl's *Kiddie Ware* depicting nursey rhymes such as *Mother Goose*, *Humpty Dumpty* and *Little Boy Blue*, are highly collectable.

Further Reference

Atterbury, P., Denker E.P. and Batkin, M., *Twentieth Century Ceramics: A Collectors Guide to British and North American Factory Produced Ceramics*. Millers, Octopus Publishing Ltd., 1999

Hible, J., Goldman Hibel, C., DeFalco, R. and Rago, D., *The Fulper Book*. Arts & Crafts Quarterly, 1992

Runge Jr., R.C., *Collector's Encyclopedia of Stangl Artware, Lamps & Birds*, 2nd Ed. Collector Books, Schroeder Publishing Co., 2006

www. fulper.net

www.stanglpottery.org

www.ragoarts.com

Earthenware plate and coffee pot decorated with the Desert Rose *pattern, designed by Mary J. Winans, diameter of plate 10⅝in (27cm), 1941*

GLADDING McBEAN COMPANY

This very popular pottery company was established by Charles Gladding, Peter McGill McBean and George Chambers, all from Chicago, in 1875. The factory was based in Lincoln, California and initially began with the manufacture of drainage pipes, later adding architectural terracotta tiles used to decorate public buildings such as the Paramount Theatre in Oakland in 1931.

From the early part of the '30s the company began manufacturing domestic tableware in its Glendale, California factory. By the mid '30s Gladding McBean was ranked as one of the top five manufacturers in America. In 1934, in line with popular trends, the company created a brand name, Franciscan Pottery, to be used for all domestic and art wares; this was changed to Franciscan Ware in 1936. The patterns were designed by Mary K. Grant, who had previously worked in New York as a stylist for Macy's and Hahn's department store, she had also designed textiles. Grant was interested in the functional aspects of pottery wares, as well as contours and the use of dramatic colours.

The first pattern range under the Franciscan Ware brand name was *El Patio*, from 1934, which was decorated in solid colours and with various patterns including *Del Mar* and *Padua*. Later in the '30s the company introduced printed patterns, *Geranium*, a stencil-style pattern, being typical.

When mix-and-match dinnerware decorated in solid plain colours became fashionable, Gladding McBean produced two ranges to keep up with its competitors. The shapes *Coronado*, designed by Mary K. Grant, and *Metropolitan*, by New York architect Morris B. Sanders, were introduced in 1935

Collection of earthenware Metropolitan *wares. Teapot and pitcher decorated with the* Tiempo *pattern, 1948; cup, saucer and creamer decorated with the* Metropolitan *pattern, 1939; and a plate with the printed* Trio *pattern, 1954, designed by Esta James, diameter of plate 9¾in (24.8cm)*

and 1939 respectively. *Metropolitan* was initially decorated in the popular two-tone colour scheme. By the late '40s the range was decorated with a single glaze and renamed *Tiempo*. In the early '50s there were a number of patterns being used, including a stylised leaf design called *Trio*, by Esta James.

In 1941 Gladding McBean introduced a translucent fine china range called *Franciscan Fine China;* this was later renamed *Masterpiece China*. The first shape was *Merced*, soon followed by *Ovide* in 1942. Over the years of production, the range included nine basic shapes and over 160 patterns designed by Otto J. Lund and George T. James. *Masterpiece China* remained in production until 1977.

Desert Rose, designed by Mary J. Winans and introduced in 1941, soon became the most popular American dinnerware pattern. In 1964 the company

proudly boasted that it had sold the sixty-millionth piece of *Desert Rose*. Other patterns launched in the '40s include *Apple*, in 1940, and *Ivy*, in 1949. Also launched in 1949 was the bone china *Encanto* shape, designed by Mary K. Grant. Offered in plain colours, such as light blue, black and dark green, the decoration was as solid coloured bodies rather than glaze colours, which had been the fashion during the preceding years.

In the early 1950s George T. James created the bone china range, *Contours*, which included forty items – such as vases, covered vessels and candleholders – decorated with six different colours and with printed patterns. He also designed the new earthenware *Eclipse* shape in 1954, which was decorated with modern patterns such as *Oasis*, *Duet* and *Pomegranate*, and the very successful *Starburst* pattern.

Examples of the earthenware Eclipse *shape designed by George T. James, decorated with the* Starburst *pattern designed by Mary C. Brown, c.1954*

In 1962, Gladding McBean & Co. mergd with Lock Pipe and Joint Co. and the Electro-Chemical Engineering and Manufacturing Corporation to form the International Pipe and Ceramics Corporation,

Plate, cup and saucer decorated with the Shalimar *pattern designed by Francis Chun, diameter of plate 10⅝ in (27cm), 1974*

which was soon renamed Interpace. In 1979 Interpace sold the Franciscan ceramics division to Josiah Wedgwood and Sons Ltd. Franciscan Ceramics ceased manufacturing in the U.S. in 1984. Production of the *Desert Rose, Apple* and *Fresh Fruit* patterns would continue to be produced in England by the Johnson Brothers division of Wedgwood alongside new patterns using the Franciscan trademark.

* *Desert Rose*, the best-selling American dinner ware pattern, is now highly collectable.
* Examples of Gladding McBean's domestic table-ware from the '30s onwards are sought after by collectors today.
* Collectors are particularly keen on George T. James' bone china series *Contours*.

Further Reference

Elliot-Bishop, J., *Franciscan, Catalina & Other Gladding McBean Wares.* Schiffer Books, 2001

Elliot-Bishop, J., *Franciscan, Hand-decorated Embossed Dinnerware.* Schiffer Books, 2004

www.gmcb.com/franciscan

Collection of stoneware shapes including a Sundial *covered casserole dish from 1937 (far left,, a* Nora *pitcher from 1954 (centre back) and an* Airflow *teapot from 1937 (front, 3rd from left)*

HALL CHINA COMPANY

The Hall China Company is probably best known today for its extensive range of teapots of all shapes and styles.

Robert Hall established the company in 1903, based at East Liverpool, in Ohio. From 1911 production concentrated on heavy-duty institutional pottery made in a traditional manner. The founder's son Robert Taggart Hall joined the business and developed a high-temperature leadless glaze requiring only one firing, thus cutting production costs considerably. That this glaze did not craze was a very important selling point. Furthermore, the pottery was extremely durable and proved ideal for domestic wares such as cookware and for catering establishments. In 1930 the business expanded and a new factory was built. In a 1935 company catalogue a range of twenty-one coloured glazes was available on a wide selection of individual items such as the *Plaza* water jug, room service wares and even the *Astoria* or *Waldorf* shaped spittoons!

The introduction of teapots came during the early part of the century; by the '20s the range was extensive and available decorated in a wide range of patterns and glazes. By the end of the 20th century, 2,000 different styles had been produced, notable examples including *Streamline* and *Surfside* from 1937, *Football* and *Donut* pitcher from 1938 and *Rhythm* from 1939. A novelty teapot was produced for the New York World's Fair in 1939/1940 embossed in gold on a blue body. The company even explained how to make a proper cup of tea in one of their advertisements.

Hall enjoyed tremendous success with a number of premium lines produced for the influential stores such as Westinghouse, Hotpoint, Sears and General Electric; contracts provided a steady run of large orders from the late '20s that continued for many years. One of the most popular of these was the

197

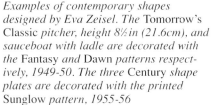

Examples of contemporary shapes designed by Eva Zeisel. The Tomorrow's Classic *pitcher, height 8½ in (21.6cm), and sauceboat with ladle are decorated with the* Fantasy *and* Dawn *patterns respectively, 1949-50. The three* Century *shape plates are decorated with the printed* Sunglow *pattern, 1955-56*

Autumn Leaf printed pattern in browns on a stippled surface created for the Jewel Tea Company from the mid '30s. This simple pattern turned out to be a best seller up until the '70s.

With such demand for Hall pottery the company undertook new developments including a new building being erected to streamline production, the introduction of dinnerware, new coloured glazes and transfer printed designs. Throughout the '30s many of the standard shapes were decorated with bright glazes rather than any overtly Art Deco styled motifs, although the *Sundial* shape bears a resemblance to streamlined Art Deco with its bright *Chinese Red* glaze, one of the most popular colours. During WWII, when the usual supply line of pottery from Europe was blocked, Hall China produced all sorts of teapots, tea urns and coffee pots that were welcomed by the trade.

The new decade marked the important contribution that Eva Zeisel made to the company with her first shape range, *Tomorrow's Classic*, which was put into production in 1952. This popular set was decorated with a range of transfer-printed patterns such as *Dawn* and *Arizona*, designed by Charles Sielger, whilst the *Fantasy* and *Frost Flowers* patterns were created by Zeisel team members Douglas Kelley, Ross Littell and William Katavolvos. It was the *Tomorrow's Classic* coffee pot that inspired Roy Midwinter to develop his own *Fashion* shape range for W.R. Midwinter Ltd. in the mid '50s. As a result of the popularity of *Tomorrow's Classic*, Hall commissioned Zeisel to create other shapes including the *Century* range, launched in 1956, which was available in solid colours or transfer-printed designs such as the *Sunglow* pattern.

During this period the company also created a set of 'refrigerator wares', for example *Tri-Tone* by Eva Zeisel, from 1954. This unusual and tasteful range included a 20-piece ovenproof cook and kitchenware line. The company also commissioned the designer Joseph Palin Thorley, an English man who had worked at Josiah Wedgwood and Sons Ltd., who created the *Granitone* range for the Sears company. Hall China continues to produce a wide range of china today.

Earthenware Windshield *shape teapot, decorated with gold spots, height 6½in (16.5cm), 1941*

- With over 2,000 different styles of teapot produced by Hall China, the serious collector is presented with quite a task. The rare designs are more sought after and therefore more valuable.
- Eva Zeisel's work is popular with collectors, in particular *Tomorrow's Classic*. Zeisel's name was printed alongside the backstamp.
- The novelty teapot for the New York World's Fair in 1939/1940 was embossed in gold on a blue body. Collectors are much keener on the 1939 edition rather than the 1940 example.
- *Autumn Leaf* created for the Jewel Tea Company from the mid '30s and *Red Poppy* made for Grand Union are both worth looking out for. Note that *Autumn Leaf* was manufactured up till the '70s, so collectors should take care to check which period examples are from.

Further Reference

Atterbury, P., Denker E.P. and Batkin, M., *Twentieth Century Ceramics: A Collectors Guide to British and North American Factory Produced Ceramics.* Millers, Octopus Publishing Ltd., 1999

Stern, B., *California Pottery: From Missions to Modernism.* Chronicle Books, 2001

Venable, C., Denker, E., Grier, K. and Harrison, S., *China and Glass in America 1880-1980; From Tabletop to TV Tray.* Dallas Museum of Art, Harry N. Abrams, Inc., 2000

Backstamps issued by Hall China, 1940s

www.hallchina.com

Collection of Fiesta *wares including a water pitcher, diameter of plate 9⅜in (23.8cm), 1936*

HOMER LAUGHLIN

Homer Laughlin is known for its excellence and originality in design for the mass market, typified by the *Fiesta* range from the '30s.

Two brothers, Homer and Shakespeare Laughlin, established the company c.1873, with assistance from their father. Initially the company operated a wholesale business selling imported pottery to American stores, but later built a white ware factory at East Liverpool in Ohio to make pots. Shakespeare Laughlin left the business in 1877. In 1896 Homer Laughlin went into partnership with W. Edwin Wells, the company's book-keeper. A year later

Earthenware commemorative plate, made for the New York World's Fair, transfer printed with gilt decoration, designed by Charles Murphy, diameter 10in (25.4cm), 1939

Homer sold his share of the company to the Aaron family. Arthur Mountford was then appointed as Art Director. The company was, at least partly, influenced by the many stores that stocked the company's wares, such as F.W. Woolworth & Co., which had 180 stores nationwide at the time. Woolworth's would have made some suggestions as to the type of products they wanted and the pricing levels. By 1916 Woolworth's was taking 40% percent of Homer Laughlin's output.

Before the start of the 20th century various tablewares and fancies were in production including vanity sets. From about 1900 to 1909 a range of new shapes were introduced including the French influenced *Angelus* shape alongside semi-porcelain dinnerware. By 1905 the company had expanded production under the control of W. Edwin Wells and Marcus Aaron. During the same year a large new factory was built in Newell, West Virginia, which included a village complex for the workers. The East Liverpool factory eventually closed in 1929.

In 1927 the English designer Frederick Hurten Rhead joined the company as Art Director, having moved to America in 1902 and working for a number of pottery companies including Roseville from 1903. His family were well-known potters and included his father Frederick Rhead and sister Charlotte working in the heart of the British pottery industry in Stoke-on-Trent. His *Liberty* shape, a reworking of the dated *Newell* shape, was decorated with a number of patterns such as *Historical America* and *Americana*, printed in pink and based on paintings by Joseph Boggs Beale, both from 1940.

The company had been experimenting with durable solid-coloured glazes for several years. The resultant colours, including red, green and brown, were first used on *Wells Art Dinnerware* by Rhead in 1930. Rhead went on to create the company's most successful range, *Fiesta*. Introduced in 1936 and patented in 1937, *Fiesta* remained in production for many years and was copied by other manufacturers. The first colours were red, ivory, yellow, blue and green, further colours, such as turquoise, were added later. The range was remodelled in red during the late '60s, being phased out in 1972. It was reintroduced in 1986 with updated shapes and glaze colours. Following the success of *Fiesta*, an alternative and cheaper range called *Harlequin* was introduced exclusive to F.W. Woolworth & Co. in 1938.

Rhead had also designed a new, functional shape, *Century*, which was introduced in 1931. Initially decorated with several transfer-printed patterns such as *Mexicana* and *English Garden*, in 1938 it was used for a new mix-and-match set, *Riviera*, which was decorated in bold solid colours. In 1939 Homer Laughlin China Co. created a commemorative plate for the New York World's Fair designed by Charles Murphy. Rhead died in 1942.

From about 1945 design matters were taken over by Donald Schreckengost. To celebrate the 75th anniversary of the company, Donald Schreckengost designed the new *Jubilee* earthenware shape range launched in 1947. *Jubilee* was introduced in four pastel colours as well as the *Epicure* and *Rhythm* sets, in 1955 and 1956 respectively, which were decorated with a range of transfer-printed patterns as well as solid colours.

Despite all the pioneering shapes and patterns that had proved so popular over many years, in 1956 the company changed direction to focus on institutional ware. In this guise, Homer Laughlin is still active today.

- Homer Laughlin's most successful range, *Fiesta*, designed by Frederick Hurten Rhead in 1936, is very popular with today's collectors. Serious collectors seek out the original colours issued in the '30s: red, ivory, yellow, blue and green. Note that the red glaze was discontinued in 1943 as the uranium oxide needed to produce the colour was unavailable due to the war.
- Look out for the commemorative New York World's Fair plate. The 1939 version is more sought after than the 1940 edition.

Further Reference

Atterbury, P., Denker E.P. and Batkin, M., *Twentieth Century Ceramics: A Collectors Guide to British and North American Factory Produced Ceramics.* Millers, Octopus Publishing Ltd., 1999

Venable, C., Denker, E., Grier, K. and Harrison, S., *China and Glass in America 1880-1980; From Tabletop to TV Tray.* Dallas Museum of Art, Harry N. Abrams, Inc., Publishers, 2000

www.hlchina.com

One of the many backstamps issued by the company, 1939

LENOX CHINA CO. INC.
Ceramic Art Company

Lenox China is one of the most important companies operating during the 20th century due, in part, to its development of innovative and high-quality table-wares made for the country's wealthiest families. Lenox successfully met the economic challenges of the '30s and '40s, going on to develop new and exciting pottery during the '50s and '60s and beyond. Lenox boasts a very keen collectors' market today.

Walter Scott Lenox and Jonathan Coxon established the Ceramic Art Company in Trenton, New Jersey in 1889. At the turn of the 20th century, with the assistance of Charles Fergus Binns, the company introduced a new ivory-coloured bone china body. Initially, only art wares were considered suitable for this body; domestic wares were limited to white bone china. However, dinnerware proved so popular that in 1906 Walter Lenox renamed the company Lenox China.

The initial patterns were individually designed and painted by skilled decorators but, as production increased, the company began to use lithographic transfers. The first successes were *Ming* and *Mandarin*, from 1917, which remained in production until the mid '60s. These were designed by Frank Holmes, the Art Director from 1905, who was responsible for many of the commercial patterns including *Autumn*, from 1919, which remains in production today. His beautifully styled *Fountain* pattern, produced for certain stores, was inspired by Edgar Brandt's iron gates at the 1925 Exposition Internationale des Arts Décoratifs et Industriels Modernes in Paris.

It was decided to improve the quality of the ware in order to rival European competitors. The company developed simple shapes made from a high-quality body and improved the glaze. In 1918 a Lenox dinnerware set was produced for the State Dining Room at the White House during Woodrow Wilson's administration. It was this high-profile commission and the resulting orders for dinnerware from all over the world that led to the company's expansion in the 1920s, including new machinery and a new showroom.

Dinner plate decorated with the Fountain *pattern, designed by Frank G. Holmes, diameter 10½ in (26.7cm), 1926*

Following WWII, John M. Tassie, who had joined Lenox in the late '30s, advised the company to reduce the number of standard patterns from approximately 400 to 47; at the same time exclusive lines for the grander stores were cancelled so that Lenox could get more of its products in to the many other shops that were keen to sell its more affordable ranges. Tassie also had a Bridal Registry set up, so

Dinner plate decorated with the Kingsley *pattern, diameter 10¼ in (26cm)*

that the cost of a dinner service could be distributed amongst the many wedding guests.

During the '50s a second factory was built in New Jersey, although production continued at the Trenton site until the mid '60s. Following the death of Frank Holmes, the responsibility for design was given to Winslow Anderson. One of Anderson's most popular patterns was *Kingsley*, which was decorated on standard shapes; introduced in 1954, it remained in production until 1980. Other patterns from the '50s include *Jewel* and *Glendale*.

During the early '60s Lenox introduced a new bone china body that would be manufactured and marketed completely separately to the main product line. This new line was launched under the brand name *Oxford* and was initially introduced with eight patterns, both plain and printed, decorated on the new *Mayfair* shape. Patterns included several banded and printed floral designs, such as *Foxcroft*, *Maldon* and *Wakefield*. This new range must have made an impact in Britain as the trade press noted that Lenox was the first American manufacturer to challenge Britain's long-standing monopoly on the production of bone china.

The company is still active today.

- Collectors are attracted to the high-quality wares produced by Lenox. Both the Art Deco tea wares and the figural work are very popular.
- The earlier patterns from the turn of the 20th century, featuring hand-painted decoration, are the most sought after today by Lenox collectors, though they are relatively expensive.
- The *Oxford* wares from the '60s and '70s are probably not as collectable as some of the earliest examples. Despite this, there are some examples worth looking out for, including the *Dimension* series from 1965 and the shape range *Innovation*, created especially for the contemporary market in 1969. Typical patterns included *Fantasies* and *Firesong*, which weren't in production long so have some collectability.

Further Reading

Atterbury, P., Denker E.P. and Batkin, M., *Twentieth Century Ceramics: A Collectors Guide to British and North American Factory Produced Ceramics*. Millers, Octopus Publishing Ltd., 1999

Denker, E.P., *Lenox Celebrating a Century of Quality 1889-1989*. New Jersey State Museum and Lenox China, 1990

Venable, C., Denker, E., Grier, K., and Harrison, S., *China and Glass in America 1880-1980; From Tabletop to TV Tray*. Dallas Museum of Art, Harry N. Abrams, Inc., Publishers, 2000

www.lenox.com

Ballerina figure designed by Patricia Eakin, height 6in (15.2cm), early 1950s

Collection of earthenware shapes from the Town and Country *range, including a teapot, height 5⅛in (13cm), cruet (salt, pepper and vinegar) and milk jug, designed by Eva Zeisel, 1945-46*

RED WING POTTERIES INC.

The Red Wing Stoneware Co. was established in 1878 and based in Red Wing, Minnesota. Like many similar manufacturers the company started business with the production of functional domestic and stonewares. From 1906, after merging with a couple of other manufacturers, the company became known as Red Wing Union Stoneware Company.

As stoneware became less fashionable in the early part of the 20th century, the company moved into the production of art wares as well as extending the range of useful wares such as ashtrays, bowls and candlesticks. A new dinnerware range was launched in 1935.

In 1936 the reference to stoneware was dropped from the company name to become Red Wing

Potteries Inc. In 1938 the company appointed Belle Kogan, who made a significant contribution to design at Red Wing. She was one of the first professional women designers in America and, over a 25-year period, created many of the important patterns produced by Red Wing. Most notable of these was her *Gypsy Trail Hostess Ware*, which included four different styles: *Plain*, *Chevron*, *Fondoso* and *Reed*. These were glazed in either pastel or bright solid colours, similar to the popular *Fiesta* range by Homer Laughlin. Kogan also had the opportunity to design a number of shapes including *Fancy Free*, launched in 1951, which was decorated with patterns such as *Desert*, a hand-painted design depicting cacti, and *Caprice*. She also designed the *Fondoso* dinnerware range in 1938.

Charles Murphy joined the company in 1940,

having previously worked for Homer Laughlin. He designed a wide range of hand-painted patterns for a series of earthenware cookie jars modelled as *Friar Tuck*, *Chef Pierre* and the *King of Hearts*, which are popular today with collectors. He left the company temporarily for war service.

In 1946 Eva Zeisel was commissioned to create a contemporary range for casual rather than formal living. *Town and Country*, launched in 1947 and now considered to be a design classic, consisted of organically shaped forms glazed in six colours: dusk blue, forest green, metallic brown, rust, grey and chartreuse.

The immediate post-war period was dominated by the designs of Charles Murphy, who had returned to Red Wing as design consultant in 1953. Over the following years he created some of the most successful lines for Red Wing, including the *Tampico* and *Capistrano* patterns decorated on the *Futura* shape in 1955, an extensive range of art wares and many patterns, such as *Brittany* and *Orleans*, for dinnerware. One of the most popular pattern ranges was *Bob White* (1955), decorated on the *Casual* shape, it included a casserole dish and bird-shaped hors d'oeuvres.

Red Wing's large production factory closed in 1967, though Red Wing Pottery continues to operate a small salt-glaze pottery, based on the original salt-glaze wares from the late 1800s.

- Collectors are particularly keen on the post-war designs, especially the cookie jars.
- Look out for the work of Eva Zeisel.

Further Reference

Atterbury, P., Denker E.P. and Batkin, M., *Twentieth Century Ceramics: A Collectors Guide to British and North American Factory Produced Ceramics*. Millers, Octopus Publishing Ltd., 1999

Venable, C., Denker, E., Grier, K. and Harrison, S., *China and Glass in America 1880-1980; From Tabletop to TV Tray*. Dallas Museum of Art, Harry N. Abrams, Inc., Publishers, 2000

www.redwingpottery.com

Collection of teawares decorated with the Lute Song *pattern, possibly designed by Charles Murphy, diameter of plate 10¼ in (26cm), c.1958-59*

Earthenware vase decorated with stylised sweet peas painted by Ed Diers, height 6½in (16.5cm), c.1905-1910

Vellum *vase decorated with purple irises on a shaded ground, height 15½in (39.4cm), c.1912*

ROOKWOOD

Rookwood Pottery is probably the best-known and one of the most important manufacturers of American art pottery produced during the early part of the 20th century. Its range of beautifully decorated Art Nouveau vases was sold in the top stores such as Marshall Field in Chicago and Tiffany of New York. Rookwood was the first art pottery from America to receive international acclaim at the Paris Exposition in 1900.

Maria Longworth Nichols set up the pottery, based in Cincinnati, Ohio, with financial support from her father in 1880. The company was named after her father's estate near the city. Three years later William Watts Taylor became manager of the pottery. In 1890 the founder and her husband moved abroad and William Watts Taylor took control of the company. Despite starting as a rather small concern, an art studio was set up in 1881. In about 1887

Albert R. Valentien was appointed as Art Director.

Many of the early wares featured under-glaze slip decoration finished in a brown glaze, which was known as the *Standard Glaze* line from about 1884 and used for over sixteen years. By 1889 new glazes, which were sprayed on to the wares, had been developed.

In about 1900 the company introduced probably its most important glaze, called *Iris*, which was used on a series of decorative wares featuring hand-painted landscapes, animals and floral motifs. Many of these early wares were marked with the year of production in Roman numerals such as 'VII' for 1907 alongside the initials of the decorator such as 'CS' for Caroline Steinle.

Under the direction of Stanley G. Burt a stunning range of a new type of matt glazes was developed such as *Vellum*, which was introduced in 1904 and shown at the Exposition in St. Louis. The glazes were used on a wide range of Art Nouveau style moulded vases, which often featured flowers and landscapes finished with additional hand-painted decoration by artists such as Sallie Toohey and Albert Pons.

From about 1912 many patterns included landscapes of trees designed by Kataro Shirayamadani who had joined Rookwood in 1887. Interestingly, at the same time, the company introduced mass-produced wares covered in matt glazes, such as green and orange, which were not signed by the artist. Rich heavy glazes over plain shapes allied with low relief modelling were a result of years of experimentation and trials to achieve this distinctive look.

In 1913 William Watts Taylor died and was succeeded by Joseph H. Gest. From 1915 Rookwood used a more durable porcelain body to manufacture vases, paperweights, flower-arranging bowls, figurines and flower frogs. This body was replaced five years later by *Jewel Porcelain*, which was used for all types of production.

Several designers worked at Rookwood during this period, including Carl Schmidt, Jens Jensen and Sara Sax. During the '20s Sax created some modern styled vases featuring stylised floral patterns that leaned towards Art Deco.

Rookwood extended its productions to include a range of animals, figures, garden ware, tiles and architectural faïence.

In 1941 the company went into bankruptcy and was bought by Walter E. Schott. Production continued through several other buyouts, finally closing in 1967.

♦ Collectors should look out for signed pieces.
♦ The earliest detailed patterns, closely associated with the Art Nouveau style, remain the most sought after by collectors today.
♦ The *Iris* range of wares (from 1893) is particularly collectable, again because of the strong connections to the Art Nouveau movement, but also because of the high quality of production.
♦ Carl Schmidt, Jens Jensen and Sara Sax all attract a following for their individual designs, fortunately most signed their work in the form of a mark, aiding identification.

Further Reference
Ellis, A., *Rockwood Pottery: The Glaze Lines*. Schiffer Books, 1995

Meredith, J., 'Rookwood, The Art of Making Fine Ceramics' in *Crockery and Glass Journal*, 1930

Rago, D., and Perrault, S., *How to Compare and Value American Art Pottery*. Millers, Octopus Publishing Group Ltd., 2001

www.ragoarts.com

Three Rockwood pieces with various glazes, centre vase finished wih a Persian blue crackled glaze, height of tallest item 9¾in (24.8cm), late 1920s

ROSEVILLE POTTERY

Roseville Pottery is famous for its stylish vases and flower containers created by a succession of talented designers. Throughout the 20th century the company produced a wide range of products finished with distinctive glazes. It is the work produced after WWI that interests collectors the most today.

Roseville was established by George F. Young in 1890 in Roseville, Ohio. Over the following years other sites were bought to increase production including two factories in Zanesville. By 1910 the entire company had moved to Zanesville.

During the early years of production Roseville commissioned the artist Ross C. Purdy to create a line of decorative wares to compete with the Rookwood company. Launched in 1900, *Rozane* (for Roseville and Zanesville) was hand-decorated with under-glaze slip painting featuring subjects such as portraits, animals and flowers. New lines were added over the following years and it was named *Rozane Royal*.

In 1900 John J. Herold was appointed Art Director and he created, amongst others, the *Rozane Mongol* range, which featured a red crystalline glaze. Part of Roseville's success was its keenness to employ several artists to design for the company including the Japanese designer Gazo Fudji, who arrived at Roseville in 1906, having previously worked at the Weller pottery. He created a number of successful lines including *Rozane Woodland*, *Crystallis* and *Rozane Fudji* from 1904.

In 1904 Frederick Hurten Rhead was appointed as Art Director. Over the next four years he produced many successful lines, such as the complex and intricate *Della Robbia* range from 1906, as well as several inexpensive lines such as *Donatello*, which was popular with the buying public. He left the company in 1908 and was replaced by his brother Harry W. Rhead.

From the early '20s the hand-thrown art wares were replaced by machine-produced examples – several in the Art Deco style. The *Futura* range, one of Roseville's bestselling designs of all time, included many different shapes and colour schemes,

Example of the popular Pine Cone *wares on a spherical, footed vase, height 6in (15.2cm), 1931*

many designed by Frank Ferrel, Art Director from 1918 to 1953. *Futura* featured various moulded decorations including floral motifs, *Dahlrose* and *Sunflower* for example.

At the same time Roseville was producing several unusually shaped vases with embossed decoration for patterns such as *Foxglove* and *Fuschia*; the thin twisting handles were prone to damage.

Pinecone, introduced in the early '30s and available in blue, brown and green colourways, was the most popular line ever produced at Roseville. Over the many years of production it was used on over 70 different shapes with a wide range of colour ways. Other notable ranges included *Rosecraft Hexagon* from 1924 and *Baneda*, featuring moulded stylised flowers, from 1933.

In 1932 Anna Young became President of the company. After her death in 1938, F.S. Clements, her son-in-law, took on the business. During the latter part of the decade the company used gloss glazes rather than the matt finishes that the company was well known for. During the '40s, lines such as *Apple Blossom*, from 1948, *Foxglove* and *Wincraft* were popular; these were less expensive than the earlier products. In 1952 the company introduced a new ovenproof tableware range called *Raymor*, designed by Ben Seibel.

Range of wares decorated with the Fuschia *pattern, height of tallest item 15½in (39.4cm), 1930s*

Roseville Pottery was sold to the Mosaic Tile Company and closed in 1954.

♦ Collectors should keep an eye out for the *Future* and *Falline* lines.

Further Reference

Atterbury, P., Denker E.P. and Batkin, M., *Twentieth Century Ceramics: A Collectors Guide to British and North American Factory Produced Ceramics.* Millers, Octopus Publishing Ltd., 1999

Huxford, S. and Huxford, B., *Collectors' Encyclopedia of Roseville Pottery Vol.II.* Collectors Books, 2001

Rago, D., and Perrault, S., *How to Compare and Value American Art Pottery.* Millers, Octopus Publishing Group Ltd., 2001

www.ragoarts.com

www.rosevilleplace.com

Selection of handled vases decorated with popular patterns including orange Windsor *(top left) and brown* Wisteria *(top right), and two candlesticks decorated with blue* Windsor, *height of tallest item 12in (30.5cm), 1930s*

Vase moulded with poppies under a fine indigo and green glaze, height 4¼in (10.8cm), c.1908-11

VAN BRIGGLE

From the very beginning of production, during the latter part of the 19th century, the Art Nouveau creations of Van Briggle have been much admired by the American pottery trade. Today these examples are highly sought after by a growing number of collectors who favour the subtle stylised forms and matt glazes. Van Briggle is the only art-pottery factory still in operation.

The force behind the success of the company was Artus Van Briggle, who had previously worked as a painter at the Rookwood Pottery. In 1893 he travelled through Europe on a painting scholarship and studied at the Académie Julian under Benjamin Constant and Jean-Paul Laurens where he saw the latest fashions in pottery decoration and the important Art Nouveau style that would later influence his approach to design. He returned to Rookwood and continued to decorate various wares for the company; in 1896 he also started to develop his own glazes.

To overcome illness he moved to Colorado Springs c.1899 and, within two years, he had set up his own pottery firm, Van Briggle, to develop new wares decorated with his new range of coloured glazes. Responsible for all the shapes, he created over 300

different moulds for vases, bowls and other decorative items, which featured low relief decorations including human figures, mainly women, and plant forms. These were finished with matt glazes from a wide range of colours, including turquoise and greens, that reflected the Art Nouveau style.

The company enjoyed great success, commercial and artistic, during the early years of the new century. His latest ranges of high-quality pottery were awarded fifteen medals at the Paris Salon in 1903. One of the most important examples of his work was *Lorelei*. Other similar patterns included the earlier *Lady of the Lily* from 1901. When the founder died in 1904 his wife Anne, herself an artist and designer, took over the running of the factory. In 1908 a new factory was built in Van Briggle's memory; two years later the company began the production of architectural tiles. These tiles, for use

Cylindrical vase embossed with tall daisies under a teal, blue and green glaze, height 7½in (19cm), 1915

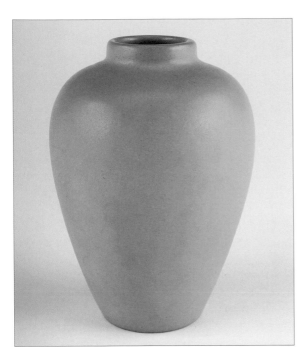

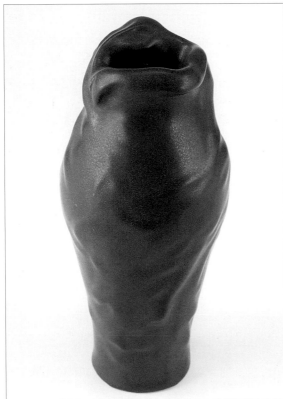

in hotels and office buildings, were decorated with typical Art Nouveau patterns, designed by Anne Gregory Van Briggle, such as stylised trees decorated with a matt glaze. Production was further extended to include the manufacture of garden furniture and of decorative tiles, a change in direction significant enough to warrant the company changing its name in 1910 to the Van Briggle Pottery and Tile Company. There was a further name change in 1913, to the Van Briggle Art Pottery.

By 1913 the pottery was struggling and the company was sold. Changing hands several times over the years, the company was eventually moved to a different site in Colorado in 1968, where it is still in production.

• The Art Nouveau designs, in particular the *Lorelei* vase, are very popular with collectors.
• The architectural tiles with typical Art Nouveau patterns, designed by Anne Gregory Van Briggle, were limited in production and are therefore much sought after by collectors today.

Further Reference
Atterbury, P., Denker E.P. and Batkin, M., *Twentieth Century Ceramics: A Collectors Guide to British and North American Factory Produced Ceramics*. Millers, Octopus Publishing Ltd., 1999

Rago, D. and Perrault, S., *How to Compare and Value American Art Pottery*. Millers, Octopus Publishing Group Ltd., 2001

Sasicki, R. and Fania, J., *The Collector's Encyclopedia of Van Briggle Art Pottery: An Identification & Value Guide*. Collector Books, 1992

www.vanbriggle.com

Top:
Earthenware vase decorated with a smooth matt mustard glaze, height 7½in (19cm), 1907

Bottom:
Example of the Lorelei *vase decorated with a persian rose glaze, height 9in (22.8cm), 1920s*

Collection of coloured wares from the '30s, including a coffee pot, cup and saucer, and plate, all decorated with the Sierra Madre *pattern from 1937; a* Montecito *shape teapot; a covered muffin dish, and a cup and saucer in the* Modern California *pattern, 1937; and a red and black carafe decorated with the* Early California *pattern, height 8in (20.3cm), from 1936*

VERNON KILNS

In 1931 Faye G. Bennison bought the tile and hotelware manufacturer Vernon China on the outskirts of Los Angeles, renaming it Vernon Kilns. Initially, Bennison used some of the old shapes left over after the purchase of the factory, however, a devastating earthquake in 1933 caused extensive damage to the stock and machinery, so the company had to start afresh. It was decided to focus on the production of earthenware rather than the more expensive bone china.

During the '30s Vernon Kilns enjoyed unparalleled success due, in part, to a progressive approach to both patterns and shapes under the Art Direction of Harry Bird. In 1931 the owner's daughter, Jane Bennison, joined the company for a couple of years having studied ceramics at the University of Southern California. She worked closely with her father and at least 24 of her designs were put into production. An art studio was set up in 1935 and, at the same time, a number of freelance designers were brought in.

Daniel Gale Turnbull, who had previously worked at the Leigh Pottery, was appointed as Art Director and took the company onto new commercial success. Whilst his patterns such as *Coastline*, *Banana Tree* and *Little Mission* proved popular, it was his *Montecito* shape range from 1935 that made the most significant contribution to the company's success. Launched c.1935, Turnbull's *Early California* range was decorated with a wide selection of patterns, such as the *Tropical Fish* design by Harry Bird, though the shape range is better known for its decoration in solid colours. *Early California* was soon followed by *Modern California*, which used the same shapes but was decorated in pastel colours. A further range of decorative wares that used these solid colours, was designed by the two sisters May and Genevieve Hamilton. As well as their *Rhythmic* dinnerware range, they created the striking *Cosmic* bowl, which bore more than a passing resemblance to the work of Keith Murray for Josiah Wedgwood and Sons Ltd. The Hamiltons' creations were marked with a special backstamp that included their names.

Example of the Salamina *pattern, printed with hand-painted decoration on an earthenware chop plate, designed by Rockwell Kent, diameter 16¾ in (42.5cm), 1937*

Freelance designer Rockwell Kent created a number of outstanding patterns for Vernon Kilns during the late '30s. One of his most important designs was *Salamina*, which depicted landscapes of Greenland with an Inuit woman. Issued in 1939, this was the only hand-painted pattern produced by Rockwell Kent; it was phased out due to WWII in 1941. Kent also created the transfer-printed patterns *Moby Dick* and *Our America*, both from 1937. The *Our America* range consisted of 30 different scenes of American life and was available in four colour-ways: blue, brown, green and maroon. Don Blading,

Group of earthenware plates, coffee pot, and cup and saucer, printed with various scenes from the Our America *series, including bread and butter plate (back row, second from left) decorated with* Mississippi River States, *large plate (back row, right) showing a view of New York City, and a large plate (bottom right) showing a view of Chicago designed by Rockwell Kent, diameter of chop plate 14in (35.5cm), 1937*

another freelance designer, created a number of patterns such as *Joy, Ecstasy, Glamour* and *Delight*.

In 1940 the company was commissioned by Walt Disney to produce a range of vases, bowls and figurines based on the film *Fantasia*. During the '40s the company produced a number of patterns that echoed the revival of the rural scenes, with patterns aptly called *Gingham, Calico, Tweed* and *Homespun*.

Despite the trade press noting that by the early '50s the factory was turning out some "three thousand dozen" pieces of dinnerware a week, the company ceased production in 1958.

♦ Look out for the range of stylish moulded wares from the '30s.

♦ Vernon Kilns produced hundreds of hand-painted patterns, including their famous plaid range.

Further Reference

Atterbury, P., Denker E.P. and Batkin, M., *Twentieth Century Ceramics: A Collectors Guide to British and North American Factory Produced Ceramics*. Millers, Octopus Publishing Ltd., 1999

Venable, C., Denker, E., Grier, K. and Harrison, S., *China and Glass in America 1880-1980; From Tabletop to TV Tray*. Dallas Museum of Art, Harry N. Abrams, Inc., Publishers, 2000

www.vernonware.com

Jap Birdimal *ewer with tubelined and painted decoration, designed by Frederick Hurten Rhead, height 8½ in (21.6cm), c.1904*

WELLER POTTERY

The Weller Pottery, founded by Samuel Weller in 1872, initially produced wares such as flowerpots and stonewares. Business was successful and, in 1890, the company relocated to a bigger factory and the range of goods was extended to include jardinières and umbrella stands. However, rather than compete with the many other pottery manufacturers producing similar goods, Weller decided to move in to the art pottery field, employing William Long to create designs for him. Long had been a director of the Lonhuda factory in Ohio, which produced a cheaper version of the art wares of Rookwood Pottery. The first range by William Long, *Louwelsa*, was launched c.1895 and remained in production for over twenty years. The *Louwelsa* range was decorated with hand-painted motifs such as flowers and finished with glazes in yellows and browns as well as other colour combinations. This success led to the similar lines such as *Turada*, designed by Samuel Weller, which was introduced in 1897.

In 1900 Charles Babcock Upjohn joined Weller as art director. He was responsible for the well-known *Dickens Ware*, which featured various scenes from the novels of Charles Dickens. Although this range was inspired by the tablewares, figurines and other items produced by Royal Doulton, Weller employed a different decorative technique, which used incised decoration, sprayed on background colours such as brown and dark blue, with slip-painted colours and finished with a glaze. Other motifs used for this range included animals, flowers and Native Americans. A second series was introduced within a few months and a third in 1904.

Another popular line, *Sicardo*, by French designer Jacques Sicard who joined the company in 1902, was applied to moulded wares and finished with a striking lustre decoration; this range was very expensive to produce. *Sicardo* came in a wide range of wares such as vases, umbrella stands, plaques and bowls. Weller also employed other designers, some of whom had worked for other leading pottery manufacturers. One of the most important was Frederick Hurten Rhead, the English-born designer, who created several successful lines such as *Jap Birdimal*, an earthenware range including designs of birds and animals. Gazo Fudji, who had previously worked at Roseville, created a new range called *Fudji*.

In 1920 Weller bought the Zanesville Art Pottery and appointed John Lessell as the new Art Director. Lessel went on the create the stunning *LaSa* pattern range, which featured hand-painted stylised trees over a lustre background. This was the last art range created by the company. Subsequently the Weller Pottery produced a wide range of vases, plates, flower bowls and jardinières featuring moulded decoration in low relief such as flowers, fruits and fish. From 1922 the company was known as S.A. Weller Company. When Samuel Weller died in 1925, the factory remained in production, and was run by his surviving family.

Following the Wall Street Crash in 1929 the Weller Pottery, like many others, suffered financially as the demand for expensive art pottery declined. The company moved production on to a single site, but could not compete with the cheaper foreign imports; the company eventually closed in 1948.

♦ Some of the rarest designs from the *Louwelsa* range such as fish, portraits and animals are sought after by collectors today.

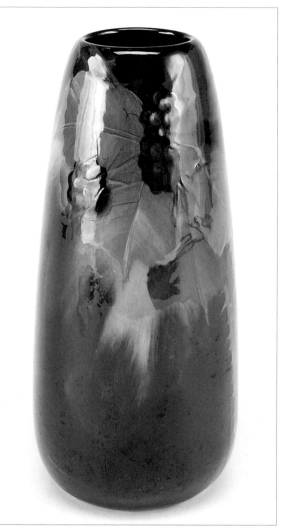

Aurelian *tapering vase decorated with berries and leaves, height 9½ in (24.1cm), c.1907-1910*

♦ Collectors are particularly keen on the third series of *Dickens Wares*; the rarest background colour was pink, items in this colourway are highly sought after.

Further Reference
Atterbury, P., Denker, E. and Batkin, M., *Twentieth Century Ceramics: A Collector's Guide to British and North American Factory Produced Ceramics*, Millers, 1999.

BIBLIOGRAPHY

General

Atterbury, P., Denker, E.P. and Batkin, M., *Miller's Twentieth Century Ceramics, A Collector's Guide to British and North American Factory-Produced Ceramics*. Miller's Publications, 1999

Benton, C., Benton, T. and Woods, G., (Eds.), *Art Deco 1910-1939*. V&A Publications, 2003

Cameron, E. (Ed.), *Encyclopedia of Pottery and Porcelain: 19th and 20th Centuries*. Faber and Faber, 1986

Casey, A., *Twentieth Century Ceramic Designers in Britain*. Antique Collectors' Club Ltd, 2001

Gallagher, F., *Christie's Art Deco*. Pavilion Books, 2000

Hannah, F., *Ceramics, Twentieth Century Design*. Bell & Hyman, 1966

Jenkins, S., *Ceramics of the '50s and '60s: A Collector's Guide*. Miller's Publications, 2001

Leibe, F. (Ed.) and Atterbury, P. (consultant), *20th Century Ceramics Antiques Checklist*. Miller's Publications, 2003

McClaren, G., *Ceramics of the 1950s*. Shire Publications, 1997

McClaren, G., *Ceramics of the 1960s*. Shire Publications, 2001

Miller, J., *Collector's Guide to Art Deco*. Dorling Kindersley, 2005

Stevenson, G., *Art Deco Ceramics*. Shire Publications, 1998

UK

Ashworth, F., *Aynsley China*. Shire Publications, 2002

Atterbury, P. and Irvine, L., *The Doulton Story*. (Booklet produced for V&A exhibition). Royal Doulton Tableware, 1979

Atterbury, P. and Batkin, M., *The Dictionary of Minton*. Antique Collectors' Club, 1999

Atterbury, P., *Moorcroft: A Guide to Moorcroft Pottery 1897-1993*. Richard Dennis, 1993

Atterbury, P., *Poole in the 1950s*. Dennis, R. and Clark, J. at the Richard Dennis Gallery, 1997

Atterbury, P., *Cornish Ware and Domestic Pottery by T.G. Green*. Richard Dennis, 2001

Batkin, M., *Wedgwood Ceramics 1846-1959: A New Appraisal*. Richard Dennis, 1982

Batkin, M., *Gifts for Good Children: The History of Children's China, 1890-1990, Vol 2*. Richard Dennis, 1996

Batkin, M. and Bumpus, B., *Charlotte Rhead Pottery*. Francis Joseph Publishing, 1999

Baynton, V., *Beswick: A Catalogue*. UK International Ceramics Ltd., 1994

Beckett, P., *A Victorian Pottery: The History of Royal Stafford and Gladstone China*. Peter Beckett, 2003

Bumpus, B., *Collecting Rhead Pottery*. Francis Joseph Publishing, 1999

Callow, D., Callow, J., Sweet, M. and Sweet, P., *The Charlton Standard Catalogue of Beswick Animals*. The Charlton Press, 1998

Casey, A., *Susie Cooper Ceramics – A Collectors Guide*. Jazz Publications, 1992

Casey, A. and Eatwell, A., (Eds.), *Susie Cooper: A Pioneer of Modern Design*. Antique Collectors' Club, 2002

Collins, M. and Collins, D., *SylvaC Animals*. SCC Publications, 2004

Eatwell, A., *Susie Cooper Productions*. V&A Publications, 1987

Eyles, D., *The Doulton Burslem Wares*. Barrie & Jenkins, 1980

Furniss, D.A., Wagner, J.R. and Wagner, J., *Adams Ceramics: Staffordshire Potters and Pots, 1779-1998*. Schiffer Publishing, 1999

Griffin, L., Alcosser, M. (Photo.) and Meisel, L. (Photo.), *The Bizarre Affair*. Thames and Hudson, 1988

Griffin, L., *Clarice Cliff: The Art of Bizarre*. Pavilion Books, 1999

Hallam, E., *Ashtead Potters Ltd. in Surrey, 1923-1935*. Hallam Publishing, 1990

Hampson, R., *Churchill China: Great British Potters since 1795*. Centre for Local History, Department of History, University of Keele, Staffordshire, 1994

Hayward, L., *Poole Pottery: Carter and Co. and Their Successors, 1873-2002*. Richard Dennis, 3rd edition

Heckford, B. and Jakes, B. (Ed.), *Hornsea Pottery 1949-1989 – Its People, Processes and Products*. Hornsea Pottery Collectors and Research Society, 1998

Hill, S., *Shelley Style: A Collector's Guide*. Jazz Publications, 1990

Hill, S., *Crown Devon: History of S. Fielding & Co*. Jazz Publications. 1993.

Hopwood, I. and Hopwood, G., *The Shorter Connection: A.J. Wilkinson, Clarice Cliff, Crown Devon – A Family Pottery. 1874-1974*. Richard Dennis, 1992.

Hopwood, I. and Hopwood, G., *Denby Pottery 1809-1997: Dynasties and Designers*. Richard Dennis, 1997

Jenkins, S. and Atterbury, P. (Ed.), *Midwinter Modern: A Revolution in British Tableware*. Richard Dennis, 1997

Jenkins, S. and McKay, S., *Portmeirion Pottery*. Richard Dennis, 2000

Jones, J., *Minton: The First Two Hundred Years of Design and Production*. Swan Hill Press, 1993

Key, G. and Key, A., *Denby Stonewares: A Collector's Guide*. Ems & Ens Ltd., 1995

Knight, R. and Hill, S., *Wileman: A Collectors' Guide*. Jazz Publications, 1995

Leith, P., *The Designs of Kathie Winkle*. Richard Dennis, 1999

Levitt, S., *Poutney: The Bristol Pottery*. Redcliffe Press, 1990

McKeown, J., *Royal Doulton*. Shire Publications, 1997

McKeown, J., *Burleigh, The Story of a Pottery*. Richard Dennis, 2003

Miller, M., *The Royal Winton Collectors' Handbook From 1925*. Francis Joseph, London, 1996

Moore, S., *Maling: The Trademark of Excellence*. Tyne & Wear Museums, 1998

Moss, S., *Homemaker: A 1950s Design Classic*. Cameron and Hollis, 1997

Myott, A. and Pollitt, P., *The Mystery of Myott: The History of Myott Pottery Stoke-on-Trent 1898-1991*. Published privately, 2003

Niblett, K., *Hand Painted Gray's Pottery*. City Museum and Art Gallery, Stoke-on-Trent, 1983

Peat, A., *Midwinter, A Collectors' Guide*. Cameron and Hollis, 1991

Prescott-Walker, R., Salmon, F. and Folkard, J., *The Wade Collectors' Handbook*, Francis Joseph, 1997

Reilly, R. and Savage, G., *Wedgwood: The New Illustrated Dictionary of* . Antique Collectors' Club, 1999

Roberts, A.H., Fielding's *Crown Devon Musical Novelties, Collectors' Handbook*. Fairview Promotions, 1998

Sandon, H., *Royal Worcester Porcelain: From 1862 to the Present Day*. Barrie & Jenkins, 1979

Scott, S., *The Charlton Standard Catalogue of Chintz*. The Charlton Press, 1999

Serpell, D., *The Carlton Ware Collectors' Handbook*. Francis Joseph Publications, 2003

Slater, G. and Brough, J., *Comprehensively Clarice Cliff*. Thames and Hudson, 2005

Spours, J., *Art Deco Tableware: British Domestic Ceramics 1925-1939*. Rizzoli International Publications, 1988

Twitchett, J. and Bailey, B., *Royal Crown Derby*. Antique Collectors' Club, 1988

Van der Woerd, A., *Shaw and Copestake: The Collector's Guide to Early Sylvac 1894-1939*. Georgian Publications, 1992

Verbeek, S.J., *The Sylvac Story*. Pottery Publications, 2002

Watkins, C., Harvey, W. and Senft, R., *Shelley Potteries: The History and Production of a Staffordshire Family of Potters*. Barrie and Jenkins, 1980

Wilkinson, V., *Copeland*. Shire Publications, 1994

Wilkinson, V., *Copeland-Spode-Copeland: The Works and Its People, 1770-1970*. Antique Collectors' Club, 1999

Europe

Brega, V., 'Le Ceramiche Robj 1921-1931'. *Leonardo Periodici*. [English translation by Gabriella Ezra Skittar]

Brunhammer, Y. and Tise, S., *The Decorative Arts in France: La Société des Artistes Decorators, 1900-1942*. Rizzoli, 1990

De Pauw, C. and Stal, M., *Catteau*. King Baudouin Foundation, 2001

Desens, R., *Villeroy & Boch, 250 Years of European Industrial History, 1748-2005*. Villeroy & Boch Aktiengesellschaft, 2005

Dufrene, M., *Authentic Art Deco Interiors from the 1925 Paris Exhibition*. Antique Collectors Club, 1997

Hellman, Å. (ed.), *Ceramic Art in Finland*. Thames and Hudson, 2005

Jackson, L., *Robin and Lucienne Day, Pioneers of Contemporary Design*. Mitchell Beazly, 2001

Living with Art: An Homage to Philip Rosenthal. Rosenthal AG, 2003

Kapp, V. and Siemen, W., *H. Th. Baumann; Design 1950-1990*. Museum der Deutschen Porzellan Industrie [Museum of the German Porcelain Industry], Hohenberg an der Eger, 1989

Opie, J., *Scandinavia: Ceramics and Glass in the Twentieth Century*. V&A Publications, 1989

America

Altman, V. and Altman, S., *The Book of Buffalo Pottery*. Schiffer Publishing, 1997

Elliot-Bishop, J., *Franciscan, Catalina & Other Gladding McBean Wares*. Schiffer Books, 2001

Elliot-Bishop, J., *Franciscan, Hand-decorated Embossed Dinnerware*. Schiffer Books, 2004

Ellis, A., *Rookwood Pottery: The Glaze Lines. Schiffer Books*, 1995

Henzke, L., *American Art Pottery*. Thomas Nelson. 1970

Hible, J., Goldman Hibel, C., DeFalco, R. and Rago, D., *The Fulper Book*. Arts & Crafts Quarterly, 1992

Huxford, S. and Huxford, B., *Collectors' Encyclopedia of Roseville Pottery*, Vol II. Collector Books, 2001

Rago, D. and Perrault, S., *How to Compare and Value American Art Pottery*. Millers, Octopus Publishing Group Ltd., 2001

Runge Jr., R.C., *Collector's Encyclopedia of Stangl Artware, Lamps & Birds*, 2nd Ed. Collector Books, Schroeder Publishing Co., 2006

Stern, B., *California Pottery: From Missions to Modernism*. Chronicle Books, 2001

Sasicki, R. and Fania, J., *The Collector's Encyclopedia of Van Briggle Art Pottery: An Identification & Value Guide*. Collector Books, 1992

Tuchman, M., *Bauer Classic American Pottery*. Chronicle Books, 1995

Venable, C., Denker., E., Grier, K. and Harrison, S., *China and Glass in America 1880-1980: From Tabletop to TV Tray*. Dallas Museum of Art, Harry N. Abrams, Inc. 2000

Periodicals

Crockery and Brass

Decorative Art, Studio Year Book

Design

Pottery and Glass Record

Pottery Gazette and Glass Trade Review

Tableware International

INDEX

Page numbers in bold type refer to illustrations